The Household Economy

Reconsidering the
Domestic Mode of Production

The Household Economy

Reconsidering the Domestic Mode of Production

EDITED BY

Richard R. Wilk

Westview Press
BOULDER • SAN FRANCISCO • LONDON

Table 4 in Chapter 5 is reprinted from Jeffery Bentley "Technical Change in a Northwest Parish" in *Portuguese Agriculture in Transition* edited by Scott Pearson, et al. Copyright © 1987 by Cornell University. Used by permission of the publisher, Cornell University Press.

Published in 1989 in the United States of America by Westview Press, Inc., 5500 Central Avenue, Boulder, Colorado 80301, and in the United Kingdom by Westview Press, Inc., 13 Brunswick Centre, London WC1N 1AF, England

Library of Congress Cataloging-in-Publication Data
The Household economy: reconsidering the domestic mode of production
  /edited by Richard R. Wilk.
    p. cm.
  Bibliography: p.
  ISBN 0-8133-7694-7
  1. Economic anthropology. 2. Home economics—Developing
countries. 3. Developing countries—Economic conditions. I. Wilk,
Richard R.
GN448.H69 1989
306.3′4—dc20   89-35017
                                                                            CIP

Printed and bound in the United States of America

(∞) The paper used in this publication meets the requirements of the American National
     Standard for Permanence of Paper for Printed Library Materials Z39.48-1984.

10   9   8   7   6   5   4   3   2   1

Contents

PART THREE
Implications of Household Processes
for Agricultural Development

Contributors

Peggy F. Barlett
Department of Anthropology
Emory University

Jeffery W. Bentley
Escuela Agricola Panamericana

David Cheal
Sociology Department
University of Winnipeg

Gracia Clark
Department of Anthropology
University of Michigan

Hilary S. Feldstein
The Population Council

Victoria S. Lockwood
Department of Anthropology
Southern Methodist University

Robert McC. Netting
Department of Anthropology
University of Arizona

M.K.G. Olsen
Bureau of Applied Research in Anthropology
University of Arizona

Susan V. Poats
The Population Council

Dianne E. Rocheleau
Ford Foundation

Henry J. Rutz
Department of Anthropology
Hamilton College

Mahir Şaul
Department of Anthropology
University of Illinois

M. J. Weismantel
Department of Sociology and Anthropology
Occidental College

Richard R. Wilk
Department of Anthropology
Indiana University

PART ONE

Introduction and Issues of Theory

1

Introduction: Dimensions and Dilemmas of Householding

Peggy F. Barlett

Comparative research in cultural ecology and economic anthropology has demonstrated the household to be a flexible component of human cultural organization, exhibiting a wide variety of forms, providing a framework for many types of activities, and responding to different pressures from the larger political economy. Though mainly seen as a dependent variable from an evolutionary perspective, the household—in all its historical complexity of norms and content in any one place and time—takes a more central and determinative role in the lives of individuals. As we are born, mature, and die, relationships within and toward households change, but the overall framework remains central to much of each individual's human experience. The authors in this volume have focused their research efforts on the little-studied internal forms and processes of households. In doing so, they challenge the traditional anthropological complacency about our descriptions of households. In this brief overview, I will summarize some of the dimensions of households and householding that have been illuminated here, thereby highlighting some of the approaches and concerns in description and analysis that broaden our thinking and will, it is hoped, improve our future research in this area. I will begin with the four dimensions of description and then turn to the focus of data collection. The broader context of social forces that affect the household will be combined with some comments on the tensions between the individual and the group. In conclusion, I will review some of the challenges that remain in spite of these new approaches to householding.

Dimensions of Description

Many authors use the term *household structure,* though the following articles do not all use it the same way or include under this heading the same data. Household structure in its broadest interpretation may be summarized by four general categories of information: personnel and household composition; production activities and the division of labor; consumption activities and inter- and intra-household exchange; and patterns of power and authority. Some attention to the first three categories are a standard part of any anthropological analysis. The age and sex composition of the household, kinship rules of recruitment, life cycle changes over time, economic activities related to production, distribution, and consumption, exchange patterns, and the disposition of the products of the economy figure in any ethnography, though they are often covered in greater detail in work by economic anthropologists. Where new insights into household processes have emerged most clearly is in the combination of these topics for a more complex description: the gendered patterns of agricultural tasks, for example, or the effect of number and spacing of children in the household, their consumption demands, and the effect on parents' economic activities and household capital accumulation. The fourth topic, the area of power and authority, which includes rights to resources and to the control of the products of consumption, is newer. Interest in this subject emerged most strongly out of the feminist critiques of traditional anthropological accounts that gloss over the inequities and power relations within the household. As the articles in this volume show, connections—between rights to land, control over labor, decision-making authority, and other aspects of power relations create very different contexts of action and meaning for each household member.

These four topical areas of description can be discussed in several dimensions. On the one hand, researchers distinguish between *the ideal and the real*. Norms of household composition may dictate who is supposed to be in household, but who is actually there is a different reality. Weismantel approaches this topic with her discussion of how the Zumbagua constitute a household ("a hearth defines a home"). The Peruvian Indians so connect the notion of family and shared eating that they may redefine kin relations between parents and children and other relatives to conform to the realities of household composition. The ways in which the process of householding is culturally constituted, interpreted, symbolized, and translated into everyday expectations are essential to a thorough study of the internal dynamics of households. At the same time, this emic reality must be contrasted with an etic assessment of the outsider's point of view, which determines the extent to which behavior conforms to the ideal.

In addition, there may be multiple version of the ideal. Many recent studies of gender and ideology have discovered that women do not always share men's conceptions, and women's distinct norms and values can be linked to the ways they guide their lives and respond to men's domination.

As Olsen points out for Slovenian households, age can be another vector for diverse values: older women's notions of the ideal extended family are not shared by younger women. With the recognition of this variation, the study of belief systems becomes at once more complicated but also more interestingly related to daily life.

In describing the "real" of household structure, anthropologists have traditionally allowed the "central tendency," the common pattern, to suffice. The growing emphasis on capturing the *diversity of behavior* behind the common pattern is one of the main thrusts that draws attention to the internal processes of the household. In her study of Tubuai, Lockwood points out that individuals, not households, choose to plant potatoes, thereby taking advantage of a subsidized government program and an opportunity to earn cash income. She demonstrates that the variation in individual access to resources, wage income, and government transfers are an important constraint on this particular economic decision. In describing the complexities of household resource management, we need to further sub-divide production and consumption processes, drawing attention to such activities as resource keeping, mobilization, and servicing.

Each household and the larger cultural content of which it is a part must be seen in its *historical context*. Many authors have documented changes in household activities and composition with the penetration of market systems and the incorporation of local areas into the world system. Şaul notes that these processes among the Bobo of Burkina Faso have allowed emergence of households as actual bounded units, distinct from the corporate lineages that dominated exchanges in the past. Bentley's description of rural Portugal reveals economic pressures that push men to migrate to find work, changing the household composition in ways that create considerable adversity for their wives.

The diachronic perspective on household structure leads not only to a discussion of global or regional context, but also to the changing form of specific household units over time. Weismantel links ". . . an apparent proliferation of household forms" in Zumbagua into ". . . a single root form," with transformations over the reproductive cycle. In her chapter, "types" of households are joined in a developmental exegesis that unites the normative expectations of change (as individual household members mature, marry, and establish their own families) with the economic pooling and productive activities that join members in different ways at different times.

Her analysis brings us to the final dimension of the description of household structure: the *quality* of household interactions, whether agonistic, cooperative, affectionate, or restrained. The reduced sensual pleasure of a cold barley breakfast in the unheated kitchen of a younger family contrasts sharply with the tangy warmth of roasting barley in the parents' kitchen. These qualitative dimensions fill out our understanding of the costs and benefits of establishing an independent kitchen. Likewise, husband-wife negotiations over labor obligations and contributions are shown among the Bobo to involve incentives as well as coercion. This latter description of husbands' demands on wives' labor illustrates the interaction of a wide range of dimensions of household structure: the expectations of wives' contributions of labor to their husbands' fields and whether and at what level these contributions are made; the variations in men's abilities to get women to work for them; the larger cultural context of considerable autonomy for men and women and the need to negotiate with spouses to obtain labor; the changes in these negotiations as both men and women have new access to cash; how these variations in women's independent economic activities have changed by generation; and the affective content of husband-wife relations.

Focus of Data Collection

The chapters in this volume show a range of specific foci of data collection, but most center on daily activities, agricultural production, marketing, or other aspects of economic decision making. Cheal argues that long-term relationships and the interactions that occur within then have the greatest influence on individuals. The concern with interactions and exchanges guides Clark's discussion of Asante traders in Ghana. In her analysis, women's exchanges with their children structure important flows of labor and capital, and a woman's independent trading enterprise benefits greatly if her husband provides regular child support and avoids demands for school fees, medical care, or other expenses.

Wilk's paper takes the traditional subject matter of economic anthropology—material goods and services—and tries to specify different organizational forms by specifying flows of cash, labor, and goods in a range of societies. His models attempt to recognize variability in frequency of flows and their rhythm and timing. Though he recognizes the need to locate each particular model in its specific economic, historical, and social context, the paper here does not attempt to do so, but instead seeks to find certain *structured forms* of flows that may recur cross-culturally.

The major contribution of such models is that they may illuminate regularities that have larger implications. As Wilk points out, the existence of a common budget pool within the household—perhaps controlled by a single decision-maker—may be correlated with the ability of such households to take advantage of opportunities for entrepreneurial investment. Such ability to mobilize resources rapidly may contribute to understanding why certain ethnic groups are able to prosper after migration while others do not.

Netting's chapter on family farmers takes a broad approach to economic activities as well, linking them to ecological processes. He argues that labor flexibility within the smallholder household is crucial to successful labor-intensive agriculture. Kin ties allow a level of recruitment, supervision, balance with off-farm work, cooperation, and work quality that out-competes other forms of agricultural production.

Rutz expands his documentation of economic flows among Fijian household members to include communicative acts. The discourse that accompanies daily life articulates the ideological underpinnings of authoritative allocation, reinforcing rights and obligation to the household head and the other members, each in unique, ranked relationships.

Several papers focus on the economic decisions that must be made in the household. Poats, Feldstein and Rocheleau document a range of differential constraints on household members in the adoption of new agricultural techniques or crop options. Their interest is to explore the complexities of choice and economic action in order to influence behavior and direct change in agricultural development projects. Behind these interventions are values that seek to channel the household structure of power and influence toward greater "equity" and broader participation in economic decisions.

In contrast, Bentley takes the position that much of economic life has only one possible alternative, and thus allocations or decisions are sufficiently constrained that choice is not always a useful perspective in which to analyze household functioning. Wilk illustrates this point by noting that some U.S. situations, "While husband and wife may end up thinking they made a decision together, they actually pursued a 'disjointed, unstructured and incremental strategy, the main goal of which was to 'muddle though,' keeping the marriage going whatever the actual decision reached." It may be that in many cultural contexts, the processes and relationships built and reproduced in the household may not lend themselves to a focus on decisions or choice.

This quote by Wilk draws attention to another important dimension of householding, the different *goals* individuals may pursue. Lockwood notes that since men have greater access to employment and cash earning on Tubuai, women desire greater discretionary income in order to raise their consumption levels. Other women, whose cash incomes are very low, have adopted potato production to try to meet basic subsistence needs. Rutz contrasts the traditional goals of a Fijian household head— to have a large retinue of dependents, to work for community or clan improvement, and to be generous to others—with the capitalist goals of wealth accumulation and standard of living. In this case, personal goals are in flux as two economic and ideological systems collide. The household becomes the "locus of tensions" between the moral economy of the "Fijian way of life" and the Western market economy.

Quite apart from culturally determined goals or individual economic strategies, there are interpersonal variations in energy level and desires to achieve certain goals. Netting notes that family farmers' production levels (after controlling for influences of resource access and Chayanovian worker-consumer ratio) are affected by personal goals. Some people aim at high productivity, some medium, and some low. Whether these variations are biochemical/genetic, psychological, or linked to some other source of diversity, they nevertheless enter into any consideration of the internal dynamics of households.

Rutz' analysis of the articulation between the world system and the household on Fiji draws attention to the larger forces at work, constraining and channeling present and determining future household structures. Regional, national, and international forces change the nature of the community in which households exists. In particular, increasing differentiation and emerging inequalities in access to land and capital, income-earning possibilities, and political power create new opportunities for certain individuals, but not the majority, with significant consequences for the household.

These chapters differ in the extent to which they focus on these forces external to the community; in some cases they are central to understanding causal processes. The cases document, however, that within the constraints of class stratification and market exchange, attention to the variation among and within households draws us to look at individual differences in personality, skills, energy, age, and gender. The range of characteristics that affect householding processes go beyond the larger economic and political forces and their local level manifestations.

Concentric Groups and Concentric Goals

Weismantel emphasizes the concentric groupings that are cross-linked by processes of production and consumption in the Peruvian case: the individual ownership of property, the household sharing of food and child care, and the extended family pooling of labor in the agricultural enterprise. The world system, the community, the household, and the individual are likewise linked in concentric groupings that trade off the complexities of economic life with other kinds of rewards.

It may be useful to think as well of *concentric goals,* that is, the way individuals have a range of culturally constituted desires and "needs" that they seek to meet through a range of relationships with nested groups. Behavioral ecology and maximization theory provide approaches to analyzing the behavior of individuals with regard to goals, but may not provide much guidance in a situation of *conflicting* goals that must be met in contexts of long- and short-term relationships with overlapping and conflicting groups. If it is true that human beings, unlike many animals, must achieve their goals through relationships and activities within groups, then positing an opposition between "the individual and the group" mis-specifies the conceptual problem. This issue may thus be redefined as nested relations between the individual and many groups (with different structures over time), for many different purposes, conscious and unconscious, complementary and oppositional, articulated and implicit, met and unmet.

Future Challenges

Several aspects of householding remain as challenges for future research. The long-term and/or daily interactions that create and validate household groupings include not only material flows, but also psychological, emotional, or affective dimensions. Even in societies which downplay emotion or socialize children to distrust others, there are important exchanges of a non-material sort which are a part of the fabric of the household. Beyond food and shelter, children need care, affection, and security for their healthy development into adults. This care provides psychic satisfactions to the caregivers as well. Between husbands and wives or elders and juniors, emotional support and approval may be an important part of the complexity that sustains hierarchical power relations. It is surely true that these psychological dimensions will vary greatly both within cultural groups and across time.

Psychologists and family therapists attempt to understand patterns of affect and bonding in households by looking at a range of observable or reportable behaviors. Communications among the individuals and the frequency and nature of such communication is one component of affection. Touching, sexuality, and other types of contact are a second. Who initiates and terminates these communications and contacts, their duration, and their content are all manifest expressions of underlying attachments. The methodological challenge of exploring these dimensions in another culture are considerable, but to the extent that we can delineate such patterns, we may increase the descriptive power or the predictive potential of our models.

Beyond emotional ties in general, another non-material dimension to households has to do with *fertility and reproduction*. Obligations to procreate, or desires to do so, are part of forming and dissolving household bonds. The existence of children has an enormous impact in most societies on the nature of the obligations among adults in a household. Continued economic cooperation between husband and wife may not be permissible without progeny, in some groups, regardless of the affective bonds that may make a husband and wife desire to remain married. Young children also constrain the time available to adults and permit (and require) certain kinds of investments on their behalf.

Greater attention to the expectations of individuals within households may reveal important patterns in the reactions to *deviation* from these norms. Consequences of deviation may be very clear or slowly evolving under circumstances of rapid change. The emotional/affective psychological consequences of variation in maintaining traditional economic arrangements within the household—and vice versa—will perhaps become particularly important as societies are transformed through larger market forces, colonialism, and other processes of historical change.

Why haven't these issues been studied in greater detail before? Part of the answer surely lies in a Western bias that sees all important cultural activity taking place in the public sphere, outside the home. But another part of the answer is that such research is methodologically very difficult. To measure these processes and flows with any adequacy, the researcher would have to gain access to many households, to assure a representative sample of the kinds of dynamics occurring. This access would have to continue for long enough to dilute the observer's impact on the process, and to gather data over a period sufficient to see daily, annual, and life-cycle variation. In addition to gaining rapport to observe such behavior and consequences, the researcher has to gather emic data to be able to articulate the actors' own understandings of the process and its meaning. Of course, such meanings may vary by at least as many people as there are involved in the household.

While recognizing that the "black box" of households is an important and fruitful challenge to increase the sophistication of anthropological research, it is also important to acknowledge that the box will be difficult to open accurately, and the potential for a thorough analysis of internal dynamics may have to come at the expense of omitting research on many other topics of importance in the group studied. It may have been appropriate for anthropologists pioneering the study of little-known groups and regions to gloss over these householding processes. It may also be a sign of the greater maturity of the field that we are, at this point, ready to refine these issues. In spite of the methodological challenges, the papers collected here show significant progress in illuminating the complexities and variety of household structures and processes.

2

Strategies of Resource Management in Household Economies: Moral Economy or Political Economy?

David Cheal

Many of the most exciting developments in studies of economic behavior today concern the ways in which resource flows are influenced by microstructures such as local labor markets, social networks and households (Roberts, Finnegan and Gallie 1985; Swedberg 1987; Risman and Schwartz 1989).[1] These developments include studies of household economies in industrial societies, which have added significantly to our knowledge of everyday life (Brannen and Wilson 1987a; Wilson 1987; Pahl 1988). In their focus on face to face relationships, and in their use of ethnographic methods, these studies often demonstrate important convergences between anthropology and sociology (Gullestad 1984; Brannen and Wilson 1987b: 12).

The significance of the new household studies for contemporary social life can be illustrated by the hypothetical case of a full time housewife, who is about to return to paid employment after raising children. She is likely to find that her immediate opportunities for wage earning are limited, because of the value that employers attach to recent occupational experience, which she does not have. Clearly, the work history of a woman in this situation cannot be explained simply by referring to models of individual choice. It is also necessary to take into account the social organization of women's caring for men and children within the home, which puts many women at a disadvantage in the labor market (Daniels and Weingarten 1984; Harris and Morris 1986; Morris 1987). Put more generally, the important point to be made here is that much economic behavior is affected by long term commitments to structures of relationships in households (Siltanen 1986; Cheal 1988: 61–62 especially).

In this chapter we are going to be concerned with two models of structures of relationships, which I refer to as "moral economy" and "political economy" (Cheal 1988: 4–16). These two models describe different kinds of structures, but they are also—perhaps they are primarily—different ways of *thinking* about structures. These different ways of thinking matter now, in ways that they did not in the past. To see how this is so, we need to remind ourselves of some of the reasons why households are so interesting to us today.

Household Resource Management

Studies of the unequal volumes of resources commanded by households in different environments have existed for a long time. Systematic investigations into the ways in which resources are handled *within* households, on the other hand, are more recent (Cheal 1989b). In much current work on household economies social analysis is pushed beyond the global resources commanded by household units, to the ways in which resources are managed by household members as they interact with one another. Such micro-analyses of economic relationships within households have been conducted by anthropologists, economists, historians and sociologists in a number of countries (Edwards 1980; Jain and Banerjee 1985; Redclift and Mingione 1985; Roberts 1986; Segalen 1986; Sharma 1986). Among the promising contributions in this field is the social anthropology of Sandra Wallman.

Wallman conceives of households as resource systems, that is to say as bounded social units possessing a variety of resources, which may be used in different ways (Wallman 1979, 1986). She identifies six kinds of resources that households need for their livelihood. They are: land, labor, capital, time, information, and social identity. Wallman claims that structures of relationships within households typically take the form of a specialization of tasks in the management of resources. Certain household members are allocated, or take over, the management of particular resources for the household. How these resource-keepers perform their tasks will clearly have important effects upon the viability of the household, and upon the well-being of all its members.

Wallman has successfully applied her approach in field research on households in London, England (Wallman 1984). Sociologists also are engaged in studying households in industrial societies, and they too are often interested in patterns of household resource management. Two main factors have brought about this enhanced interest in households. One is that there is now more concern with adverse effects of contemporary economic changes, and with the ways in which individuals respond to those changes (Caplovitz 1979; Smith, Wallerstein and Evers 1984; Gallie

1985; Smith 1987). The nature and level of household supports can facilitate or hinder individual strategies for coping with change, and how individuals respond is often influenced by the quality of relationships with other household members (Moen, Kain and Elder 1983; Morris 1985; Pahl 1987).

The second reason for increased interest in household economies is a greater awareness of the disadvantages and deprivations experienced by women, who do most of the day-to-day housework (Eichler 1973; Meissner et al 1975; Delphy 1984; Finch 1985). In the western industrial societies, the new awareness of women's burdens is partly due to the effects of demographic change. Increased longevity for women has meant that poverty in old age is more and more a phenomenon of poor widows. Also, increased divorce has meant that much larger numbers of children now experience poverty at some point in their childhood, as a result of being supported not just by one parent only, but usually by the lower earning parent (that is, the mother). Both of these consequences of change are related to the gendered division of labor within the household, through the latter's effects upon financial welfare (Dulude 1984; Sidel 1986; Millar 1988).

As a result of the various developments noted above, perceptions of households have become increasingly diverse, and sometimes contradictory. On the one hand, the cooperative management of resources for the improvement of members' collective quality of life appears to be a distinctive achievement of many households (Rosen 1987). On the other hand, there is also evidence of conflict, domestic violence, and privileges for some members amidst the poverty of others (Pahl 1980; Land 1983; Ayers and Lambertz 1986; Glendinning and Millar 1987). At this time it is clearly necessary to find ways of describing households which do not assume that they are harmonious systems, but which leave the exact nature of their effects open, to be determined in each case (e.g. Cheal 1989b; Wilk this volume). In this chapter the different possibilities within household economies will be described through contrasting models of moral economy and political economy.

Models of Moral Economy and Political Economy

The concept of a moral economy was first introduced by the historian E.P. Thompson, in connection with his studies of transitions from pre-capitalist to capitalist societies (Thompson 1971). In pre-capitalist societies, economic exchanges appear to be regulated by traditional norms that define both an individual's social status, and the support to which he or she is entitled in order to maintain an appropriate level of subsistence (Scott 1976). This concept of a moral economy has important similarities with the standard model of the household in sociology and in anthropology. In economic anthropology, households have usually been understood as intimate economies based on sharing, rather than on the economic exchange that is found in more distant relationships (e.g. Price 1975). Rights to goods and services are therefore thought to be defined by social obligations rather than by calculations of returns, and they are described as being patterned by the role structure of the group. This conventional view of households can be summarized in a model of the household economy as a moral economy, comprised of five interrelated characteristics.

Moral Economy

1. The actions of individuals in their capacities as household members are motivated by a desire to produce socially preferred (i.e. moral) relationships between the incumbents of different social categories, such as roles which define the domestic division of labor.
2. Insofar as all members act in this way, transactions between them will take the form of a ritual interaction order of approach and avoidance, in which the possibility of conflict is minimized. Furthermore, fears of provoking jealousy, and felt needs to maintain enduring relationships of cooperation and solidarity, result in explicit ideologies of mutual support in transactions between household members.
3. Within a moral economy, a rational individual will use all available means to maintain the framework of ritualized relationships, which is the source of long term economic security. Any disruption to the accepted balance of well-being will be remedied by compensatory transactions.
4. Resources become available to individuals through a socially defined process of mobilization and distribution. It is therefore the forms of institutionalized interactions that structure the directions in which resources flow. Rules of category membership, and the extent of available resources, together determine the net gains and losses that individuals receive from their transactions.
5. In order to ensure the participation of others in such transactions, household heads engage in verbal and non-verbal discourses that construct the meaning of the household as the natural center of economic life. Within the relational culture of the household economy, the pattern of resource flows is accepted as taken-for-granted reality.

Depictions of households as moral economies can be found in several of the discussions presented in this volume. For example, Weismantel shows how the distribution and consumption of food constitutes the household as an emotionally significant unit in Zumbagua. The preference for maintaining structures of relationships between household members is very strong in Zumbagua. We see this in the way that a newly married couple only slowly relinquish their roles in the households of their parents. Even when a new household has established its independence through the production of hot meals, ritual gifts of food from one kitchen to another continue to symbolize enduring intimate ties with the parental household, and those ties are only gradually allowed to become less close. According to Weismantel, such unity in food consumption expresses the intention to continue to share in the pooling of labor for production. Shared meals, which are the principal goals of household resource management in Zumbagua, imply a commitment to work together in the future.

Weismantel's account suggests that there is little conflict or overt struggle in Zumbaguan domestic life. Nevertheless, it appears that in order to establish their independence, recently married women must resist the efforts of their mothers and mothers-in-law to maintain control over their children and over their production of cooked food. Preferences for individual autonomy would seem to be present in each succeeding generation, even in such closely knit families as the ones described by Weismantel. Indeed, some desire for personal independence is presumably necessary in any society if new households are to be established at all.

In places where desires for personal autonomy are much stronger than they appear to be in Zumbagua, preferences for early independence by adult children may lead to open struggles between the generations. Olsen's description of changing household composition in Slavonia illustrates this point very clearly (this volume). Over the past century, Slavonian households have fallen in size from large extended family units to small extended family households and nuclear family households. This change was associated with the transition from peasant farming to an industrial mode of production. At the same time, new ideas of personal autonomy were introduced. Amounts of disposable wealth increased, and as they did individuals began to look to their own self interests, and to calculate the gains that might be made from household partition. A struggle between the generations ensued. Young men and their wives tried to set themselves up in independent households with as much personal property as possible. The premature partitioning of the household was resisted by the older generation, and rivalry between siblings manifested itself in a competitive struggle over the division of household resources.

According to Olsen, the new desires for autonomy did not entirely replace the old ideals of household integrity and their emphasis on the

group rather than the individual. Nevertheless, it seems clear that a
fundamental change in the principles of household organization did take
place with industrialization. That change can be described as a shift from
a moral economy to a political economy. Given sociologists' special
interests in industrial societies, it comes as no surprise that models of
political economy have been applied extensively in sociology, including
the study of households (Swedberg 1987; Cheal 1989a). The form of
the household economy as a political economy is specified in the following
model.

Political Economy
1. The actions of individuals are motivated by the rational pursuit of
   their self interests, in whatever context they find themselves.
2. Insofar as all individuals act in this way, transactions must take
   the form of exchanges of values. Participants in exchanges seek to
   obtain the best possible outcomes for themselves, and exchange
   relations are therefore competitive. The opposition of interests
   within the exchange process may result in an implicit negotiation
   of advantage, explicit bargaining, or open struggle.
3. Rational individuals will use all available means to pursue their
   personal interests. The net gains and losses that individuals receive
   from their transactions will therefore be determined by differences
   in manipulative skills, and by differences in the possession of
   resources that generate inequalities in power.
4. Resources become available to social actors through a social process
   of the division of labor and its products. Modes of production
   and appropriation, including property rights, therefore structure
   the directions in which resources flow.
5. In order to ensure the collusion of the powerless in unequal or
   otherwise disadvantageous exchanges, those who possess symbolic
   resources expound ideologies which mystify the true nature of
   exchange transactions. If revolutions in social consciousness occur
   that expose the underlying politico-economic realities, then force
   will be used to maintain existing systems of relations.

In this volume Lockwood presents a strong argument for the relevance
of the political economy model to households on the island of Tubuai.
Her particular concern is not the struggle for power between the
generations but the system of gender stratification, in which men and
women have different economic interests. Lockwood's analysis of the
political economy of intra-household gender relations focuses on the
sexual division of labor, and on corresponding relations of production,

patterns of resource control, and differential authority and decision-making power.

According to Lockwood, male domination in commodity producing peasant households is based in the control of cash-earning activities by men. On Tubuai, the introduction of new cash crops and wage employment was assimilated into a pre-existing household economy, in which men and women occupied different positions. Women's work is concentrated in or near the household, and includes food preparation, household maintenance and childcare. Men's time is therefore released for productive tasks requiring greater physical mobility, and men have been able to invest more labor than women in commercial agriculture and wage work. As a result, men usually control the cash incomes derived from household production, even when women's labor has contributed to the value of the products.

In the political economy of the Tubuai household, men and women are recognized as having separate economic interests. Individuals of either sex may claim the right to dispose of crops which they have planted, and typically Tubuai husbands and wives keep their incomes from cash crops separate. They consider the funds which they control to be their own, which has the systemic consequence of producing gender inequalities in consumption. Since men control the larger incomes, they are in a better position to purchase goods for themselves. Men and women in Tubuai tend to have different consumption preferences. Men's interests lie in liquor, gambling, and consumer goods that are exciting or entertaining. Women, on the other hand, are more interested than men in spending money on clothing and school supplies for children, as well as consumer durables that make household production more efficient. Not surprisingly, women are likely to be dissatisfied with their husbands if the latter do not consult them about personal expenditures. The principal dynamic factor in the household economy in Tubuai, it seems, is a political economy of interest opposition.

Parallel Systems of Household Organization

In this chapter we have shown that household economies can be described by two general models of structures of relations. The model of a moral economy and the model of a political economy that have been presented here differ in several respects. In an ideal-typical sense they identify contradictory bases of social organization. From the perspective of moral economy, household resource management is generated by shared meanings that govern the interactions between individuals occupying defined social statuses in a system of mutual aid. From the perspective of political economy, on the other hand, the organization of the household is determined by the negotiation of personal interests, within a socially distributed balance of power. The former model presumes the existence of consensus and cooperation, whereas the latter model assumes that dissensus and division are to be expected.

In later chapters the reader will find much evidence of the different images of households described by these contrasting models. For present purposes, it remains to ask one important question. Are models of moral economy and political economy mutually exclusive ways of describing households? Are they, perhaps, objective evolutionary structures that apply to unique household forms in different kinds of societies, and in different historical epochs? Or are they parallel systems of social organization, that are found to differing degrees everywhere?

There is much evidence to suggest that models of moral economy are most applicable to households involved in subsistence agriculture, whereas models of political economy have a special relevance for households involved in the exchange of labor and other commodities for money. (Such exchanges can be found in both capitalist and socialist societies, and under conditions of industrial or agricultural commodity production.) However, it would be inadvisable to leap from that evidence to a modernization theory in which the pre-commodified household = moral economy, and the commodified household = political economy. The reason for this is spelled out very clearly in Rutz's description of households among the urban middle class in Fiji (this volume). Under modern conditions, the Fijian household economy is structured by *both* principles of moral economy (the "Fijian way") and principles of political economy (the "money way").

The urban middle class depends heavily upon money incomes for household maintenance, including the purchase of houses. In Fiji, in most cases, the wage of the household head is insufficient to meet house purchase payments, and he must rely upon negotiated contributions from other household members. Co-resident daughters and sons, and their spouses, are therefore called upon to assume varying portions of household costs.

Although all employed members are expected to contribute to household maintenance, they do not benefit equally from the accumulation of capital which their payments make possible. Houses are usually owned outright by male heads, who usually cede them to their oldest sons. Daughters, and junior sons and their wives, recognize that the contributions they make to the purchase of "their" home are most unlikely to help them achieve personal financial independence. Indeed, the use of their wages in this way must make such independence less likely with each passing year. As a result, subordinate household members are frequently tempted to avoid meeting their monetary commitments to the household. Since they control their own incomes, and usually have their own bank accounts, these middle class Fijians are able to conceal portions of their incomes, which they retain for personal enjoyment.

At one level, we can see that the middle class household economy in Fiji is constituted by principles of political economy. Household resource management is subject to the calculation of individual interest, especially in the form of opposed interests of brothers and sisters, and of older and younger brothers. Yet, Rutz insists that this type of household is not organized simply as a political economy of opposition.

In Rutz's account of the Fijian middle class, there is little evidence of household fission in which young wage earners lay claim to financial independence by setting up their own households. Rather, it appears that subordinate members are usually persuaded by a rhetoric of loyalty and cooperation. Household heads articulate a discourse of authoritative allocation, which defines loyalty and cooperation as the taken-for-granted means by which the needs of every individual will be met. According to Rutz, the traditional Fijian discourse of resource management constructs an alternative source of meaning to that of the market economy of capitalist society. It ensures that the continuous recognition of extended kinship ties through norms of inclusion, and norms of exclusion (or closure) generate a system of reciprocal intergenerational transfers within the enduring social unit of the household. Within the discourse of Fijian custom, institutionalized descent ties modify market-based constructs of individualism in the direction of a moral economy of ritual obligations.

Conclusion

It seems that we are not, after all, bound to choose between moral economy and political economy as mutually exclusive principles for analyzing informal transactions (see also Cheal 1988; Etzioni 1988). Instead, we may find when all the evidence is in, that structures of moral economy and political economy are typically parallel systems of household organization. We can usefully conceive of the models presented here as contrasting sets of rules and resources, that are selectively drawn upon by social actors to achieve their purposes at hand, under conditions when no single strategy provides a permanent best solution.

The conclusion advanced here relies heavily upon studies of societies that have only recently been affected by the expansion of commodity production and wage employment. Shifting relations between structures of moral economy and structures of political economy are probably most evident in such circumstances. However, the insights gained from these studies are not likely to be limited to developing countries. They may also have something very important to say about everyday life in our own society. It may be that patterns of household resource management in contemporary North America are not well described either by a monolithic model of moral economy, or by a monolithic model of political economy. If so, then there is a need for social scientists from all disciplines to find out how these different sorts of rules are invoked, for they are likely to have quite different kinds of effects upon different categories of household members.

Notes

1. The author's work on households is supported by the Social Sciences and Humanities Research Council of Canada, Strategic Grants Program in Family and the Socialization of Children (Grant No. 498-85-0004 and Grant No. 498-86-0004).

References Cited

Ayers, Pat, and Jan Lambertz. 1986. "Marriage Relations, Money, and Domestic Violence in Working-Class Liverpool, 1919–39," in Jane Lewis (ed.), *Labour and Love*. Oxford: Blackwell. Pp. 195–219.

Brannen, Julia, and Gail Wilson, eds. 1987a. *Give and Take in Families*. London: Allen and Unwin.

_____. 1987b. "Introduction." in Julia Brannen and Gail Wilson (eds.), *Give and Take in Families*. London: Allen and Unwin. Pp. 1–17.

Caplovitz, David. 1979. *Making Ends Meet*. Beverly Hills: Sage.

Cheal, David. 1988. *The Gift Economy*. London and New York: Routledge.

_____. 1989a. "Theoretical Frameworks," in G.N. Ramu (ed.), *Marriage and the Family in Canada Today*. Scarborough, Ontario: Prentice-Hall. Pp. 19–34.

_____. 1989b. "A Value-Added Model of the Household Economy." Prepared for the Annual Conference of the British Sociological Association, Plymouth.

Daniels, Pamela, and Kathy Weingarten. 1984. "Mothers' Hours," in Patricia Voydanoff (ed.), *Work and Family*. Palo Alto, CA: Mayfield. Pp. 209–231.

Delphy, Christine. 1984. *Close to Home*. Amherst: University of Massachusetts Press.

Dulude, Louise. 1984. *Love, Marriage and Money*. Ottawa: Canadian Advisory Council on the Status of Women.

Edwards, Meredith. 1980. "Economics of Home Activities." *Australian Journal of Social Issues* 15: 5–16.

Eichler, Margrit. 1973. "Women as Personal Dependents," in Marylee Stephenson (ed.), *Women in Canada*. Toronto: New Press. Pp. 36–55.

Etzioni, Amitai. 1988. *The Moral Dimension*. New York: Free Press.

Finch, Janet. 1985. "Work, the Family and the Home." *International Journal of Social Economics* 12: 26–35.

Gallie, Duncan. 1985. "Social Change and Economic Life." *Quarterly Journal of Social Affairs* 1: 61–86.

Glendinning, Caroline, and Jane Millar, eds. 1987. *Women and Poverty in Britain.* Brighton: Wheatsheaf.

Gullestad, Marianne. 1984. *Kitchen-table Society.* Oslo: Universitetsforlaget.

Harris, Christopher C., and Lydia D. Morris. 1986. "Households, Labour Markets and the Position of Women," in Rosemary Crompton and Michael Mann (eds.), *Gender and Stratification.* Cambridge: Polity Press. Pp. 86–96.

Jain, Devaki, and Nirmala Banerjee, eds. 1985. *Tyranny of the Household.* New Delhi: Vikas.

Land, Hilary. 1983. "Poverty and Gender" in Muriel Brown (ed.), *The Structure of Disadvantage.* London: Heinemann. Pp. 49–71.

Meissner, Martin, Elizabeth Humphreys, Scott Meis, and William Scheu. 1975. "No Exit for Wives." *Canadian Review of Sociology and Anthropology* 12: 424–439.

Millar, Jane. 1988. "The Costs of Marital Breakdown," in Robert Walker and Gillian Parker (eds.), *Money Matters.* London: Sage. Pp. 99–114.

Moen, Phyllis, Edward Kain, and Glen Elder. 1983. "Economic Conditions and Family Life," in Richard Nelson and Felicity Skidmore (eds.), *American Families and the Economy.* Washington DC: National Academy Press. Pp. 213–254.

Morris, Lydia. 1985. "Responses to Redundancy." *International Journal of Social Economics* 12: 5–16.

———. 1987. "The Household in the Labour Market," in C.C. Harris (ed.), *Redundancy and Recession in South Wales.* Oxford: Blackwell. Pp. 127–140.

Pahl, Jan. 1980. "Patterns of Money Management within Marriage." *Journal of Social Policy* 9: 313–335.

———. 1988. "Earning, Sharing, Spending," in Robert Walker and Gillian Parker (eds.), *Money Matters.* London: Sage. Pp. 195–211.

Pahl, Ray. 1987. "Does Jobless Mean Workless? Unemployment and Informal Work." *Annals of the American Academy of Political and Social Science* 493: 36–46.

Price, John. 1975. "Sharing: The Integration of Intimate Economies." *Anthropologica* 17:3–27.

Redclift, Nanneke, and Enzo Mingione, eds. 1985. *Beyond Employment.* Oxford: Blackwell.

Risman, Barbara, and Pepper Schwartz, eds. 1989. *Gender in Intimate Relationships.* Belmont, CA: Wadsworth.

Roberts, Bryan, Ruth Finnegan, and Duncan Gallie, eds. 1985. *New Approaches to Economic Life.* Manchester: Manchester University Press.

Roberts, Elizabeth. 1986. "Women's Strategies, 1890–1940," in Jane Lewis (ed.), *Labour and Love.* Oxford: Blackwell. Pp. 223–247.

Rosen, Ellen. 1987. *Bitter Choices.* Chicago: University of Chicago Press.

Scott, James C. 1976. *The Moral Economy of the Peasant.* New Haven: Yale University Press.

Segalen, Martine. 1986. *Historical Anthropology of the Family.* Cambridge: Cambridge University Press.

Sharma, Ursula. 1986. *Women's Work, Class, and the Urban Household.* London and New York: Tavistock.

Sidel, Ruth. 1986. *Women and Children Last*. New York: Viking Penguin.

Siltanen, Janet. 1986. "Domestic Responsibilities and the Structuring of Employment," in Rosemary Crompton and Michael Mann (eds.), *Gender and Stratification*. Cambridge: Polity Press. Pp. 97–118.

Smith, Joan. 1987. "Transforming Households: Working-Class Women and Economic Crisis." *Social Problems* 34: 416–436.

Smith, Joan, Immanuel Wallerstein, and Hans-Dieter Evers, eds. 1984. *Households and the World-Economy*. Beverly Hills: Sage.

Swedberg, Richard. 1987. "Economic Sociology." *Current Sociology* 35: 1–215.

Thompson, E.P. 1971. "The Moral Economy of the English Crowd in the Eighteenth Century." *Past and Present* 50:76–136.

Wallman, Sandra. 1979. "Introduction," in Sandra Wallman (ed.), *Social Anthropology of Work*. London: Academic Press. Pp. 1–24.

———. 1984. *Eight London Households*. London and New York: Tavistock.

———. 1986. "The Boundaries of Household," in Anthony Cohen (ed.), *Symbolising Boundaries*. Manchester: Manchester University Press. Pp. 50–70.

Wilson, Gail. 1987. *Money in the Family*. Aldershot: Avebury.

3

Decision Making and Resource Flows Within the Household: Beyond the Black Box

Richard R. Wilk

Introduction

This paper is an experiment growing out of dissatisfaction with anthropological treatment of the household as an economic unit. Households are a problem for anthropologists for a number of reasons, historical, sociological and intellectual. In avoiding some of these problems, in going around them, we have left some significant gaps in ethnographic and ethnological knowledge. Our most glaring failure is the comparative study of household budgets, including the flows of resources and decisions about how to allocate and consume them.

In the meantime, other social scientists rush in where anthropologists fear to tread. Undeterred by epistemological uncertainty, sociologists, social psychologists, and a host of others in applied fields like consumer research, home economics, and family therapy have busily worked on the issues of how households make decisions, manage their budgets, organize their labor and time, and negotiate power and authority. Because most of this research reduces culture to a system of norms and roles, and fails to look beyond the American mainstream, it may seem naive and unsatisfying to anthropologists.

I do not pretend to command this vast and complex literature. But one goal of this paper is to tease out some of its major strengths and weaknesses, to show what is lacking and where anthropology can make a contribution. We certainly do not need to reinvent the wheel, but to mix a metaphor, we do not have to jump on a broken-down bandwagon either.

The more substantive goal of this paper is to suggest some tools and standards of comparison for household economies and budgets. Anthropology has a rich vocabulary of terms for describing and comparing kinship systems and behavior, but very few that can be applied to household systems. I will put some concepts borrowed from ecology to use in suggesting how this particular gap can be filled.

The Black Box

The problem of household budgeting and decision making was forced on me during ethnographic research on the adaptations of Kekchi Maya swidden farmers in southern Belize to economic change (Wilk 1981, 1984, 1986, 1989). Some households were taking advantage of new economic opportunities, growing new crops using agrochemicals, expanding their cash crop production, setting up small retail shops, trading in hogs, and buying trucks for hauling freight. Other households with the same family composition and the same access to labor and basic resources, spent most of their cash income on consumer goods and foods. Each household made different decisions about mixing subsistence production and participation in the cash economy, but some were actively accumulating capital while others did not.

I could find no differences in 'entrepreneurial spirit' between the members of the two kinds of households, nor were there sharp difference in desires for cash income or consumer goods. Rather, what enabled some households to invest their cash income in new economic enterprises, appeared to be the way they managed their household economies. Simply put, some households pooled their labor and money and channeled it into productive investments, while other households did not. Within the same culture, with the same set of kinship roles and the same normative values of how household members should behave, there was still variation in household behavior. I could not reduce this variation to individual personalities, to differential exposure to external norms, or to different modes of articulation with capitalist forms of production.

A number of authors have focused attention on the structural problems that households face in combining subsistence production with market-oriented farming or wage labor (eg. Collins 1986; Meillasoux 1981; Adams 1988; Painter 1984). World-systems theorists have recently identified the household as the crucial social unit where pooling of different forms of income from household and non-household production reproduces labor (Smith et al. 1984; Young et al. 1981). Recent marxist and feminist literature gives a great deal of attention to the division of labor within the household, and at the ways that power and production roles change during proletarianization (eg. Hartmann 1981; Minge 1986; Creighton 1980). Yet others have looked at the changing economic basis of power and inequality in the household (Young et al. 1981; Curtis 1986; Bould 1982).[1]

This work makes important points about what households do, how they fit into larger-scale processes, and how their economic and social functions change over time. But the details of what goes on inside households, of how they manage and combine their production, exchange, investment, inheritance, sharing, minding, pooling, preparing, and consuming, are rarely the central focus (see Van Esterik 1985: 79). Anthropology has tended to treat each of these activities and functions separately, leaving their conjunction untouched. Households end up being treated as things instead of activities and relationships (Wilk and Netting 1984).

Obstacles

The different behavior of Kekchi households can only be explained by what takes place inside them, in the intimate space of 'householding.' But we cannot break open the "black box" of the household simply by refining existing typologies. Households that may look the same, with the same number of members and the same kinship structure, at the same stage of the developmental cycle, can have very different economic structures. They may organize their work, and apportion costs and benefits quite differently.

Two theoretical issues block an analytical approach to intra-household processes. First is the question of whether or not households function as corporate social units. Do the members of households act in their own self interest, or are they behaving in an altruistic (or dominated) way, acting to further the interests of the group at the expense of their own (see Laslett 1984; Creighton 1980; Anderson 1971; Peters 1986)? The first option suggests that the individual should be the unit of study, and the second implies that we can treat the household as an economic unity, a proxy individual with what economists call a joint utility function (Becker 1981; see Folbre 1984 for discussion).

The "new home economics" based on neoclassical approaches to individual behavior, has tried to show that household behavior, and the gender-based division of labor within the household, can be generated from individual rational goal seeking (eg. Blau and Ferber 1986). While this mode of analysis has led to some convincing arguments about, for example, the costs and benefits of raising children (Schultz 1981; Caldwell 1981), values and utilities are assumed to be exogenous. The question of where the values come from is left out of the analysis completely, a crippling problem when studying social change.

The anthropological view has tended to stress altruism, rather than self interest, as the basis of household behavior. Sahlins' 'domestic mode of production' defines domestic behavior as inherently unselfish, founded on generalized reciprocity and uncalculated pooling (1972: 196). Individuals use a different economic logic, founded on morality rather than self interest, in dealing with their close kin.

For anthropologists, therefore, raising the issue of intra-household resource distribution leads into uncomfortable territory. It requires that we pry into the details of altruism, generosity, kinship, and the moral basis of social life (see Bloch 1973). The degree to which individuals are willing to submerge their own interests in that of a collectivity is often a matter of principle instead of the object of empirical research. Medick and Sabean label the two poles of opinion as interest and emotion, and find they are often treated as opposites, when in fact all domestic life is composed of both in a rich dialectic (1984: 10–16).

Marxist analysis has tended to focus on issues of class and increasingly gender, in determining how households respond to economic change. But the world systems theorists and dependencistas still tend to assume that within the household a moral or pre-capitalist economy prevails. The survival of peasant enterprises and simple commodity production and the continuing subordination and exploitation of the peasantry depend on the household's non-capitalist rationality (see Lehman 1986). In contrasting this literature with traditional neoclassical approaches, however, Folbre observes that:

> Whether or not peasants and capitalists, households and firms . . . respond in similar ways to economic constraints, it is not clear whether they respond as individual households or as members of economic classes, or both. But both theoretical perspectives tend to treat the household in much the same way as traditional Neoclassical economists treat the capitalist firm—as a black box whose internal workings are uninteresting and irrelevant. (1984: 23)

This lack of attention becomes especially crippling in trying to understand issues of equity and inequality. Who gets the benefits of increased income? Who will eat and who will go hungry? Van Esterik says "The subject has become everyone's "Black Box"—the great residual category." (1985: 79)

The second obstacle is the problem of setting boundaries around the household unit. How can we talk about what is inside the household if we can't agree on the boundary between inside and outside? What functions or attributes can provide a uniform guide to membership? As Laslett (1984) and Sahlins (1972) point out, there is no society in which households are totally isolated and self-sufficient. Households are always connected to each other, and penetrated by other affiliations through age, kinship, gender and class. In a number of cultures, especially those in west Africa, individuals may belong to a number of domestic units. The actual conjugal unit may be of little economic importance in their lives (eg. Woodford-Berger 1981; Guyer 1981, 1986). The slippery and insubstantial nature of many households leads many to question its corporate nature and its usefulness as a unit of analysis (see Wilk and Netting 1984).

The focus on the household as the unit of production and distribution often appears, in this light, to be ethnocentric.

> . . . many analysts of the peasant economy and household production appear to be mesmerized by the concrete existence of the household as a social form in all strata of the socioeconomic structure, in many historical and economic circumstances. This leads to. . .the treatment of the household as a black box. The changing nature of the production, distribution and consumption relations within the household, especially as they are affected by its position in the overall socioeconomic structure, or the changes in that structure over time, are rarely dealt with in many of these models. (Whitehead 1981: 89)

These problems challenge us to refine our concept of the household and re-examine its definition, and in doing this we need to pay much closer attention to what goes on among household members. We need to see the household as social relations and practices that integrate a number of functions and activities, distributing the products of labor, and allocating work and resources. A focus on integrative activities, on the ways that things are shared, and the ways decisions are made, is logically inseparable from the issue of household boundaries.

The inner workings of the household have not been completely ignored by ecological and economic anthropologists. Attention has been paid to the ways that the labor of household members is managed and apportioned to various tasks (eg. Barlett 1982; Maclachlan 1983), the ways that property and wealth are managed and transmitted between household members (egs. Goody 1977; Carter 1984), the ways that food is apportioned among members for consumption (eg. Van Esterik 1985), and the ways that rights to the use of household resources are divided between members (eg. McMillan 1986).

Nevertheless these separate pieces have not been assembled into a model of the household as a system. In anthropology, the beginnings of such a household ecology can be found in studies of consumer/worker ratios in households, Chayanovian balancing of labor and resources, and the juggling of waged and unwaged labor in 'simple commodity production' (all in some way building on Sahlins' discussion of the domestic mode of production [1973]). These studies are implicitly concerned with the balance of resources, labor, and consumption within households, and recognize that the household is not a closed system. But the 'domestic mode of production' has itself not been cracked open, and the conceptual tools of ecological anthropology have not been applied to the contents.

What is peculiar is that anthropology has developed comparative techniques and terminology for almost every aspect of human culture *except* the daily conduct of household relationships and the handling of funds. There is no comparative 'Home Economics' on a par with comparative studies of systems of production. It seems odd that the very heart of domestic life, the daily activities and interactions that are the 'habitus' of the household, is not an ethnological subject in and of itself.[2] We need a systematic language to fill this gap. Useful concepts can be found in the work on household decision making in consumer research and the ecological study of energy and resource flows within ecosystems.

Household Decision Making

Anthropological interest in household decision making can be traced back to studies of post-marital residence choice (eg. Korn 1975; Goodenough 1955; Barth 1967; Ross 1973). More recently, the study of economic change and innovation has led many to study of choice and decision making (see Cancian 1972; Barlett 1980, 1982, Orlove 1980). Formal modeling and graphic methods have been used to show the crucial factors affecting decisions.

But the range of choices analyzed in this way has been limited, concentrating on discrete choices among defined alternatives, or on the allocation of a finite quantity (especially labor and land) among a number of alternative uses (Nardi 1983). "Strategies" are often post-hoc deductions based on actual performance, rather than something discovered through ethnography (Schmink 1984: 95). These unitary strategies conceal dissent, confusion, and the complex processes by which goals are set and solutions are structured (Mathews 1987).

While decision theorists in anthropology treat households and individuals as the crucial players in economic adaptation, group decision processes have largely been ignored. Often a single individual in the household is singled out as the decision maker; between the farm and this lone farmer, the household gets squeezed out (eg. Gladwin and Zabawa 1987). The household is depicted as a single entity, or the kinds of interactions between members are subsumed under the term of 'generalized reciprocity,' assuming that everything is shared equally in a primitive Communism, while the term exchange is reserved for what goes on between households (Hardesty 1977: 82).[3]

Consumer researchers have given close and detailed attention to a particular kind of household decision making—purchasing behavior—in Euro-American households (O'Connor et al. 1983; Davis 1976). They have been motivated by the desire to predict purchasing behavior, especially in response to recent changes in American household composition and organization (see Roberts and Wortzel 1984). In the process they have generated a wealth of concepts and tools that can be used to study cross-cultural household patterns.

At its best, consumer research approaches ethnographic detail in discussing the ways that purchasing decisions are made within households. Topics include the different means of group decision making, including bargaining, consensus-making, and negotiation, and the variety of means which husbands and wives use (from threats to barter) to influence each other (Spiro 1983; Ferber and Lee 1974). The research asks what kinds of household decisions are made by a group ("syncratic" or consensual), and which kinds are made by husband or wife alone ("autocratic" or accommodative) (Ferber 1973; Bonfield et al. 1984; Green et al. 1983; Douglas-Tate et al. 1984). These sophisticated typologies of modes of decision making, conflict, and the different roles played within household often draw on game theory and cognitive studies of choice. A major research question is why some households are characterized by conflict and disagreement, while others handle decisions in a routine fashion, why some households are highly structured and others are informal (reviewed in Bonfield et al. 1984).

Some of the more interesting studies propose that American households cope with disagreement by specialization, with husbands and wives each taking different roles at different points in the decision process, for example, initiator, shopper, gatekeeper, and information seeker (Sternthal and Craig 1982; Hempel 1974; O'Connor et al. 1983). Park suggests that some important decisions that appear to involve both husband and wife are not made jointly at all; instead the individuals pursue their own decisions, while attempting to minimize conflict, in a recursive, discontinuous process (1982). While husband and wife may end up thinking they made a decision together, they actually pursued a "disjointed, unstructured, and incremental strategy," the main goal of which was to "muddle through," keeping the marriage going whatever the actual decision reached (1982: 52). Thus, household decisions are seen as inherently bivocal and recursive; they are simultaneously concerned with their ostensible object, and with maintaining or changing the household itself.

This school of research also has its problems. Though self-reports of decision making are unreliable and spouses rarely agree on what happened, most studies use self-reported survey responses instead of recording actual behavior. The resulting models depict household decision making as a linear process with a beginning and an end, rather than as parts of continuing social relationships.

A more fundamental problem stems from the intellectual roots of this research in social psychology and social exchange theory. The source of variation is always sought in measurable variables like age, occupational status, and income. Strategies of decision making are often simplistically classified as either husband dominant, wife dominant, or joint. Then exchange theory (Heer 1963; Spiro 1983) or resource theory (Blood and Wolfe 1960; Davis 1976; O'Connor 1963; Rodman 1972) is used to explain patterns of occurrence. The gist of both theories is that the balance of power and influence belongs to the spouse who brings the most economic and educational resources into the marriage (see Oppong 1970; Scanzoni 1972). These common sense notions (similar to those of the 'new home economists') contradict anthropological studies that find household roles and power firmly entrenched in wider cultural and social concepts like gender and age (eg. Hartmann 1981; Curtis 1986; Leacock 1986). Those studies that recognize the cultural nature of household roles tend to reduce it to a single unidirectional variable, often called 'traditional role ideology' (Davis 1976; Green et al. 1983; Kenkel 1961).

The lack of a concept of culture or social structure cripples the consumer research approach to household decision making and economic allocation.[4] Lacking a comparative sample of households in other cultures, or a concept of corporate social structure as instituted process, each actor is seen as an isolated economic node, guided only by norms and values. The major mode of analysis is to classify the nodes into empirical 'types,' which are then correlated with an arbitrary selection of economic and social constructs and measures, called 'variables' (Ferber 1973; Roberts and Wortzel 1984).[5]

To summarize, consumer research has elaborated a set of concepts and tools for understanding certain kinds of household decision-making in a narrowly defined cultural context. Anthropologists would find many of the goals of consumer research in studying American households to be rather trivial (for example, the question of who holds the balance of power in decisions to buy soap). Nevertheless, the descriptive tools and vocabulary they have developed can form the basis for cross-cultural studies and ethnological analysis of group decision-making, even if consumer researchers have not taken on this task themselves. I will not pursue this further here, but will instead move on to borrowing some more familiar tools and concepts from ecological anthropology.

An Ecological Approach

Ecological anthropology offers concepts and tools that can be used to study the internal operations of households and the ways they change. Most of these ideas come directly from biological ecology, but like most ecological anthropologists I will treat them as heuristic tools and analogies (Moran 1984a: xv).

The boundary problem mentioned above has been persistent in household studies. How can we treat households as corporate budget units when they are so interconnected and their boundaries are permeable? If instead we treat households as *systems* analogous to ecosystems, the problem of the discreteness of the household becomes less pressing, and even expectable. Ecosystems are not naturally bounded units either. We put arbitrary lines around sub-units for analytical purposes (Moran 1984b: 19, 1982: 9–11). Closure can never be assumed, though degrees of permeability can be defined. An analogy between ecosystems and household systems therefore suggests that we should place boundaries where we want during our analysis, as long as we remember the boundaries are arbitrary (even if they are emicly specified), and specify the flows across them (Golley 1984: 44).

Ecology also offers tools for describing discrete systems and the ways they inter-relate, without obscuring the dynamic and changeable nature of those relationships. A principle method is formal modeling (Smith 1984: 53, Moran 1982), using a variety of graphic and statistical methods to simplify and represent the systems under study. While biological ecology has tended to concentrate on models of energy flow, and some ecological anthropologists have also modeled the flow of energy within cultural systems (Ellen 1982: 96–109), other kinds of human interactions can be modeled. A major goal has been to make the models less static, and more useful in depicting socially relevant flows and connections (for example Foster's use of network models [1984]). The rest of this paper will draw selectively on consumer research and ecological anthropology to model intra-household processes in several ways. Some of the symbols I use are loosely based on those of Odum (1971 also Moran 1982: 82–90).

Figure 3.1 is a model of the flow of resources, and the major decision points in the Anglo-American household, as usually assumed in consumer research and home economics (eg. Fitzsimmons and Williams 1973; Ferber 1974), and in some anthropological studies (Lorensen et al. n.d.). Flows of cash and labor from household members enter a single general

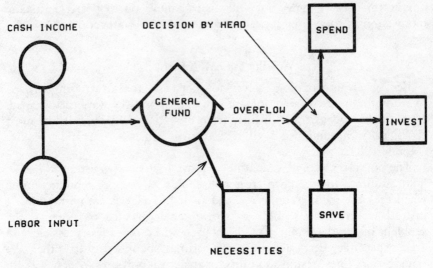

CASH INCOME

DECISION BY HEAD

SPEND

GENERAL FUND

OVERFLOW

INVEST

LABOR INPUT

NECESSITIES

SAVE

DETERMINED BY ENGEL'S LAW

Figure 3.1 The Normative model of the American household, as usually assumed in the social sciences.

fund (using Odum's symbol for a 'storage' function). A proportion of this fund is drained off for necessities (determined by 'Engel's Law', which states that the proportion of income spent on necessities goes down as the total income goes up), and the leftover, the overflow, is apportioned to different uses by the household head, or the 'family financial officer,' to use the language of consumer research (Prais and Houthaker 1971).

This model lies behind the research agenda of consumer research, and many problems stem from using it as a model for all households. The crucial node is the decision box, and most consumer research is concerned with how this allocation function works. Most 'resource theory' in consumer research looks for linkages between who produces the inputs to the general fund, and who gets to allocate those resources (eg. Davis 1976), or at the ways that household members interact in making those allocation decisions (eg. Olshavsky and King 1984). Anthropologists and economists have often assumed that household budgets also take the form of a general fund or pool. McGuire et al. (1986) see household change in Mexico as a product of changes in the kinds of contributions to the pool (ie. cash vs labor), as well as in the kinds of kin who are contributing to and drawing from the pool (men, women and children). In other words, they are not concerned with the shape and nature of

OBLIGATED FUND MODEL OF HOUSEHOLD BUDGET

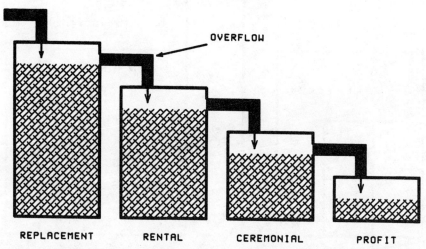

Figure 3.2 Household budgets as a series of funds, as proposed by Wolf (1966). Overflow from each fund goes into the next lowest in priority.

the pool, only with the kinds of things going into it and who provides them.

This 'general fund' model of household budgets has been challenged by anthropologists working in Africa, who have found the notion of a single household fund or pool, and a single nexus for allocation decisions to be inaccurate, and deceptive in understanding household change (see Moock 1986, Guyer 1981, 1986). Their objection has much wider applicability, because some degree of individual ownership and self-provisioning is found in every culture studied by anthropologists (eg. children often procure food that is not contributed to the household pool). The single household fund is as difficult a concept as the idea of perfect altruism or complete self-interest.

More accurate models for the ways that household funds are differentiated can be found implicitly in the work of several anthropologists. Figure 3.2 is derived from Eric Wolf's (1966) proposal that the the peasant household maintains a series of different funds, each obligated for a particular purpose. He implies that they are hierarchically arranged by order of priority, as I have shown here with the notion of overflow. Once the most basic fund is filled, the overflow goes to the next, and so on, leaving discretionary funds for the last. This model implies that for peasants the allocation of funds is largely pre-determined, and that the only place for the exercise of decision making power is with the small 'profit' fund left when the crop is in.[6]

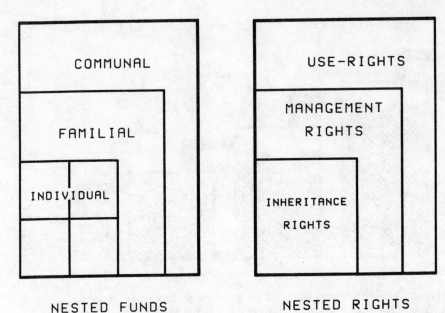

Figure 3.3 Two ways to model household economies as a series of nested boxes. On the left, funds are held individually or pooled at the familial or household level. On the right, the household is differentiated into concentric spheres of rights to household resources.

However, this model also implies that the rights to household funds are equally shared among all household members. Figure 3.3 shows two ways to model total household resources as a series of nested boxes. On the left we have a system of nested funds, as found in some African households (see McMillan 1986). A pool of land, money, food, and goods belongs to an entire multiple-family household, and then each nuclear family unit within the household has its own pool. Finally, each adult also controls personal property and funds. As Whitehead points out, inequality between the sexes may be manifested when women are expected to donate their earnings to the household pool, while men get to keep their earnings and spend them at their own discretion (1981).

But ownership and control of property are not absolutes. On the right is an adaptation of Goody's idea that large households are often internally differentiated by different kinds of rights to real property (1973). For example, in 17th century rural Japan (Smith 1959), all household members had rights to the use of houses, tools, and land, but only collaterals of the male household head had the right to be heard in management decisions, and only some patrilineal descendants of the head had rights of ownership extending into the future through inheritance. Both of these nested models carry clear implications for studies of decision making, ranking, and authority.

Even these divisions are not sufficient in many cases. In much of west Africa, the ownership and management of real property is not vested in the household at all, but in the lineage, and individual funds are not in any way nested inside household funds. Ashanti households described by Abu (1983) are modeled in Figure 3.4. Lineages own property, individuals own property, and in many cases married couples also acquire household property. These funds are distinct, but there is a degree of overlap and transfer by virtue of an individual's participation in all three at any one time. Lineages are linked to each other by a series of individual and household funds.

Maps of funds are static and say little about the flows between funds and people, and about the purposes for which the funds are used or obligated. Figure 3.5 is a flow chart for an Ashanti household at the stage when children (represented at the right), are too young to work. This model shows the flows of work and funds and makes the decision points clear, disclosing an asymmetry where men and their lineage do not contribute equally with women to the maintenance of children.

Still, this model makes no clear distinction between different kinds of funds. Figure 3.6 is modified to show that there are both capital funds used infrequently to buy goods, and operating funds used daily to buy food. Men contribute to a household fund of capital and permanent goods of value, while women do not (Abu 1983). Women put more into the household maintenance fund than their husbands. Both husband and wife eat out of this fund, which the wife controls. Obviously this flow chart would be considerably more complicated if step-children and polygynous marriages were included, and if the contributions of grown children to the household budget were added, but even these simple charts provide a basis for comparing the dynamics of different household forms.

In some societies (for example the Japanese Dozoku, urban Ashanti and Effutu fisherfolk in Ghana), there is no communal household property at all. With duolocal residence, husband and wife do not even share the use of a house. In these cases, conjugal economic relationships are best modeled as exchanges (as suggested in Clark 1986). Figure 3.7 shows the flow of labor, goods and cash in marriages among the coastal Effutu in Ghana (Hagan 1983). Males live in patrilineal mens' houses, while women live in matrilineal women's houses. Children live with the mother until about age ten, when boys go to live in their father's house. Husbands and wives have two different kinds of exchange relationship. During the fishing season the husband gives his share of the fish he catches (with

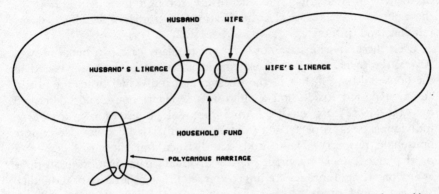

Figure 3.4   A model of property owenership in Ashanti marriage from Abu (1983). Individual and household funds link property-owning lineages.

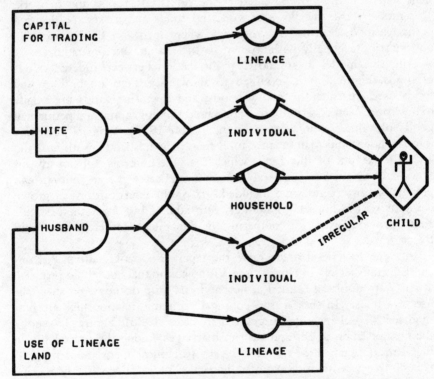

Figure 3.5   Flows between different funds in Ashanti marriage, showing the unequal contributions to child care between husband and wife.

FLOWS TO DIFFERENT KINDS OF FUND IN ASHANTI MARRIAGES

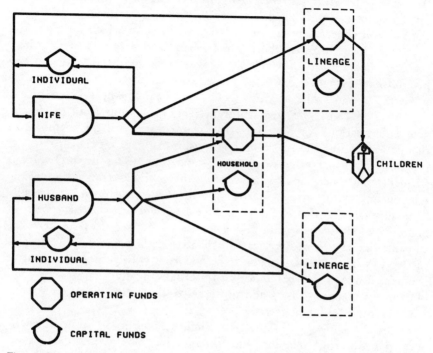

Figure 3.6 Ashanti marriage, showing different kinds of funds, and flows of resources between them.

MARITAL EXCHANGE AMONG THE EFFUTU

Figure 3.7 Marriage modeled as a series of exchanges, among the Effutu fisherfolk (from Hagan 1983). There is no household fund.

his agnates) to his wife, who smokes and markets them. At the end of the season she gives him the cash value of the fish (discounted below open market price). This delayed exchange is counted as a debt if its not paid on time (there are many other cultures in which husband and wife make loans to each other). The husband and wife also have a direct exchange relationship in which she provides one meal a day to him and his sons, in exchange for cash. He is also supposed to give her cash payments towards the feeding, schooling, and medical costs of his daughters and his younger children. The most important *productive* economic relations for both men and women are with the members of their lineages, but the marriage relationship forms a crucial link in the processing and marketing of a seasonal and variable resource. Divorce is frequent, and men and women often have single-stranded exchange relationships with partners outside the marriage, as shown on the left.

It may appear that we are dealing here with two basic types of household; one like the Effutu which has no household pool or fund, and one like the Euro-American single-account household. But most of the world's households actually lie in between, with some communal or conjugal funds, and other funds that are individually managed. A combination of mapping funds and flows helps distinguish between various kinds of mixed-fund households.

Figure 3.8 shows a working-class English household (summarized by Segalen 1986: 266). The husband splits his income, keeping part for his own personal discretionary fund, and giving the rest to his wife as a housekeeping fund for food and daily expenses. Part of his discretionary income goes for personal items like beer and tobacco, and another part goes for periodic household expenses like large bills, furniture, or educational costs. His personal expenditures are his own business, but the control of the household fund is negotiated between husband and wife. The wife's wage goes into the "housekeeping money" (which presumably pays the costs of substituting services like child care for her own labor). Children's wages go to the mother, who puts some in the housekeeping money, and returns some as allowance. This model is a much more accurate representation than Figure 3.1, and it shows that the issue of control is more complex than is often assumed; there are both group and individual decisions. The model also serves as a better basis for predicting what will happen if some of the flows change (see Whitehead 1981).

These maps of exchange relationships are especially useful in understanding households in parts of the world where long-term wage migration is common. In the rural Caribbean, for example, men may leave and send cash payments to a number of households where they have children,

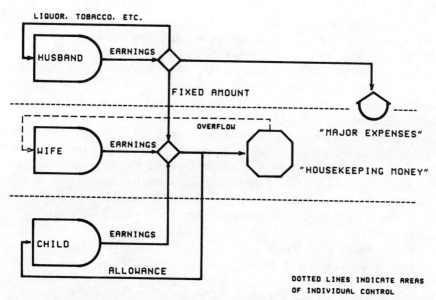

Figure 3.8 A model of funds in a working-class English household, as discussed by Segalen (1986). The dotted lines show the boundaries between areas of individual control.

sisters, or parents, and women may leave their children with a caretaker and do the same (good examples are Rubenstein 1987 and Palacio 1982). Households that may look the same in terms of social *structure* (ie. the number of people and their relationships to each other) may actually prove to have quite different economic structures, when mapped out in this way.

Conclusion: A Return to the Kekchi

This discussion is meant to be provocative rather than conclusive. My goal is to show that households can be productively seen in other ways than just through lists of activities, members, inputs and outputs. In particular, we need to differentiate cash, labor, and material flows, and to define (and perhaps create symbols for) more kinds of funds and decision processes. It should be possible to distinguish the degree to which the household budget and household processes are *structured* as opposed to being amorphous. For example, Segalen (1986: 269) finds that lower middle class French households have very organized budgets, while upper middle class households handle every expenditure through a separate decision process. She also points out that models must incorporate aspects of rhythm and timing if they are to be complete.

Another issue that needs further investigation is that of real vs ideal behavior. Abbott (1976) found that there were consistent and patterned differences between cultural ideals and actual practice in the gender-based division of authority in Kikuyu households. Yet even her measures of 'real' were self-reported behavior. There are actually three levels of data that need to be taken into account therefore; the stated cultural ideal, the self-reported instance (how people perceive their own actions), and the actual behavior. We should not expect congruence between any of the three levels. The major challenge remains the elicitation and recording of actual decision-making behavior. Discourse analysis may be our most powerful tool in this task (eg. Mathews 1987; Gaskins and Lucy 1986).

The ultimate goal of this attempt at a household ecology is not just a cross-cultural catalog of the various forms that households can assume. As Firth pointed out in his study of Tikopia, households adapt to changing circumstances by changing their internal arrangements, their structures of sharing and decision making, to serve new purposes (see Lees and Bates 1984). Economic change leads to alterations in boundaries, in the economic bargains and balances between household members, in the allocation of labor and resources to different funds, and in the economic roles taken by different people (McKee 1986 and Jones 1986 for excellent examples). By adding this kind of analysis to existing studies of household decision making, households can be seen to do much more than passively adapt to changing environments.

In the Kekchi case, and perhaps in others (Hyden 1986; Rudie 1971) the form of the household ecology actually restricts and channels the household's ability to adapt to new circumstances, and affects the kinds of strategic choices made by members. To return to my brief example at the beginning of the paper, I should ask once again, why some Kekchi households are able to pool resources and allocate them to productive investment, while other households do not.

One part of the problem is that money, labor, and food are not equivalent within the household economy. As money becomes more important in the household, it provides an uncontrolled and therefore objective standard of value that undercuts existing concepts of equivalence (Wilk 1989; Maher 1981). As the cultural definitions of costs and benefits change, the balances and bargains that underlie the household economy are also changing. Monetary values have certainly penetrated some households more quickly and deeply than others. A crucial event is often when sons who still live in the household take wage-earning jobs. Parents must then decide how to treat those earnings, and reach some accommodation with the son about them.[7] But even among the households where some members earn wages, there is a good deal of variation in how wages, income from crops sales, and subsistence production are pooled and managed. The two most common Kekchi systems are shown in Figures 3.9 and 3.10.

In Figure 3.9 we have a patriarchal system where the male household head controls a single central fund which includes most agricultural products, cash from selling crops, and the cash income earned by all members, including children. He allocates some of the agricultural products and some cash income to an operating fund which is managed by his wife. She transforms the agricultural products into food, and spends the cash on clothing and other consumable goods as needed. The labor she spends in raising pigs does not result in autonomous cash income, for the money from selling pigs goes into the central fund. Similarly, sons' cash earnings go into the central fund, where they are allocated by the male household head.

Decision making about expenditures from the central fund in these households tends to be authoritarian, and wives and children often resort to overt bargaining to get cash for their own personal use ("I will provide meals so you can participate in the ritual dance, if you will give me money for the childrens' schoolbooks."). The man has a general obligation to meet his family's needs, but these needs are vague and nonspecifically defined, and are often themselves the subject of dispute. Because women and children lose control over the products of their labor when they contribute to the central fund, both try to divert some of their production into their own individual fund; sons keep some of their earnings for themselves, and women sell small amounts of eggs, forest and craft products, and food in order to get their own cash.

In Figure 3.10, the central fund and the operating fund have been merged, and management is not patriarchaly controlled by the male household head. All household members contribute to the single fund, and share rights to its use. Each decision is a matter of joint management, conceived as a group decision over group resources, rather than as a process of bargaining between individuals over funds controlled individually. While the operating fund could be analytically separated, because it is not emicly separate, goods and money can flow back and forth between them on an ad hoc basis. School supplies, for example, are paid from the household general fund, rather than from the wife's operating fund. Paying for school supplies is therefore a household decision, rather than an occasion for the wife to ask the husband for money.[8]

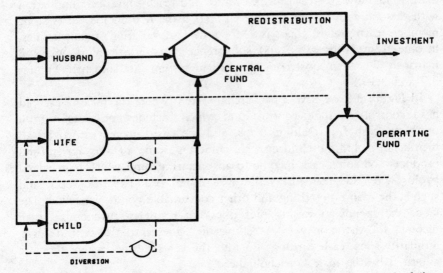

Figure 3.9 Kekchi households with central funds under the control of the male household head.

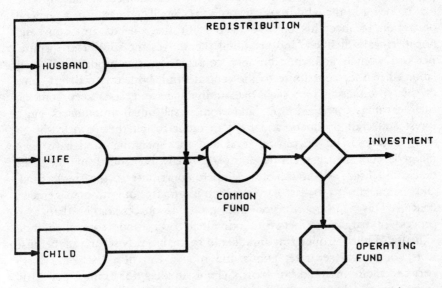

Figure 3.10 Kekchi households with a central fund that is treated as a common fund under the joint control of all household members.

In households with budget structures like Figure 3.10, all household members have a say in the management of the central fund, but this greater participation is balanced by less autonomy. The male household head is less autonomous in controlling household resources, and women and children do not have their own individual funds to manage as they want.

In the short run the patriarchal household budget is capable of motivating and concentrating its resources for particular goals, like buying young hogs to feed, or box hives for keeping bees. But these projects run into problems, because while they require the help and labor of all household members, they are not household projects, but those of the patriarch. The patriarch must now convince, cajole, threaten, or bargain to get his wife and children to tend the hogs, separate the honey, or process the cocoa. What is their incentive? Only the promise that some of the increased income will improve their standard of living, but they have only vague 'moral' claims on this fund. Often the new income just goes back into the business—his business. The result is resistance; everyone is reluctant to contribute their labor, their products, or their money to the household pool. In the long term, wives and daughters cut back their labor in household production, and hoard whatever resources they can keep for themselves. Sons work on their own fields if they can, and they keep aside their profits or their wages. Each person tries to conceal at least a portion of their income. As soon as sons have a chance, they leave the household to set up their own farm, so they will have some control over the products of their labor. As a business, the household fails in the long run because it provides no incentives to its members.

In the long run the most successful households have adopted the second form of budgeting. In these households there is more overt discussion of goals and expenditures. The household may be slow to take new opportunities or expand its enterprises in response to changes in the market or the labor supply. But when the members of the household agree to pursue a strategy, from buying a horse to transport crops, to planting several acres of cocoa, or opening a small village shop, they act together. The consequence is that each household member is more willing to contribute extra work time, extra effort, extra attention, to the project.

Many Kekchi men begin projects with income-earning in mind, but later abandon them because they did not have time to manage them during the dry season when they have to devote full time to subsistence farming. They were unable to get their wives and children committed to the project. Managing both income-generating projects and subsistence production, in this environment, requires a great deal of coordination and informal task-sharing that must be based on mutual interest. Households that organize their budgets along the centralized lines depicted in Figure 3.10 have an easier time promoting this mutual interest. Household ecology is therefore a crucial variable in the economic success or failure of households. Articulating two economies, subsistence and cash, is a difficult and complex management task that places very specific demands on the household budgeting process.

My analysis of Kekchi household budgeting turns some of Sahlins' ideas about the dynamics of the domestic mode of production around. Sahlins argues that generalized reciprocity within and between households—pooling—reduces the incentive to produce (1973: 84–88,94). Households set their production targets in relation to other households, below their optimum capacity. The mechanical solidarity of the household encompasses a simple gender-based division of labor that is linked to low work intensity. Sahlins implies that relations of authority and inequality, of coercion, extraction and competition, provide the incentive for increased production. While the issue of how demand for goods is generated and mediated within the household remains unsettled (and important), the Kekchi case shows that in specific circumstances, more equal pooling of household labor and resources may increase production, and authoritarian relationships may lead to a long-term decline.

My fieldwork among the Kekchi did not concentrate on budgeting and this sketch is based largely on anecdotal material and study of relationships between fathers and sons (see Wilk 1989). A true test of the hypothesis would require a census of family budget strategies and a long-term correlation of these strategies with various indices of economic success. Nevertheless, this mode of analysis points out the need to go beyond the study of personality or of the composition of households in understanding economic and social change. It may be that a great deal of household-centered research has focused on the wrong variables. Perhaps studies of household typology and change would be more productive is they shifted from descriptions of kinship composition, and household size or developmental cycles, to patterns of sharing, exchange and decision making.

Acknowledgments

A preliminary draft of this paper was read at the 1987 American Anthropological Association Meetings, in a symposium on intra-household processes. The revision has benefited from the comments and papers presented by the others in that symposium. The paper also depends heavily on insights accumulated while working with Robert Netting on other papers, and on his comments on an earlier draft. Ben Orlove, Henry Rutz, and Peggy Barlett have also made extremely helpful comments. Please do not place any burden of responsibility for the ideas and arguments presented here on any of those who have helped.

Notes

1. Much of the recent literature on the role of households in capitalist penetration has little historical depth, counterpoising the timeless encapsulated self-sufficient household of pre-capitalist times with the households of a fully-monetized proletariat or marginal peasant society (eg. Wallerstein 1984). My historical study of the Kekchi economy found, on the contrary, that their households had been mixing various forms of subsistence farming, cash crop production, and wage labor for at least 400 years (Wilk 1986). Yet Kekchi villages still seem traditional and unacculturated, and each time a new wave of peripheral-capitalist development washes over them, it appears to be the first time they have emerged from the primeval forest.

2. I have appropriated Bourdieu's (1977) term here with some understanding of its implications. I find his concept fruitful in understanding how seemingly corporate and structured aspects of households exist without being normatively determined.

3. The issue has some theoretical weight since it is parallel to the controversy about group selection in evolutionary ecology. What is the unit of human adaptation (see Lees and Bates 1984)? Some researchers feel that treating the household (or any group) as an adaptive unit raises the issue of altruism. In rejecting altruism or group selection, they assume that groups themselves do not adapt, except through the cumulative action of individuals or the manipulative actions of powerful individuals (Ellen 1982: 246). In this way the issue of what goes on inside households, the most fundamental human social group, questions and threatens some of the core concepts of ecological and economic anthropology, and poses difficult problems about the origin, structure, and function of all social groups.

4. It is clear that people working on household decision making are aware that something is lacking in their analysis. This is reflected in the somewhat confused response to understanding changes in household decision making that are occurring because of increasing female participation in the workforce (Hill and Klein 1973; O'Connor 1983; Douglas-Tate et al. 1984; Rodman 1982).

5. Without serious cross-cultural experience or a concept of culture, consumer researchers have not even asked the question of whether ideology and customary rules, or economic rationality and pragmatic practice are the primary cause of household and family behavior, an issue that anthropologists are deeply concerned with (Yanagisako 1984; Bourdieu 1977). The cross-cultural research done by consumer researchers seems concerned mainly with finding differences in the relative power of husbands and wives; researchers assume that the variables established in North American studies are cross-culturally valid. Sometimes the typology of cultures used to 'explain' differences in decision making is dangerously simplistic and naive (eg. Green et al. 1983).

6. This model, as well as the previous one, assumes that there is a sharp dividing line between luxuries and necessities, when in fact the definition of what is necessary is largely itself a cultural matter.

7. The disposition of cash earned from selling crops is much less problematical for Kekchi households. Crop surplus falls within the traditional definition of the male economic sphere, and male household heads retain rights to them whether they are sold or not.

8. Both of these budget arrangements are 'traditional.' Neither is a recent product of capitalist penetration, for the Kekchi have been producing for the marketplace for hundreds of years. Instead the two forms of budgeting are perceived as two forms of marriage, resulting from differences in personality, relative ages of spouses, the different political positions and ambitions of men and women, and such accidents as birth order.

References Cited

Abbott, S. 1976. "Full-Time Farmers and Week-End Wives: An Analysis of Altering Conjugal Roles." *Journal of Marriage and the Family* 38: 165–174.

Abu, K. 1983. "The Separateness of Spouses: Conjugal Resources in an Ashanti Town," in C. Oppong (ed.), *Female and Male in West Africa*. London: George Allen and Unwin. Pp. 156–168.

Adams, Jane. 1988. "The Decoupling of Farm and Household: Differential Consequences of Capitalist Development on Southern Illinois and Third World Family Farms." *Comparative Studies in Society and History* 30: 453–482.

Anderson, Michael. 1971. *Family Structure in Nineteenth Century Lancashire*. Cambridge: Cambridge University Press.

Barlett, Peggy. 1980. "Introduction: Development Issues and Economic Anthropology," in P. Barlett (ed.), *Agricultural Decision Making*. New York: Academic Press. Pp. 1–18.

_____. 1982. *Agricultural Choice and Change*. New Brunswick, N.J.: Rutgers University Press.

Barth, F. 1967. "On the Study of Social Change." *American Anthropologist* 69: 661–669.

Becker, Gary S. 1981. *A Treatise on the Family*. Cambridge, Mass: Harvard University Press.

Blau, F. and M. Ferber. 1986. *The Economics of Women, Men, and Work*. Englewood Cliffs: Prentice-Hall.

Bloch, Maurice. 1973. "The Long Term and the Short Term: The Economic and Political Significance of the Morality of Kinship," in J. Goody (ed.), *The Character of Kinship*. Cambridge: Cambridge University Press. Pp. 75–87.

Blood, R. O. Jr. and D.M. Wolfe. 1960. *Husbands and Wives*. New York: The Free Press.

Bonfield, E., Kaufman, C., and S. Hernandez. 1984. "Household Decisionmaking: Units of Analysis and Decision Processes," in M. Roberts and L. Wortzel (eds.), *Marketing to the Changing Household*. Cambridge, Mass.: Ballinger. Pp. 231–263.

Bould, Sally. 1982. "Women and the Family: Theoretical Perspectives on Development." Working Paper 13, Women in International Development Program, Michigan State University.

Bourdieu, Pierre. 1977. *Outline of a Theory of Practice.* Cambridge: Cambridge University Press.

Caldwell, John. 1981. *The Theory of Fertility Decline.* Homewood, Illinois: Irwin Publishers.

Cancian, Frank. 1972. *Change and Uncertainty in a Peasant Economy: The Maya Corn Farmers of Zinacantan.* Stanford: Stanford University Press.

Carter, A. 1984. "Household Histories," in R. Netting, R. Wilk and E. Arnould (eds.), *Households: Comparative and Historical Studies of the Domestic Group.* Berkeley: University of California Press.

Clark, Gracia. 1985. "Domestic Work and Trading: Pressures on Asante Wives and Mothers." Paper presented at the annual meeting of the Society for Economic Anthropology, Urbana-Champaign.

Collins, Jane. 1988. "The Household and Relations of Production in Southern Peru." *Comparative Studies in Society and History* 28(4): 651–671.

Creighton, Colin. 1980. "Family, Property and Relations of Production in Western Europe." *Economy and Society* 9: 129–164.

Curtis, Richard. 1986. "Household and Family in Theory on Inequality." *American Sociological Review* 51: 168–183.

Davis, Harry. 1976. "Decision Making within the Household." *Journal of Consumer Research* 2: 241–260.

Douglas-Tate, M., J. Peyton, and E. Bowen. 1984. "Sharing of Household Maintenance Tasks in Married-Couple Households," in M. Roberts and L. Wortzel (eds.), *Marketing to the Changing Household.* Cambridge, Mass.: Ballinger. Pp. 205–216.

Ellen, Roy. 1982. *Environment, Subsistence, and System.* Cambridge University Press: Cambridge.

Ferber, Robert and Lucy Lee. 1974. "Husband-Wife Influence in Family Purchasing Behavior." *Journal of Consumer Research* 1: 43–50.

Ferber, Robert. 1973. "Family Decision Making and Economic Behavior: A Review," in E. Sheldon (ed.), *Family Economic Behavior: Problems and Prospects.* Philadelphia: Lippincott. Pp. 29–64.

Fitzsimmons, C. and Williams, F. 1973. *The Family Economy: Nature and Management of Resources.* Ann Arbor: Edwards Brothers.

Folbre, Nancy. 1984. "Cleaning House: New Perspectives on Households and Economic Development." Paper Presented at the XII International Congress of the Latin American Studies Association, Albuquerque, New Mexico.

Foster, B. L. 1984. "Family Structure and the Generation of Thai Social Exchange Networks," in R. Netting, R. Wilk and E. Arnould (eds.), *Households: Comparative and Historical Studies of the Domestic Group.* Berkeley: University of California Press.

Gaskins, S. and J. Lucy. 1986. "Passing the Buck: Responsibility and Blame in the Yucatec Maya Household." Paper Presented at the meetings of the American Anthropological Association, Philadelphia.

Gladwin, C. and R. Zabawa. 1987. "Transformation of Full-Time Family Farms in the U.S.: Can They Survive?" in M. Maclachlan (ed.), *Household Economies and Their Transformations*. Lanham: University Press of America. Pp. 212–227.

Golley, Frank. 1984. "Historical Origins of the Ecosystem Concept in Biology," in Emilio Moran (ed.), *The Ecosystem Concept in Anthropology*. Boulder: Westview Press. Pp. 32–50.

Goodenough, W. 1955. "A Problem in Malayo-Polynesian Social Organization." *American Anthropologist* 57: 71–83.

Goody, J. 1973. "Strategies of Heirship." *Comparative Studies in Society and History* 15: 3–20.

Green, R., J. Leonardi, J. Chandon, I. Cunningham, B. Verhage, and A. Straieri. 1983. "Societal Development and Family Purchasing Roles: A Cross-National Study." *Journal of Consumer Research* 9: 436–442.

Guyer, Jane I. 1981. "Household and Community in African Studies." *African Studies Review* 24: 87–137.

_____ . 1986. "Intra-Household Processes and Farming Systems Research: Perspectives from Anthropology," in J. Moock (ed.), *Understanding Africa's Rural Households and Farming Systems*. Boulder: Westview Press. Pp. 92–105.

Hagan, G. 1983. "Marriage, Divorce and Polygyny in Winneba," in C. Oppong (ed.), *Female and Male in West Africa*. London: George Allen and Unwin. Pp. 192–203.

Hardesty, D. 1977. *Ecological Anthropology*. New York: John Wiley and Sons.

Hartmann, Heidi. 1981. "The Family as a Locus of Gender, Class, and Political Struggle: The Example of Housework." *Signs* 6: 366–394.

Hareven, Tamara. 1982. *Family Time and Industrial Time*. Cambridge: Cambridge University Press.

Heer, David. 1963. "The Measurement and Bases of Family Power: An Overview." *Marriage and Family Living* 25: 133–139.

Hempel, D.J. 1974. "Family Buying Decisions: A Cross Cultural Perspective." *Journal of Marketing Research* 11: 295–302.

Hill, R. and D. Klein. 1973. "Towards a Research Agenda and Theoretical Synthesis," in E. Sheldon (ed.), *Family Economic Behavior: Problems and Prospects*. Philadelphia: Lippincott. Pp. 371–404.

Hyden, Goran. 1986. "The Invisible Economy of Smallholder Agriculture in Africa," in J. Moock (ed.), *Understanding Africa's Rural Households and Farming Systems*. Boulder: Westview Press. Pp. 11–35.

Jones, C. W. 1986. "Intra-Household Bargaining in Response to the Introduction of New Crops: A Case Study from North Cameroon," in J. Moock (ed.), *Understanding Africa's Rural Households and Farming Systems*. Boulder: Westview Press. Pp. 105–123.

Kenkel, W. F. 1961. "Husband-Wife Interaction in Decision-Making and Decision Choices." *The Journal of Social Psychology* 54: 255–262.

Korn, S. R. D. 1975. "Household Composition in the Tonga Islands: A Question of Options and Alternatives." *Journal of Anthropological Research* 31(3): 235–260.

Laslett, Peter. 1984. "The Family as a Knot of Individual Interests," in R. Netting, R. Wilk and E. Arnould (eds.), *Households: Comparative and Historical Studies of the Domestic Group.* Berkeley: University of California Press. Pp. 353–382.

Leacock, E. 1986. "Postscript: Implications for Organization," in E. Leacock and H. Safa (eds.), *Women's Work: Development and the Division of Labor by Gender.* Massachusetts: Bergin and Garvey. Pp. 253–265.

Lees, Susan and Daniel Bates. 1984. "Environmental Events and the Ecology of Cumulative Change," in Emilio Moran (ed.), *The Ecosystem Concept in Anthropology.* Boulder: Westview Press. Pp. 133–159.

Lehman, David. 1986. "Two Paths of Agrarian Capitalism, or a Critique of Chayanovian Marxism." *Comparative Studies in Society and History* 28(4): 601–627.

Lofgren, Orvar. 1984. "Family and Household: Images and Realities: Cultural Change in Swedish Society," in R. Netting, R. Wilk and E. Arnould (eds.), *Households: Comparative and Historical Studies of the Domestic Group.* Berkeley: University of California Press.

Lorensen, S., A. Murphy, and H. Selby. n.d. "Household Budgetary Strategies in Urban Mexico: Mediating the Income-Consumption Nexus." Unpublished paper in possession of the author.

Machlachlan, Morgan. 1983. *Why They Did Not Starve.* Philadelphia: ISHI.

Maher, V. 1981. "Work, Consumption and Authority within the Household: A Moroccan Case," in K. Young, C. Wolkowitz and R. McCullagh (eds.), *Of Marriage and Market: Women's Subordination in International Perspective.* London: CSE Books. Pp. 69–87.

Mathews, H. F. 1987. "Predicting Decision Outcomes: Have We Put the Cart before the Horse in Anthropological Studies of Decision-Making?" *Human Organization* 46(1): 54–61.

McGuire, R., J. Smith, and W. Martin. 1986. "Patterns of Household Structures and the World Economy." *Review* 10(1): 75–97.

McKee, K. 1986. "Household Analysis as an Aid to Farming Systems Research: Methodological Issues," in J. Moock (ed.), *Understanding Africa's Rural Households and Farming Systems.* Boulder: Westview. Pp. 188–198.

McMillan, Della. 1986. "Distribution of Resources and Products in Mossi Households," in A. Hanson and D. McMillan (eds.), *Food in Sub-Saharan Africa.* Boulder: Lynne Rienner.

Meillassoux, Claude. 1981. *Maidens, Meal and Money.* Cambridge: Cambridge University Press.

Minge, Wanda. 1986. "The Industrial Revolution and the European Family: 'Childhood' as a Market for Family Labor," in E. Leacock and H. Safa (eds.), *Women's Work: Development and the Division of Labor by Gender.* Massachusetts: Bergin and Garvey. Pp. 13–24.

Moock, Joyce. 1986. "Introduction," in J. Moock (ed.), *Understanding Africa's Rural Households and Farming Systems.* Boulder: Westview. Pp. 1–10.

Moran, Emilio. 1984a. "Preface," in Emilio Moran (ed.), *The Ecosystem Concept in Anthropology.* Boulder: Westview Press. Pp. xiii–xvi.

_____. 1984b "Limitations and Advances in Ecosystems Research," in Emilio Moran (ed.), *The Ecosystem Concept in Anthropology.* Boulder: Westview Press. Pp. 3–32.

_____. 1982. *Human Adaptability: An Introduction to Ecological Anthropology.* Boulder: Westview Press.

Nardi, Bonnie. 1983. "Goals in Reproductive Decision Making." *American Ethnologist* 10(4): 697–714.

Odum, H. T. 1971. *Environment, Power, and Society.* New York: Wiley-Interscience.

O'Connor, P. J., G. L. Sullivan, D.A. Pogorzelski. 1983. "Cross Cultural Family Purchasing Decisions: A Literature Review." *Advances in Consumer Research* 10: 59–64.

Olshavsky, R. and M. King. 1984. "The Role of Children in Household Decisionmaking: Application of a New Taxonomy of Family Role Structure," in M. Roberts and L. Wortzel (eds.), *Marketing to the Changing Household.* Cambridge, Mass.: Ballinger. Pp. 41–52.

Oppong, C. 1970. "Conjugal Power and Resources: An Urban African Example." *Journal of Marriage and the Family* 32: 676–680.

Orlove, Benjamin. 1980. "Ecological Anthropology." *Annual Review of Anthropology* 9: 235–273.

Painter, Michael. 1984. "Changing Relations of Production and Rural Underdevelopment." *Journal of Anthropological Research* 40: 271–292.

Palacio, J. 1982. "Food and Social Relations in a Garifuna Village." PhD. Dissertation, University Microfilms: Ann Arbor.

Park, C. 1982. "Joint Decisions in Home Purchasing: A Muddling-Through Process." *Journal of Consumer Research* 9: 151–162.

Peters, Pauline. 1986. "Household Management in Botswana: Cattle, Crops, and Wage Labor," in J. Moock (ed.), *Understanding Africa's Rural Households and Farming Systems.* Boulder: Westview Press. Pp. 133–154.

Prais, S. J. and H. S. Houthakker. 1971. *The Analysis of Family Budgets.* Cambridge: Cambridge University Press.

Roberts, Mary and Lawrence Wortzel (eds.). 1984. *Marketing to the Changing Household.* Cambridge, Mass.: Ballinger.

Rodman, H. 1972. "Marital Power and the Theory of Resources in a Cross Cultural Context." *Journal of Comparative Family Studies* 1: 50–67.

Ross, Harold. 1973. *Baegu: Social and Ecological Organization in Malaita, Solomon Islands.* Urbana: University of Illinois Press.

Rubenstein, H. 1987. *Coping with Poverty: Adaptive Strategies in a Caribbean Village.* Boulder: Westview Press.

Rudie, Ingrid. 1970. "Household Organization: Adaptive Process and Restrictive Form: A Viewpoint on Economic Change." *Folk* 12: 185–200.

Sahlins, M. 1972. *Stone Age Economics.* Chicago: Aldine.

Scanzoni, J. 1972. *Sexual Bargaining: Power Politics in the American Marriage.* Chicago: University of Chicago Press.

Schmink, M. 1984. "Household Economic Strategies: Review and Research Agenda." *Latin American Research Review* 19(3): 87–102.

Schultz, T.W. 1981. *Economics of Population.* Reading, Mass.: Addison-Wesley.

Segalen, Martine. 1986. *Historical Anthropology of the Family.* Cambridge: University of Cambridge Press.

Sirgy, M. J. 1984. *Marketing as Social Behavior.* New York: Praeger.

Smith E. 1984. "Anthropology, Evolutionary Ecology, and the Explanatory Limits of the Ecosystem Concept," in Emilio Moran (ed.), *The Ecosystem Concept in Anthropology.* Boulder: Westview Press. Pp. 51–86.

Smith, Joan., I. Wallerstein and H. Evers (eds.). 1984. *Households and the World Economy.* Beverly Hills: Sage Publications. Pp. 23–36.

Smith, Joan, I. Wallerstein and H. Evers. 1984. "Introduction," in J. Smith, I. Wallerstein and H. Evers (eds.), *Households and the World Economy.* Beverly Hills: Sage Publications. Pp. 7–13.

Smith, T.C. 1959. *The Agrarian Origins of Modern Japan.* Palo Alto: Stanford University Press.

Spiro, Rosann. 1983. "Persuasion in Family Decision-Making." *Journal of Consumer Research.* 9: 393–402.

Sternthal, B. and C. Craig. 1982. *Consumer Behavior: An Information-Processing Perspective.* Englewood Cliffs: Prentice-Hall.

Van Esterik, P. 1985. "Intra-Family Food Distribution: Its Relevance for Maternal and Child Nutrition," in *Determinants of Young Child Feeding and their Implications for Nutritional Surveillance.* Ithaca, NY: Cornell International Nutrition Monograph Series, Number 14. Pp. 74–149.

Wallerstein, Immanuel. 1984. "Household Structures and Labor-Force Formation in the Capitalist World-Economy," in *Households and the World Economy.* J. Smith, I. Wallerstein and H. Evers (eds.) Beverly Hills: Sage Publications. Pp. 17–22.

Whitehead, Ann. 1981. "'I'm Hungry, Mum': The Politics of Domestic Budgeting," in K. Young, C. Wolkowitz and R. McCullagh (eds.), *Of Marriage and Market: Women's Subordination in International Perspective.* London: CSE Books. Pp. 88–111.

Wilk, Richard. 1981. "Agriculture, Ecology And Domestic Organization Among The Kekchi Maya." Ph.D. Dissertation, University Microfilms, Ann Arbor.

———. 1983. "Little House in the Jungle." *Journal of Anthropological Archaeology.* 2(2): 99–116.

———. 1984. "Households in Process: Agricultural Change and Domestic Transformation among the Kekchi Maya of Belize," in R. Netting, R. Wilk and E. Arnould (eds.), *Households: Comparative and Historical Studies of the Domestic Group.* Berkeley: University of California Press.

———. 1987. "The Search for Tradition in Southern Belize: A Personal Narrative." *American Indigena* 47(2): 77–95.

———. 1989. "Houses as Consumer Goods: The Kekchi of Belize," in Benjamin S. Orlove and Henry J. Rutz (eds.), *The Social Economy of Consumption.* Lanham: University Press of America.

Wilk, Richard R. and Robert M. Netting. 1984. "Households: Changing Form and Function," in R. Netting, R. Wilk and E. Arnould (eds.), *Households: Comparative and Historical Studies of the Domestic Group.* Berkeley: University of California Press.

Wolf, Eric. 1966. *Peasants*. Englewood Cliffs: Prentice Hall.

Woodford-Berger, Jane. 1981. "Women in Houses: The Organization of Residence and Work in Rural Ghana." *Antropologiska Studier* 30–31: 3–35.

Yanagisako, Sylvia. 1984. "Explicating Residence: A Cultural Analysis of Changing Households Among Japanese-Americans," in R. Netting, R. Wilk and E. Arnould (eds.), *Households: Comparative and Historical Studies of the Domestic Group*. Berkeley: University of California Press.

Young, K., C. Wolkowitz and R. McCullagh. 1981. *Of Marriage and Market: Women's Subordination in International Perspective*. London: CSE Books.

PART TWO

Case Studies of Household Decision Making, Resource Flow, and Power

4

Making Breakfast and Raising Babies: The Zumbagua Household as Constituted Process

M. J. Weismantel

The household is the fundamental unit of Andean social structure. In the classic 1977 Bolton and Mayer volume on kinship, for example, Mayer refers to it as the basic unit of production, distribution and consumption in Tangor (1977: 61); for Bolton, who calls it "the dominant social unit," its importance in Qolla social structure ". . . cannot be overstressed" (1977: 217). Any attempt to describe the domestic economy of Zumbagua, an indigenous parish of the Ecuadorian Andes, must similarly begin with the household.[1]

However, to assert the primacy of the household may mystify more than clarify, if the household and the domestic activities that are its focus are taken as self-evident.[2] As Yanigasako (1978) has suggested, both the category household and ". . . the somewhat impenetrable label of 'domestic' activities," need to be explored (Yanagisako 1978: 164). Several papers in this volume critique the pervasive notion of the household as a "black box" (see Lockwood, Wilk, Barlett, as well as Rutz's comments on Wallerstein).

Before we can assume that we know what households are, and how they vary across cultures, domestic activities must be disentangled from one another and analyzed separately and in their relationship to one another. Wilk (this volume) points out that anthropological studies that touch on aspects of household life remain "fragmented and single-stranded" in their depiction of the household itself, and do not focus on the totality of intra-household processes. For the Andes, although scholars have documented the relationships of the household to other households, to descent and inheritance, and to the organization of labor,

analysis of the household itself, its constituent relationships and reproductive processes, remains largely absent from the ethnographic literature.

This chapter analyzes the economic processes through which the
household is constituted in an indigenous area of the northern Andes.
In so doing, it addresses a problem which has emerged in the literature
on household-level analysis. This is the issue of boundaries, raised by
both Wilk and Clark in this volume. As I discuss below, during my
fieldwork in Zumbagua I found the exact limits of the household to be
quite difficult to identify. Wilk comments that the slippery boundaries
of the household can lead scholars to question its usefulness as a unit
for analysis. But the Zumbagua household is not merely an analytical
construct; Zumbaguans themselves consider it to be at the center of
domestic life and indeed as the foundation of society. What the elusive
quality of household boundaries suggests is not that they do not exist
or that they are not important, but rather that what makes Zumbagua
households matter is that they are so deeply interpenetrated with other
households and with other social forms. As Clark's analysis of the Asante
demonstrates, links between households and boundaries within them are
integral to domestic life, and the very fluidity of social arrangements,
which can seem to the analyst to indicate weakness or insubstantiality,
may in fact contribute to social cohesiveness.

In Zumbagua, two points are necessary to understand the role of the
household in domestic life. The first is that the household is not so
much a static social unit defined by co-residence as it is a set of ongoing
economic activities, a relation of production, consumption and reproduction. The second, related aspect of the Zumbagua household is that
the process of social reproduction of the household, through its division
into new households, is not only necessary to long-term social survival
but is a constant and intrinsic aspect of the household formation itself.

When these two crucial aspects of Zumbagua household formation
are taken into consideration, the relationship of the household to other
households and to other social units becomes clearer. The household
emerges as one of three critical forms in Zumbagua domestic economy:
the individual, the household and the family. Close attention to the
relationship between these three units reveals the processes of social
reproduction and makes possible for Zumbagua the kind of description
asked for by Cheal (this volume): ". . . ways of describing households
must be found which do not assume that households are integrated
systems, but which at the same time do not reduce the study of households
to the study of individuals . . ." For Zumbagua, we can define an
economic system in which the various activities associated with production,
reproduction and consumption are allocated between the three units of

individual, household and family in such a way as to insure a tightly integrated yet flexible whole.

Anatomy of the Household:
The Developmental Cycle

Zumbagua (Cotopaxi Province, Canton Pujilí) is a rural parish located on the western edge of the Cordillera Occidental at approx. one degree South, with altitudes ranging from 3200 to more than 4000 m, well above the upper limits of maize cultivation. Most residents of the parish live in rural dwellings scattered over the ten thousand-odd hectares of the parish. The local economy is based primarily on the cultivation of barley, fava beans, potatoes and onions on lower slopes, together with sheep and llama pastoralism in the high páramos; each of these zones comprises roughly half of the total area of the parish, with settlement being concentrated in the lower elevations. The households in which its more than thousand-odd inhabitants live combine this largely subsistence agriculture with a variety of wage-earning activities, the most significant of which is male temporary migration to the capital city of Quito; other strategies include wage labor on small agricultural enterprises on the western slopes, and involvement in the transportation of contraband liquor. The area is characterized by extreme poverty relative to other highland populations, and by the existence of a strong local indigenous culture typified by the Quichua language, a characteristic clothing style (especially handwoven striped ponchos), and an elaborated fiesta cycle.

The dwellings that make up a Zumbagua household consist of a series of one-room buildings around a patio. These fall into two basic categories: cooking buildings, or kitchens, and non-cooking buildings, which are primarily storage rooms. Every household contains a minimum of one kitchen and a storage room, but additional buildings, which serve as dormitories, are added during periods of expansion. The existence of a household is defined by the presence of a kitchen. The word "kitchen" in itself implies much more than a room where food is prepared. It is here that meals are made and eaten, male and female heads of the household sleep and live, baths are taken, the family meets, guests are entertained, decisions made, wakes held, babies born and the sick nursed back to health. Other buildings are storage rooms and sleeping places; only the kitchen is a home. In addition, only kitchens are warm: the hearth is the only source of heat in Zumbagua homes. Cats, guinea pigs and convalescent sheep demonstrate their innate grasp of the role of the kitchen in the Zumbagua household by their refusal to live in any other building, while chickens and dogs, less privileged, spend most of their lives attempting to join the circle around the kitchen hearth.

Zumbagua households have a long life-cycle, undergoing several distinct phases. At first, there is a married couple and their children. They all sleep in the kitchen together. In later years, the children, as they mature, may begin to sleep in the storage room or to build small separate dormitories. Finally, when they marry, if they do not join their spouse's family they will build more substantial dormitories within their parents' household, bordering the same patio as the kitchen in which they were born. That kitchen remains the hearth where they eat their meals, and where their own first children are born.

The married children cook, eat, work and play with their parents for a number of years. Not until a young couple has several children over the age of five will they consider establishing their own household by building a separate kitchen. Ideally, the youngest child never leaves home; the natal household finally enters a last phase in which the youngest couple and their children sleep in the central, kitchen building while an elderly parent inhabits a small dormitory nearby.[3]

The lengthy transition from dependent child to independent parent implied by this pattern is not surprising, given the propensity in Andean society for transitions between social states to be extremely gradual. Life crises typically take the form of lengthy processes of becoming, rather than the sudden transitions of status characteristic of other societies, including our own. In Zumbagua, as elsewhere in the Andes, birth is only one step in a process that begins with conception and only very gradually produces a child with a firmly established biological and social existence. Birth and baptism are separated by a period of varying length in which the infant is referred to as an auca, a wild unsocialized creature, and during which its death is not treated as the death of a human being. Even after baptism, babies and very young children announce by their easy nudity, loose ungendered clothing and matted uncut hair that, until the ritual of first haircutting, they are not fully human in the social sense. Olivia Harris suggests that in the Bolivian Andes, "The process by which a new-born individual becomes a fully socialized human being," represented ". . . in terms of the child's progressive ability to speak," is a very gradual one which does not end at the haircutting ceremony, but continues throughout the transition to adulthood, as verbal and cognitive abilities continue to develop (1980: 72).

At the other end of life, Andean texts describe the transition from life to death as a similarly drawn-out process. The film "Spirit Possession of Alejandro Mamami" depicts a man gradually and very consciously approaching and even creating his own death from old age (1974). In the Ecuadorian Andes, Rivet (1926) speaks of the wake beginning before physical death has occurred; throughout the Andes, after interment an elaborated series of commemorative celebrations are held at eight days, one year or other intervals, continuing the rite of passage. These practices, together with the pan-Andean feeding of the dead on All Souls', reveal the Andes as typical of those cultures van Gennep describes as deliberately drawing out the transition from life to death (1960: 163).

If Andeans appear reluctant to pin down the moment of an individual's entrance into and departure from the world, it is not surprising that entrance into the civil state of marriage, the marker for transition to adulthood, is likewise not always accomplished in a single day. Various authors have discussed the notion of "trial marriage," *sirvanakuy* or *watanaki* (including Carter 1977; Price 1965; Mishkin 1946). Bolton suggests that Qolla marriage is best "conceptualized as a complex sequence of interactions and decisions rather than as an event."(1977: 217) In Zumbagua, young adults are encouraged to move slowly throughout the process of courtship and marriage, and to delay final decisions about commitments even after the birth of a child. Ultimately, the delay of the civil and/or religious ceremony for a period of months or years after co-habitation serves to prolong the process still more, a strategy parallel to the spacing of birth and baptism.

Like the life cycle of the individual, the developmental cycle of the Zumbagua household is one of prolonged transitions. A woman giving birth to the fifth child of her marriage confided to me, "Ours is a very new marriage." "Really?" I asked, surprised. "Oh, yes," she replied, "only seven years old, and just separated from tayta-mama's house for two."

Dissection: Constituent Processes

For the analyst, a basic grasp of the developmental cycle of the Zumbagua household, as described above, reduces an apparent proliferation of household forms into the more manageable pattern of a single root form that undergoes several phases in its reproductive cycle. However, representation of the household as a formal constellation of related individuals is indicative of the anthropologist's role as passive outsider. We now turn from description of form to analysis of the interlocking set of constitutive processes that create relations between members and thus define the roles of individual, household and family.

Yanagisako (1978:166) states that domestic activities are commonly grouped into two primary types, one having to do with social reproduction, the other with the production and consumption of foods. At a less elevated level of analysis, my first major achievement in disentangling Zumbagua households came when I learned to separate eating and sleeping from one another. Until then, I had unthinkingly assumed that these two activities were always found together as aspects of domestic life performed under one roof by those who considered themselves members of the same household. By separating them as analytical categories, I was able to grasp a fundamental principle of Zumbagua household organization: Zumbagua slows down the separation of new households from old ones by letting go of domestic activities one by one, rather than all at once.

Once married, it is assumed that a couple will sleep together, in their own house, under a separate roof from their parents. It is equally taken for granted that they will eat together with the parents in whose compound they live (whether residence is virilocal or uxorilocal). From the bowl of hot water for morning ablutions to the last tidbit eaten just before going to bed, newlyweds share the older couple's hearth. Sharing meals means sharing intimacy, especially during the meals eaten in pre-dawn darkness and late at night; these casual, cozy, sleepy occasions seal those who share them into a single social unit.

In the most literal sense, the warmth of these meals, eaten around the glowing hearth at which they were cooked, contrasts sharply with the cold and dark of the newlyweds' own little house, which has no source of heat or light. There physical intimacy provides the only warmth, and sexual intercourse replaces the social intercourse of the kitchen. It is from these beginnings, however, that the germ of a new hearth is created. As children are born and mature, the new couple will establish their own kitchen. This progression from the marriage bed to the founding of a kitchen is amply celebrated in Zumbagua verbal symbolism, and the jokes and teasing to which young married couples are subjected makes frequent use of metaphors of warmth, heat, and cooking.

The separation of food and sex enabled me to understand the physical layout of Zumbagua households much more readily, and to distinguish older household compounds with their multiple storage houses and dormitories from newer households where everyone sleeps in the kitchen house. There are many variations on this pattern. Newly married couples sometimes build their dormitory houses outside the family compound, while couples making their first kitchen sometimes build them as close to the original kitchen as possible, as though to reassure the family that the social and emotional distance between them remains negligible. Nevertheless, the most important fact about any couple whose parents are still living is whether or not they have their own hearth. No matter what the distance from the older kitchen, if they do not cook, they still begin and end each day with their parents; no matter how close, the establishment of a separate hearth marks a significant move away.

This splitting of the activities of sleeping and eating, independence in the former being the prerogative of any married couple, while the latter is not, is the most important division in Zumbagua domestic activities. However, it is only the first cut in the dissection of the household. If we are to understand the further differentiation of married couples into newly married, then progressively more well-established households, and ultimately, after generations, into senior households for their own families, we must differentiate further categories within each of these two major activity complexes of nourishment and reproduction. For the household, food involves two major sets of activities, production and consumption, while the social reproduction of new individuals requires two other spheres of activity, those of procreation and childrearing. As marriages mature, the allocation of each of these activities changes.

For a young couple, only the physical acts involved in reproduction are purely their own concern. Social reproduction, the raising of a child, occurs within the extended family, where the young parents themselves are still considered immature and incapable of taking full responsibility for an infant. This stage is a further evolution of the couple's relations before marriage, a time when even sexual activity and sleeping were separated, sexual intercourse being conducted in secret away from the household. Children produced during this first, premarital period are raised in the mother's own natal household, and are treated as her mother's children rather than hers. Should she later marry the father of the child and want to take the child with her, she will very likely have to fight her kin. Similarly, the young woman does not control the rearing of the children she bears in the second phase, the early years of marriage. These children, born and nurtured in the kitchen of her mother-in-law, are subject to the senior woman's authority at all times, just as she is.

For many women, motherhood is a continuum from an early child she bore but did not raise, a second and often a third child over which she had little control, and finally a series of older children that she raises in her own home. At this point, her control over children peaks, then begins to diminish: she appropriates her unmarried daughters' children as her own, and dominates the children of her young daughters-in-law, but progressively sees the next generation of mothers take control of the raising of their own children and grandchildren.

By the time a couple has several children and finally builds their own kitchen, all of these activities, sleep and sex on the one hand, procreation and child-raising on the other, will have finally become united into a single set of domestic activities conducted within their own household. But if these activities have now been united, the activities involved with nourishment have been split apart.

At first, consumption itself is divided for the new household: not all the food they eat is cooked in their own kitchen. The woman who moves from her parents' or in-laws' house to her own kitchen at last has her own hearth.[4] However, the number of meals that she cooks there may be very small at first. On most days, she still works in collective endeavors with other family members. As a result, the main meals of the day, the large daytime *almuirzus*, are cooked and eaten in the kitchen of the oldest couple, together with everyone who has shared the work in the fields. Often, preparing that meal, or helping to prepare it, is part of a woman's daily tasks.

In contrast to the days before she had her own kitchen, a woman in this phase of her career does cook the smaller meals eaten in darkness at the beginning and end of the day. Here she is faced with a new problem, for the mainstay of these meals are sweet porridges made of freshly ground and toasted barley, and new kitchens do not have the equipment to make them. There is an unmistakable relationship between the developmental phase of a household's social form and the kitchen equipment it possesses. In a household in the most expanded phase in its life-cycle, with in-laws and grandchildren in residence, the kitchen will be graced with the presence of two *kutana rumis* (big grinding stones) on the kitchen floor. The early morning meal in such a household is prepared the "right" way, the "old-fashioned" way: the barley is toasted, ground and sifted just before the porridge is made.

It is easy to prepare the morning meal freshly from scratch in a big household with one woman to do the first grinding and another to do the fine grinding and the sifting, leaving the senior woman to toast and boil and fill the bowls, handing them to a young granddaughter to carry to the men. Mornings in such a kitchen represent the ideal of Zumbagua family life, with tasks shared among many hands, each individual feeling her/himself surrounded by the bustle and hum of social and productive activity and all the sensory stimuli that Zumbaguans associate with home and the sharing of meals.

A woman who runs a kitchen with only young children to help her cannot achieve this ideal. Most newly-established kitchens don't even have a *kutana rumi*; the woman must go back to her mother's or mother-in-law's in the midafternoon to grind barley for the next day's meals. Or the gift of labor may be reversed: after so many years of grinding barley at the older couple's home, an established woman may be awakened by a child bearing a bowl of barley flour from the "big" house, ground by a grandchild or new daughter-in-law.

The early-morning meals prepared in the new kitchen consist of hot sweetened water to which a woman adds the cold, pre-ground barley prepared elsewhere. The brief boiling of water does little to heat up her house, and the cold barley has little taste or smell, compared to barley just toasted, which fills the whole house with the heat of its toasting and the strong aroma. As a result, the contrast between the "cold" house of a young marriage and the "warm" house of the well-established family, which had marked the beginnings of their marriage, continues to plague the couple in these first years of having their own kitchen, even though they now have their own hearth. The new household is still part of the larger family, and as such remains dependent on the elder household. The political and emotional relationship to parents is acknowledged through small rituals of deference and respect, while a continued economic dependence is reinforced through the location of strategic resources near or in the senior compound: a well, a livestock shelter, or in this case the kitchen grinding stone.

Gifts of food between the two households are the primary tangible sign of their interrelationship. The older household may send ingredients for the making of a meal, as in the example above, but they frequently send an entire pot of already-cooked food, steaming hot. Nor is the movement of cooked food unidirectional. Typically, every time a meal is prepared in the new kitchen a pot of food is sent to the old kitchen, while the parental household does the same. This constant exchange of cooked food signifies the continued closeness of the two households, and serves to reassure the old household that the new one still considers itself part of an undivided affective and economic whole.

Ultimately, this unity in food consumption expresses the intent to share fully in food production. For while the establishment of a new hearth allows a couple to eat separately from the rest of the family, they continue to work the fields and herd the flocks together with the parents and siblings whose hearth they recently shared. When a couple finally establishes its own kitchen, the mother or mother-in-law may lose direct control over some of the younger woman's kitchen activities, but she can still expect to coordinate tasks with the fledgling households scattered around her in the management of the farmstead as a whole. One or two people to herd sheep; one or two to go up to the páramo, the highest ecological zone, to cut grass for fuel and other uses; one to feed the pig and the dogs, clean house and cook the midday meal, doing a little weeding in the field near the house in the meantime. The organization of farm tasks almost necessitates the participation of women from several households, negotiated between the members of the family within a loose framework of senior authority, sometimes controverted by considerations such as wealth or physical or emotional strength.

In the sphere of food production, the relevant social unit is not the household, the small co-residential group that shares a hearth, but the family, the larger group defined by descent and enlarged by marriage. The pooling of labor is one of the major functions of both family and marriage in Zumbagua. Work parties are made up of parents and children, siblings and siblings' spouses. More distant relations, *compadres* and hired laborers are called in only when absolutely necessary, and most families prefer to work without them. New couples strive to represent themselves to both families as having added a new partner to the food production effort, rather than diminishing it; and on the occasion of establishing a new kitchen, they must again work hard to convince their family that they remain willing contributors.

In fact, these households do continue to work in the fields and pastures as they did before. One reason for the stability of the labor pattern is that the establishment of a new household does nothing to change the ownership of land and animals, or the relationships by which they are worked and managed. The Zumbagua household is not, in and of itself, a unit of ownership of assets. Neither marriage nor the establishment of a new household initiates the fusing of the agricultural assets of husband and wife. Ownership of agricultural assets—land and animals— is reckoned strictly on the individual level. As is found in many parts of the Andes, inheritance is bilateral, and all children ideally receive equally from each parent (although a de facto preference for males is common). The transfer of property occurs gradually during a child's lifetime, with major gifts occurring at the child's marriage and the parent's death—another example of the Andean propensity for slow and steady transitions. This transfer has two phases. Until marriage, or perhaps more accurately, until the birth of children, the parent retains control of the greater part of the property. In this first period, gifts to the child are less a significant economic transfer than a tool in socialization.

"Wise" parents gradually give control of some portion of their property to their children, teaching them responsibility. The first major transfer of property usually occurs at marriage, but gifts of livestock begin when a child is young. Among the sheep a family herds, the guinea pigs underfoot in the house, the dogs in the patio, one or two belong to a child, who learns the joys and anxieties of ownership as their charges prosper or die, and bears the brunt of another's anger when a sibling's sheep strays while in their care. Even very young children may be "given" (mingana) one row of plants in a field. They are encouraged to care for their plants, and to go out to the field each morning to inspect them, as adults do. They begin to feel pride in their contributions to the family's wealth. As the children become adolescents, they sell an occasional sheep to purchase their own clothing, and volunteer to contribute guinea pigs when the family participates in food gift exchanges with another household, thus beginning to invest in social networks of their own. After marriage, the relationship between adult children and aging parent begins to reverse itself, as parents' physical strength declines and adult children's needs increase until ultimately, the aged parent becomes a dependent.

While these characteristics of Andean social economy have often been noted, what I want to emphasize here is the pattern of totally individualized ownership that this system creates, a characteristic of all Zumbagua families regardless of the age of their members or the stages of household development. Agricultural assets are identified with specific owners down to individual guinea pigs and even specific plants in a field. While the unperceptive onlooker may see a teenage girl going off herding in the morning as someone "tending her family's animals," the girl herself perceives the flock as made up of individually-owned animals, jointly tended. Two levels of social organization are involved here: the individual, who owns assets, and the family, which pools labor to manage the assets of its members. The household as a unit enters into neither side of this equation. Marriage changes the organization of production insofar as the new affine joins the labor pool of her/his spouse's family, and gains the labor of the spouse for her/his own family in return. Initially, a family only indirectly enjoys the assets of an affine, through opportunities to share in the products of their land, animals or income through meals, gifts and ritual occasions. Only when the relationship of marriage produces children is property redistributed. But before or after marriage, before or after the establishment of a new household, a young adult owns certain pieces of property which are worked by the entire family, with whom the products are shared.

The foregoing analysis of household organization leads to a rejection of the definition of the household as a bounded unit. The individual, not the household, owns assets, land or animals. Nor does the household function as a unit of agricultural production, for most families consist of separate households that work together in agriculture. The household is not a discrete unit of consumption, for younger households remain partially dependent upon their parent kitchen, and all households within a family share cooked food to a greater or lesser degree. It would appear that while the extended family is a meaningful unit, the household is not. Few in Zumbagua, however, would agree with this assessment, and there are good reasons why this is so.

One significance of the household lies in the simple fact that, over time, just as every marriage bed generates a kitchen, every household should become a new family. Andean families do not survive more than three generations. Gradually, despite the importance of the natal family for adults, and the long period of residence within the extended family experienced by newlyweds, couples do eventually become heads of their own families, and gradually detach themselves from their family of orientation.

This process sometimes appears in the anthropological literature as a simple transition at the death of the parents. The family disbands, the land is divided and the economic relationship between the siblings changes from one of generalized reciprocity to one of limited and balanced reciprocity. In Zumbagua, however, this process is so gradual that at any given point in time, few families find themselves living as adult siblings in clearly separate households and exchanging labor in a formalized manner, or as an extended family living as a single household and engaging in a generalized sharing of all consumption and production activities. Rather, those two extremes are ideal states between which clusters of related households are constantly moving, each household at its own pace. At any given moment, some hearths are growing in strength, adding new members, and others are fading as younger, stronger households in the family grow.

It is in these processes of reproduction and transformation that the significance of the household becomes clear. For middle-aged households dissociating themselves from their parents, the ultimate goal is withdrawal from the labor pool. But the means for achieving this lie largely in the narrowing and formalizing of food consumption activities shared by the households of the family. It is in this realm of the consumption of food that the household, which seemed to disappear when we looked closely at its functions of production and reproduction, re-emerges as a key social unit.

Definition: Consumption, Production, and Reproduction

In Zumbagua, the hearth defines the home. It supplants the marriage bed as the symbol of conjugal living, and the bond of blood as the emblem of parenthood. In Zumbagua relatedness means eating together. The central importance of the sharing of cooked foods can perhaps be most clearly seen in the creation of kinship relationships, especially in the adoption of children.

There is a general feeling that no home should be without children, both for affective reasons and because their labor is necessary in running a household. Physiological incapacity to reproduce is overcome by social mechanisms. By redistributing children among extended and fictive kin, the demands on each household are matched to its ability to provide. Older, more established households are homes to more young children than new ones, and poor families often give children away. Over the years, patterns of living, working and eating create family structures that differ substantially from actual consanguineal kinship.

If a woman's granddaughter lives with her for a number of years, she comes to be referred to as her "daughter." Similarly, a biologically unrelated boy becomes the "son" of those who raise him. Actual blood ties are not forgotten, although they are seldom referred to. But if a child has not been raised by blood relatives, s/he does not consider them collectively as family, nor their houses as homes. Blood creates individual ties, but only the sharing of food creates membership in a household and a family. The word *viñachishca* is used to refer to children raised within a household despite the absence of a blood bond, and it emphasizes the nurturing and growing of children: their feeding.

It is the sharing of cooked food that defines Zumbagua social groups, from the household to the community. Among all the meals cooked within a household, the widest group ever fed from a single hearth is the enormous mass assembled at weddings or wakes. At the other extreme are the "sweet" meals of barley porridge eaten in the darkness of early morning and late night. If a single parameter were chosen to define the boundaries of the household, it would surely be these latter occasions, the smallest and most private of meals. The domesticity of these scenes marks their social insignificance as specific events, while at the same time their daily repetition places them at the core of Zumbagua life.

These core meals identify a core group, the household in its most minimal definition. Surrounding this group are blurred sets of larger groups, first the other kitchens still interdependent with the core on a daily basis, then the kitchens of older, more independent family members, whose sharing in the agricultural tasks of the family still involves them in many midday meals. Beyond this are family members who have established still more distant relationships, compadres, and finally the community with which meals are only shared at the major celebrations of a lifetime.

This use of the shared meal to define a social group is carried into the realm of production. In Zumbagua, as throughout the Andes, the sharing of agricultural labor is accompanied by the sharing of meals. Further, there is an assumption that people who eat *almuirzu* together on a regular basis do so because they are a family. Since the family is by definition the unit of agricultural production, the work team, these shared meals imply a commitment to work together in the future, even though the meal is primarily an acknowledgment of work already performed. The same logic motivates the transformation of food consumption patterns between emergent and older households. Rituals of consumption do not merely symbolize relations of production, but actually cause them to happen, and changes in the former must precede changes in labor organization.

During a couple's dissociation from the natal family and the final transformation of a household into the core kitchen for a new extended family, their goal is independence in production. But the means through which independence is expressed, executed and finally accomplished lie in the realm of food consumption, and specifically in the sharing of cooked food. These changes cannot be enacted in the harvest-day *almuirzu*, which must be eaten jointly by all those working together. Rather, change involves small day-to-day alterations in the movement of food between kitchens, the effects of which will only be seen in future years.

These changes are best understood if we look at the entire range of food sharing patterns. At one end of this continuum are the very small children within a house, who freely partake of any food they desire, fishing tidbits out of adults' bowls, stealing treats out of the larder, secure in the knowledge that any food found anywhere in the household is theirs. At the other end is the *compadre*, with whom the sharing of cooked food is typically a formal affair narrowly associated with specific favors and especially with prestations of labor, although good *compadres* also lubricate the relationship with occasional gifts of uncooked foodstuffs delivered to one another's households.

To establish independence from the natal family, one moves from one end of this continuum, the total dependence of the child, to the other. From the sociological perspective, *compadre* relationships are best understood as modeled on those of adult married siblings. But from the perspective of a maturing adult it may be more accurate to say that one wishes to model one's relationship with one's siblings, which tend to be ambiguous, emotional and conflict-ridden, on those far more clearly defined ties established with *compadres*. Delicately, carefully, and over the years the new household changes the movement of food to other households of the family from a constant flow of cooked meals to a more limited exchange. Meals are shared when major agricultural tasks are performed, and frequent, generous gifts of uncooked foodstuffs are made, but the hearth is sealed off, and the other households are excluded from the everyday meals prepared there. At the end of this process, the everyday deliveries of pots of soup, ground barley, and tidbits are a thing of the past.

The sealing off of the hearth as the key step in establishing independence, reveals the centrality of the cooked meal within domestic life, and re-establishes the primacy of the household as the basic social unit. In the realm of consumption, the individual disappears (no one in Zumbagua eats alone), and while larger groups exist, the household is primary. As this discussion has indicated, in this domestic economy the ability to control consumption implies the ability to engineer changes in production as well. And as the sequence of childrearing demonstrates, control of social reproduction rests more securely in the household than even in motherhood itself.

In Zumbagua, then, two contradictory tendencies act on the definition of the household. On one hand the household is emphasized as a discrete and economically significant unit, the focal point for individual identity and the basic component within the extended family. On the other, the boundaries between households are deliberately blurred by a prolonged process of staggered separation through which new households emerge. These characteristics are born of basic principles upheld in Zumbagua, including a disinclination to make sudden transitions in social state, and a strong determination to protect individual ownership of assets while enmeshing every individual in a large, complex network based on the sharing of labor. The very slowness of household reproduction acts to enlarge and complicate this socioeconomic network, by its tendency to involve people with the meals, children and lives of more than one household at a time.

Analysis of the separate processes making up the domestic sphere has led us to first dismantle the household completely, but now to reinstate it as one of the most significant of a series of concentric social and economic groupings. Other social units—the individual as the locus of ownership of assets and the family as the productive team—are integral to the domestic economy, but consumption, social reproduction and exchange remain firmly tied to the domain of the household. This underlying structure is clearly understood by all participants, but the organization of everyday domestic practice acts to blur the boundaries not only between households but between individual, household and family as discrete levels of organization, and between production, consumption and social reproduction as socioeconomic categories. In Zumbagua daily life, domestic processes emphasize a social whole which is experienced as more complex, satisfying and meaningful than the sum of these parts.

In conclusion, the Zumbagua household is not so much a formal residential structure but a constituted process, made up of activities ranging from the mundane tasks of making breakfast to the critical social undertaking of making and raising a baby. Its identity as a social unit derives from the constant repetition of domestic activities in all their reassuring sameness, but the most constant factor in Zumbagua household life is the steady accretion of minute alterations in everyday domestic habits, out of which come the major transitions of an individual lifetime, as well as the evolution of new households and families.

As I demonstrate in this paper, the starting point for analysis of domestic economy and social organization should be the actual processes and relations of production, reproduction and consumption. My analysis begins with these constituent processes: growing food, raising and eating it, conceiving, giving birth to and raising children. Such an analysis provides a concrete understanding of domestic life and its underlying social and economic structures, and provides a basis for defining individual, household and family. In addition, in the case of Zumbagua, close attention to the details of everyday domestic life—grinding barley, cooking porridge, minding children—reveals the importance of the processes of reproduction and transformation through which existing households are maintained and new household created.

Not only the domestic economy but the social fabric itself and the lived experience of Zumbaguans is constituted out of everyday practice, and this practice must be the starting point for analysis. This approach replaces the sterile quests for elusive boundaries between artificially construed social units with an understanding of the role of fluidity and transformation in the creation and maintenance of social units. This kind of process-oriented analysis allows us to see that the most significant thing about the boundedness of units like the household is that they create the possibility of movement, sharing and exchange. In Zumbagua, households and families are produced through the movement of goods and labor: people create families through the exchange of work on individually-owned property, and daily reproduce their households by sharing the products of their land and labor.

Notes

1. The data presented in this paper is based on fifteen months' fieldwork done in 1983–4, together with a three-month preliminary reconnaissance of the province in 1982 and a brief (80-day) re-study in 1985. The main project was funded by a Fulbright-Hayes dissertation research grant, while support for the two smaller field trips was provided by the University of Illinois.

2. A second and perhaps more serious problematic, which space does not permit me to directly address in this paper, lies in the tendency of anthropology to assume an ahistorical uniformity of social forms within cultural areas like the Andes. This paper presents those aspects of Zumbagua household structure of most relevance for the Andes as a whole, and does not deal, except in passing, with certain important features related to the specific history and current socioeconomic situation of the parish. Social forms in the parish bear the marks of historical forces, most notably the political economy of the hacienda which dominated the region from the early 17th century until 1965, as well as the recent semi-proletarianization of the economy. Contemporary problems include the relations between subsistence-farmer wives and wage-worker husbands, which I have dealt with elsewhere (Weismantel 1986, 1989, 1988a, 1988b), and the reshaping of the Zumbagua household and extended family as a result of these relations, a topic which I will address in a later paper.

3. This prolonged period of residence within the family of orientation, in which Zumbagua differs from Andean residence patterns described elsewhere, may be attributable to social conditions that emerged in the latter years of the hacienda. Although the initial shortage of labor on Andean haciendas continued

for several centuries, by the beginnings of this century haciendas like Zumbagua had no new *huasipungos* (a form of peonage in which usufruct of small plots of land was given in exchange for labor) to offer young couples born on the hacienda. (See Weismantel 1989: 60–66; also Crespi 1968: 68–69 and Prieto 1980: 106 for other examples from the Ecuadorian Sierra.) No data exists on Zumbagua social structure at that time, but the emergence of a residence pattern of patri- and matrilocality replacing neolocality hardly seems surprising given the unavailability of new house plots.

4. This is a long-awaited moment for many young women, and one which can sometimes be hastened by using a wage-earning husband's savings to build a cement block home. Such a move earns the censure of older family members, whose unhesitating assertions that the woman is responsible points to a shared knowledge of the unenviable position of young wives within their mother-in-law's kitchen (See Weismantel 1989: 171–176).

References Cited

Bolton, Ralph. 1977. "The Qolla Marriage Process," in Ralph Bolton and Enrique Mayer (eds.), *Andean Kinship and Marriage*. American Anthropological Association special publication no. 7, Washington, D.C.: AAA. Pp. 217–239

Carter, W.E. 1977. "Trial Marriage in the Andes?" in Ralph Bolton and Enrique Mayer (eds.), *Andean Kinship and Marriage*. American Anthropological Association special publication no. 7, Washington, D.C.: AAA. Pp. 177–216

Crespi, Muriel Kaminsky. 1968. "The Patrons and Peons of Pesillo: A Traditional Hacienda System in Highland Ecuador." Ph.D. dissertation, University of Illinois at Urbana-Champaign.

Harris, Olivia. 1980. "The Power of Signs: Gender, Culture and the Wild in the Bolivian Andes," in Carol P. MacCormack and Marilyn Strathern (eds.), *Nature, Culture and Gender*. Cambridge: Cambridge University Press.

Mayer, Enrique. 1977. "Beyond the Nuclear Family," in Ralph Bolton and Enrique Mayer (eds.), *Andean Kinship and Marriage*. American Anthropological Association special publication no. 7, Washington, D.C.: AAA. Pp. 60–80

Mishkin, Bernard. 1946. "The Contemporary Quechua," in Julian H. Steward (ed.), *Handbook of South American Indians. Vol. 2, The Andean Civilizations*. Bureau of American Ethnology Bulletin 143. Washington: Smithsonian Institution. Pp. 411–470

Price, Richard. 1965. "Trial Marriage in the Andes." *Ethnology* 4(3): 310–322.

Prieto, Mercedes. 1980. "Haciendas estatales: Un Caso de ofensiva campesina 1926–1948," in *Ecuador: Cambios en el agro serrano*. Quito: FLACSO-CEPLAES. Pp. 101–132.

Rivet, Paul. 1926. "Coutumes Funeraires des Indiens de l'Equateur." *Congres International d'Histoire des Religiours*. Paris. Pp. 376–412.

Spirit Possession of Alejandro Mamami. 1974. Film Produced by Filmakers Library, NY.

Weismantel, M.J. 1989. *Food, Gender and Poverty in the Ecuadorian Andes.* Philadelphia: University of Pennsylvania Press.

_____. 1988a. "The Children Cry for Bread: Hegemony and the Transformation of Consumption," in Benjamin S. Orlove and Henry J. Rutz (eds.), *The Social Economy of Consumption.* Lanham: University Press of America. Pp. 105–124.

_____. 1988b. "Mishqui Women, Jayaj Men: Gender and Semiproletarianization in the Ecuadorian Andes." Paper presented at the Annual Meetings of the International Society for Rural Sociology, Bologna.

_____. 1986. "Wanlla: Desire and Demand in the Contemporary Peasant Household." Paper presented at the Annual Meetings of the Association of Consumer Research, Toronto, Canada.

Yanagisako, Sylvia Junko. 1979. "Family and Household: The Analysis of Domestic Groups." *Annual Review of Anthropology* 8: 161–205.

5

Eating the Dead Chicken:
Intra-Household Decision Making
and Emigration in Rural Portugal

Jeffery W. Bentley

In 1983, while helping a Portuguese farmer carry a rye-cleaning machine to his threshing floor, we accidentally set the machine down on a half-grown chicken and killed it. The farm couple glanced at each other, and without a word, the man picked up the chicken and handed it to his wife. That night we ate the chicken for dinner. There was really no decision to make: the farmer had accidentally killed a chicken he would rather not have killed, but once it was killed the only logical choice was to cook the chicken and eat it.

Household members often reach a consensus easily, because frequently one choice is the only logical one. In a previous paper on the relationship between agricultural change and emigration, I assumed that decisions to buy labor-saving agricultural machinery were based on economic factors such as the household's supply of capital and labor. The declining supply of labor (a result of out-migration) motivated many households to buy labor-saving machinery. Households of different economic means behaved differently, in predictable patterns, according to their supply of the factors of production (land, labor, and capital). I considered each household a single decision-making unit, reaching decisions according to relatively obvious choices, to the benefit of most or all household members (Bentley 1987).

Background. Case material comes from my fieldwork (June-November 1983, April-November 1984) in the *freguesia* (smallest political-administrative unit, glossed here as "parish") of Penabranca (fictitious name), in the Northwest Portuguese province of Entre Douro e Minho (the Minho). Penabranca covers about 10 square kilometers of hilly woods and cropland on the eastern edge of a plateau, 15 kilometers from a

TABLE 1

Distribution of Crop Land and Cattle by Household

farm size	number of households	average herd size	average size of holding in hectares
no land	95	0	0
below .5 ha	84	.060	.164
1 to 2 ha	22	3.091	1.406
2 to 4 ha	16	5.750	3.043
4 to 7.5 ha	8 a)	13.375	5.712
Total	253 b)	1.221	.619

a) One farm in the parish is owned and managed by a man who was born in the parish, and inherited the farm. He lives in the nearby city, but visits the farm daily. This farm is included in this table, but has no resident household members, and so is excluded from the remaining tables in this chapter, and from other sociological discussions of the parish's 261 households.

b) Nine households deleted from sample because of insufficient data.

regional city of 70,000 inhabitants. Most of the land lies between 300 and 400 meters above sea level. In 1984 Penabranca had a population of 1109 people, in 261 households.

Major commodities produced in the parish are milk, corn, wine, rye grass and potatoes. Rye, olive and fruit trees, beans and vegetables (especially kale) are also grown. Rainfall of about 2000 mm per year falls mainly in the winter, with little yearly variation in amount of precipitation (Stanislawski 1959: 39). Summer crops must be irrigated from springs, wells or streams.

Because Penabranca is so close to the city, people can live there and commute to work in town, generally by bus or motorcycle. Penabranca is not unusually close to a city, compared with other rural Minhoto parishes. The central Minho is completely suburbanized, with over 250 people per square kilometer (Guichard 1982). Agriculture now makes up an important minority fraction of its total economy. Although farms are divided into a large number of different parcels, land fragmentation is not the barrier to production that it is commonly made out to be (Bentley 1986, 1987a).

Table 1 shows the unequal distribution of land and cattle in Penabranca. The upper 10% of the households farm 60% of the farmland.

In the early twentieth century most of the people were landless, or nearly landless. They worked as sharecroppers (*caseiros*) as agricultural day laborers (*jornaleiros*) and as farm hands (*criados*) for the farmers and large land owners.

In the mid 1960s France opened its doors to emigrant workers, and men from Penabranca poured across the border, including many sharecroppers and day laborers. Traditional patterns of labor use and social relations changed dramatically. Between the 1960s and the 1980s the number of sharecroppers declined from 20 to six, and agricultural labor became scarce (Bentley 1987; Caldas 1981).

Emigrants emerged as a new, generally wealthier, social group (Brettel 1979, 1983). Many of the emigrants never visit Portugal. They are bitter about the poverty of their youth, and wish to live in France until they die.

Other emigrants return to Penabranca each August. They live abroad eleven months of the year with their household, and return to a large, modern house that stands empty most of the year. Most of them hope to retire in Penabranca, although few of their children wish to leave France.

Other emigrants are married men, who do not take their families with them to France. The wives of these men stay in Penabranca to tend their small farms or fields, seeing their husbands once a year.

Many other men have also left agriculture to work local construction jobs, often building houses for emigrants. Agricultural work in Penabranca and the Minho has become increasingly feminized (Brettell 1982; Goldey 1981). By 1984 three-fourths of the parish's agricultural work force was female. Men have only stayed on about 30 of the largest farms, so daily farm chores are performed by women, especially on the smaller farms. Many other women spend hours daily cultivating large gardens and tending rabbits, pigs, and chickens. Tasks requiring big crews, like planting or harvesting, are often done on holidays or Saturdays when the male kin are home to help.

Choice and Decision

In this chapter I wish to suggest that although decisions can be classed according to the amount of choice implicit in a decision, and the participants involved, cultural values help people discard or fail to consider certain alternatives, allowing many households to opt for long-term separation through the emigration of one household member.

Obvious Choice, Petty Decision. Many examples could be added to the dead chicken story, to suggest that many decisions have but one viable choice. Potatoes are almost always planted and harvested when men are not at their construction jobs. I asked one farmer how she decided when to plant potatoes. "We sat around the table after dinner one night," she said, "and decided to plant on April 25 (the anniversary of the 1974 Portuguese Revolution) because my husband had the day off."

Obvious Choice, Big Decision. The petty decisions of everyday life—like eating chickens or planting potatoes—are not the only ones which may have only one logical choice. Consider the decision of the last of the parish's "big farms" (5.6 ha of fields; 14 ha of forest) to buy a tractor. The principal farmer lived with his wife, his elderly father, mother and his celibate father's brother. Generally his mother tended the young couple's two daughters while the others worked the farm. They had plenty of labor for farm work, but as the elders of the household neared age 70, and would soon retire from the most vigorous activities, the man confided to me that he was afraid that his wife would have to stay home and care for the old people, and he would be unable to tend the farm alone.

A year after we had this conversation, the household bought a tractor, a major labor-saving device. They sold some standing timber to pay for it. Although they were surprised to find out how fast a tractor burns up diesel fuel, they were delighted with how much work the tractor saved. While this household had been able to put off the decision to mechanize, the decision was inevitable because the short supply and high cost of labor (due in large part to out-migration) ruled out older solutions like renting out part of the farm to sharecroppers, getting live-in farm hands, or hiring enough day labor to make up the deficit (Bentley 1987; Caldas 1981: 212; Goldey 1981: 127).

One-Sided Decisions, No Choice Offered. At other times, a decision is made unequally, by one person, and other household members do not participate in it. In 1922 a man from Penabranca emigrated permanently to France (after serving there in World War I), leaving a wife and four-month-old son. In 1979, after an absence of 57 years, the old man came home, a return-migrant Rip van Winkle. His son had grown up, married, had had a son and died after falling from a tree. The grandson was a grown man with a family, still living in the old man's house. Although his wife didn't recognize him, the prodigal was accepted back into the household. His wife died soon afterwards, and he was cared for by his elderly daughter-in-law. The migrant had raised another family in France, lost contact with his family in Portugal, but had eventually come home to live out his last years. His household was affected by his decision to break relations with the family, and by his decision to return, although they did not participate in either decision.

Muddling Through. Some decisions resemble a "muddling through" (Park 1982) process more than others. As household members acquire new experience they may change their position on an issue. In 1978, one of the returning emigrants decided to grow improved seed potatoes.

Villagers were just starting to plant improved seed potatoes, with chemical fertilizer, and many did not know what high yields they would get. The returning emigrant wanted to buy four bags of seed potatoes. His wife thought that four bags were far too many, so he bought three instead. That fall she was so pleased with the potato harvest that after that, he recalled with a smile, his wife would let him plant as many potatoes as he wanted.

Participants

Participants are one of the most important of the components of the speech act, as defined by Hymes (1974). The above examples suggest that there are household decisions made by one person and household decisions reached by two or more. This section examines the interaction of two or more household members reaching a decision together. The previous example focused on the husband-wife pair, who reached a decision (to plant more potatoes) to the advantage of both by waiting and acquiring more information. The following example shows that husband-wife decision making is not necessarily so cordial.

Husband and Wife Conflict. In the 1940s when her children were small, a woman I will call Anastácia had grown tired of not being able to feed her children. She borrowed 20 escudos and bought a tray-full of (fresh) sardines to sell. Her husband didn't want her to sell sardines, and they had an argument over it, but in the end she did what she had decided to do. She made 20 escudos the first day. "I was so happy," she said, "now I have money to feed my children."

Eventually Anastácia's husband could not find work, and decided to sell sardines too. "That's fine," Anastácia told him, "because you can make a lot of money, but you're not following me. You have to get your own route." They kept their money separately.

He wasn't successful and came to Anastácia to borrow money. She laughed when she told me she had retorted, "What for, to spend it on whores?" In 1957 this man emigrated to Africa. He wrote for a couple of years and then disappeared.

In this case the husband and wife did not reach a decision, and the wife sold sardines as she wished. In some cases though, a husband's opinion is reluctantly heeded. In 1984 one woman complained that her husband didn't want her to sell bread on Sundays. He worked a construction job, and she worked on her parents' small farm. "He says he doesn't want me to wear myself out," she said, "but look at me working here in the fields." (Implying that what he really objected to was the freedom of movement she would have selling bread door to door.)

Mother-Daughter Conflict. People of the same sex can generate as much heat and as little light while reaching a decision as can people of opposite sexes. In 1962 a couple of agricultural laborers decided they could no longer afford to feed their six year old daughter, and sent her to live as a farm hand (*criada*) with a nearby farm family. The farmer made her work so hard it was nearly impossible for her to go to school. She had to cut a large basket of grass for the cows every morning before school, so she was often late. She never finished third grade. Every year the farmer gave her a dress, which with her daily soup and bread was her only pay.

Eight years later while home for Christmas (her one day off a year) she told her mother she was never going back to work for that farmer. Her mother beat her with a stick. After the beating the young woman ran away for the day. While tearfully explaining the problem to a neighboring farmer, he asked her to come live with his family. This second farmer payed her a little money, and taught her how to drive a tractor. When she was 22 she was able to get a salaried job on a small commercial farm.

Mother-Daughter Solidarity. Although much of the marketing literature focuses on the husband and wife pair (Park 1982, Davis 1976, Spiro 1983) other people may be involved in reaching a decision. In cases where husband and wife are at disagreement, a grown daughter may join her mother in making the decision.

A farmer and her daughter had spent the day planting potatoes. When the old woman's husband came home from his construction job he complained about the variety they had planted. The women argued back together, pointing out that there wasn't much to be done about the matter now, since the potatoes were already in the ground. The man soon realized he was out-numbered and quietly withdrew from the discussion.

In another case a man came home complaining that someone had knocked a stone wall over on the pipe that carried water from their spring to the house. He wanted to call in the rural guard. His wife and daughter argued that that would only make the vandals more angry, and would not do any good anyway. Eventually they swayed him.

Offering an Opportunity to Other Household Members. Not all household decisions are contentious. Some decisions sprout from an opportunity tendered by a household member. In 1961 a childless widower, living with his third wife and his wife's 18 year old niece, hit upon an idea to have his wife's niece marry his own brother's son, to take over the farm and provide him with old age care. He proposed the idea to his 31 year old nephew, who had been working in France for three years, offering to give him two fields, and sell him the rest of the farm over time, if he would marry the young woman. The nephew was not going to inherit much of his own father's farm, since the bulk of that farm was going to be inherited by his younger brother, who had married first and moved his wife into his parent's household. The sibling who marries first generally becomes the major heir if his/her spouse moves into his parents house with him or her (Bentley 1986, 1987; Silva 1983). The nephew and the young woman married during one of the nephew's visits from France and he worked abroad the next 16 years to buy the rest of the farm and a tractor. Although the couple had to decide to marry of their own accord, the idea was first proposed by another household member.

Intermediate Conclusion. Many decisions have only one rational option. Other decision-making events are unequal; one member exercises a decision which the others adapt to. In other cases, household members are able to muddle through to a consensus. Many decisions are made between husband and wife, but not always. Sometimes a decision is made by a woman and her daughter, and imposed on the husband. Some decisions are offered as opportunities to other household members, who have to decide whether or not to accept them. Decisions may be made in a spirit of cooperation or of conflict. Of course the amount of conflict the ethnographer perceives is likely to diminish with time. One may observe more conflict watching a household squabble over the dinner table than any of the participants would report later. But some decisions do persist as conflicts in the memory and talk of the people involved.

Emigration

Cultural values, held by all villagers (men and women) are important for reducing the field of choices, hence reducing the amount of potential conflict. In the case of eating the dead chicken, a set of common sense cultural values are called into play that classify accidentally killed animals and half grown chickens as acceptable food. These cultural values allow people to rule out other possibilities (throwing the chicken away, feeding it to the dog, etc.) and reach a decision rapidly, with little or no discussion. Cultural values can also reduce the field of choice for big decisions. The following section discusses how the values of this very Catholic little community allow villagers to reach one of the biggest decisions a household can make: to send the principal wage earner abroad, alone, for most of his career, to earn money for the household. The following case history frames the emigration experience in human, individual terms.

Deciding to Emigrate. Many villagers discuss the extreme poverty before emigration as a major factor in deciding to emigrate. They tell how

many people were involved much of the time in marginal tasks that are
the symptoms of under-employment, like scouring the forest for acorns,
to sell to large farmers as hog feed, and saving household ashes to sell
to farmers as fertilizer. Farmers reminisce that before emigration people
would be waiting at the threshing floor every morning at 5 o'clock
looking for work, and farmers picked the ones they wanted and sent the
rest away. Informants say there was widespread begging and occasional
starvation. Guerreiro says that before emigration when there was a bad
harvest there was no food, and people offered a day's labor for a piece
of bread and water, and that some women prostituted themselves for a
kilo of sugar (Guerreiro 1981: 195–96).

In 1956, a couple I will call Fernando and Maria were married. They
were in their mid 30s, and not from wealthy families. Maria had inherited
a cottage with a tiny garden. The couple moved into Maria's house,
with Fernando's father, who died two years later. By the time Fernando
and Maria's second daughter was born in 1959, they could no longer
live on the money they made as agricultural day laborers.

They decided together that Fernando should emigrate to France, to
send money home. Emigration was illegal, so Fernando had to sneak
across two borders before he reached France, where one could "walk
into the arms of the gendarme" to receive work papers (cf. Guerreiro
1981: 283–299). Fernando was gone for three years without coming
back. Finding steady work was hard. He would find a job, at low pay
and just be getting ahead when he would lose that job. He wasn't able
to send money home. Maria still recalls with pain the hunger of those
first months. She said, "He was gone from the fifth of February to the
12th of May, without sending home a dime." Maria grew enough kale
in the garden to make a little pot of soup every day, until Fernando
was able to send money home. Eventually they saved enough money to
buy a big house and about a hectare of land. In 1981, after 22 years
abroad, Fernando retired, and came home to live the life of a semi-
retired, small-scale dairy farmer (Carvalho et al. 1982: chapter 3).

This case is reasonably representative of Penabranca's migration patterns.
Two of the cases presented earlier—of the man who emigrated to France
for 57 years and then returned, and the man who abandoned his wife
to go to Africa—are both unusual because in one case the man abandoned
his family while away and in the other the man abandoned his family
permanently. Other villagers expressed contempt for the behavior of both
men. The ancient World War I veteran was even criticised to his face
in my presence. It is far more common to eventually return, either with
savings, or to send money home before returning.

The people of Penabranca have heart-felt values about household
formation, especially marriage. Three values that allow long-term migration

of husbands without disolving their marriages are firm marital commitment with no possibility of divorce, marital economic fidelity, and hard work with deferred gratification.

Marital Commitment. Marriage is generally contracted between people of roughly similar economic status (O'Neill 1984, 1987; Guerreiro 1981: 51). As one middle-aged woman put it, "If I were poor and you were rich you wouldn't want me." Courtship is long, often for six or eight years, involving so much conversation that courtship itself is called "talking." People describe the length of the courtship: *"Falemos oito anos"* (we talked for eight years). (In the rural dialect spoken around Braga the regular preterite, first person plural suffix of -ar verbs is -emos, not -amos.) Courting couples visit on Sundays after mass, generally sitting within sight of the young woman's home—but out of earshot, talking for hours. Only after a number of years, and rarely, is the couple allowed to spend any time alone together.

Post-marital residence is neo-local for most of the poorer people, but the rule for the large farm households is to form a stem family household (Bentley, 1986; O'Neill 1984, 1987; Willems 1962; Silva 1983; Rowland 1986; cf. Dias 1981: 185). The lengthy courtship prepares couples for a long-term commitment. Divorce is never an alternative, and there have been no divorces in the recorded history of the parish.

Economic Marital Fidelity. Minhotos do not have exceptionally romantic notions of marriage, and the cozy, sexy part of marriage is considered to last for about a year. These values are reflected in three verses collected by Guerreiro in the Upper Minho:

Se o amor fosse no fim
Como era no começo,
Eu dizia à minha mãe,
Que me casasse no berço.

If love were at the end
As it was in the beginning,
I would say to my mother,
Marry me from the cradle.

Casadinha de três dias,
Ela lá vem a chorar,
Coitado de quem nas cria
Para outro as castigar.

Only married for three days,
Here she comes to weep,
The poor one that raises them
For another to punish them.

O primeiro ano é cara con cara,
O segundo é cu con cu,
O terceiro: "Puta, que tenho eu?"
"Que trouxeste tu?"

The first year it's cheek to cheek,
The second it's ass to ass,
the third: "Puta, what have I got?"
"What did you bring?"

(Guerreiro 1981: 52–53)

The word "puta" (whore) is a common swear word—in a region where swear words are used frequently. It is used to show general displeasure and in this case does not mean that the husband is calling his wife a whore.

While love may not be the tie that binds, shared cultural values are. In spite of a sexual double standard, in which only women are really expected to remain faithful, husbands and wives expect a strict economic fidelity from their spouses. While men are away in France they may visit prostitutes, but not very often, because it is irresponsible to spend money on personal entertainment. When men send money home to their wives they expect that the money will be saved for major purchases (land, tractors, houses)—or simply left in the bank for undetermined future use (Portela 1981)—but that the household members who stay in Portugal should feed themselves as much as possible with their garden or farm produce (Goldey 1981: 115).

Hard Work and Deferred Gratification. The villagers share the intensive farmer's work ethic with small-scale, peasant farmers everywhere, whether Protestant or not (Netting 1988, 1974; see also Rhoades and Thompson 1976; Netting 1981; Leach 1968). Farmers commonly work from sunup to sundown, and although they do not work in the fields on Sundays, they often use Sundays to repair equipment. Male off-farm workers usually work on their family's land on Saturdays and after work (Bentley 1987). Women work all their waking hours. Penabrancans are experts at not spending money. They virtually never eat in restaurants, or go to movies, and rarely buy new clothes. Clothing and equipment are repaired over and over again, so that there will be money for major purchases.

Out-migration has been a theme of Portuguese life for centuries, with a major movement to Brazil in the 1910s and a much larger migration to Western Europe (especially France) in the 1960s (Serrão 1981, especially Fig. II, pp. 48–49). By 1973 Serrão estimates that there were nearly a million Portuguese in Western Europe, most of them in France (see Table 2). The population of Portugal was 8,889,392 in 1960 (Instituto Nacional de Estatstica 1964) and in 1984 was widely assumed to be over 10 million, due to the return of hundreds of thousands of colonists and refugees from Africa after 1974.

Migration is predominantly a male activity. The general pattern is for men to go to Western Europe (especially France) while the women and children stay in Portugal to work the land (Serrão 1982: 119–127; Brettel 1982: 19–22; Guerreiro 1981: 183). Table 3 shows that most of the migrants from Penabranca are men. Women who emigrate generally go a few years after their husbands, and generally come from households with little or no land to tie them to their home village.

Out-migration from Penabranca has been high. The parish population remained the same between 1950 (1,098) and 1980 (1,110) due to the high amount of out-migration, which reached a peak of 402 net out-

TABLE 2

Portuguese Emigrants in Europe in Mid-1973

France 773,000
Germany..110,000
Spain 26,300
England 16,250
Luxembourg 16,100
Holland 8,700
Belgium 7,100
Switzerland 6,100
Italy 4,100
Sweden 1,550

Total 969,200

Source: Serrão 1982: 66 (Table 13)

TABLE 3

Years Spent Abroad, by Gender and Type of Residence

	number	average number of years abroad
women currently or previously living abroad, from resident households (1)	28	8.7
men currently or previously living abroad, from resident households	136	11.6
women currently abroad, from emigrant households (2)	21	14.8
men currently abroad, from emigrant households	20	20.3

Source: Author's census

1) Resident household: one of the 261 households in Penabranca in which one person or more resides throughout the year, although one person or more may be an emigrant, absent for most of the year.

2) Emigrant household: one of the 21 households in Penabranca, censused by the author, in which no one resides throughout the year. Most of these households live in France and only visit their homes in Portugal in August. Many plan to eventually retire to these houses.

TABLE 4

Net Number of Out-Migrations from Penabranca

```
1920s ............... 8
1930s .............. 69
1940s .............. 42
1950s ............. 103
1960s ............. 402
1970s ............. 115

total ............ 740
```

Source: Bentley 1987: 171 (Table 9.2)

TABLE 5

The Whereabouts of People Born in 1954 or Before,
As Reported by their Parents Living in Penabranca in 1984

```
In their parents' household ................... 19   (7%)
In Penabranca, not in parent's household...... 66  (23%)
In the Minho, but not in Penabranca .......... 39  (14%)
In Portugal, but not in the Minho ............ 19   (7%)
In other countries ........................ 138  (49%)

Total ...................................... 281 (100%)
```

migrations from the parish in the 1960s (see Table 4). In 1984, half of the people (born in 1954 or earlier) whose parents still live in Penabranca lived abroad (Table 5).

Most of the Portuguese men in France work in heavy industry, especially construction (Serrão 1982: 66; Guerreiro 1981: 156). While working abroad the men say that they "live like slaves" to save as much money as possible (Brettell 1982: 65). Returned migrants told me that while they worked construction jobs they generally lived in barracks, or crowded into tiny apartments. If they worked building houses they would build the garage first, and live in it while they built the rest of the house. The wives of these men live quiet, industrious lives in their absence, working long hours in the fields and spending virtually no money on themselves, even for food.

The Results. After many years abroad, the migrant generally builds a new house in Penabranca, or remodels an old house, if the household has been fortunate enough to inherit one. My census of the community revealed 97 new housing starts since 1960—all but 33 for households with some emigration experience. Some writers share the opinion of the old-money Portuguese that the "emigrant houses" are gaudy, "new symbols of dubious taste" (Lucas 1983: 166). The houses are often massive, two-story monuments, complete with brass and marble exterior stair-cases and six colors of tile blanketing the outside walls. Inside they tend to be comfortable.

The critics of the neo-Portuguese architecture ignore what it means to the people who build it. As the former landless laborers, sharecroppers, and the smallest farmers, who left their homes with little or nothing, it means a great deal to show their neighbors and former employers that they have been successful (Brettell 1982: 65, 1983: 179; O'Neill 1987: 245–46).

Building a house allows them to play the role of employer (O'Neill 1981: 65). They generally hire another villager as contractor, who works on the house with a crew of two to six men for about two years, often finishing the house in the last few years of the migrant's foreign sojourn. By bringing back blueprints from France and using colorful materials— in contrast to the somber granite houses of the large farmers—the return migrant demonstrates that he owes his success to years of working in a foreign country, not in staying behind to earn the low wages of the Portuguese worker or the low returns to labor of the smallest farmers. (For information on wages and returns to labor see Bentley 1987; Monke 1987; Pearson et al. 1987.)

The first goal of most migrants is to save money to build a house or remodel their existing house (Brettell 1982: 46; Rodrigo 1981: 403; cf. Dias 1981: 60). Likewise, one of the first major expenses of successful farm families is modern plumbing in their old farm houses. The purchases that Portuguese villagers commonly make—new houses, hot and cold running water, and land for growing food—suggest that they buy things that benefit all household members more or less equally. This contrasts with other areas, Belize for example, where rural men are more likely to spend money on themselves alone (Wilk 1988).

The out-migration of men is seen by the villagers as a very responsible act, because they are leaving to earn money for their families. Brettell refers to Portuguese laws that restricted female emigration "particularly women whose husbands, for whatever reasons, preferred not to have their wives join them in France" (1982: 33). The reasons are generally that they want to avoid the expense of a family in France; they want to keep the land at home in cultivation; and they want their children to grow up Portuguese.

Discussion

The ideology of the Catholic marriage and the high value placed on frugality and hard work are part of the village morality that maintain a trust relationship between a husband and wife when they are separated for years. Regardless of the factors that a couple weighs when deciding that the man should emigrate, because of the cultural values that they share they know that they can count on each other to maintain their economic partnership in spite of their separation.

Tension. The local moral code that allows households to use long-term emigration as a successful economic strategy also exacts a cost. Although many people grow old and comfortable with their spouse, other people find themselves trapped in an unbreakable marriage with someone they can no longer tolerate. Of the 261 households in Penabranca in 1984 I knew of three elderly couples who were still married but longer lived together. Two were return migrants. One man had moved into a separate cottage and avoided any contact with his wife. Another moved into a house across the lane but continued to take his meals with his wife, their daughter and son-in-law. Another man felt humiliated because there was some suggestion that his wife had been sexually unfaithful to him while he was in France (Blok 1981), so although he continued to live in the same house he kept his own room, ate elsewhere, and never worked alongside his wife. Ten years before I lived in Penabranca an emigrant (whose wife had stayed in Portugal) killed himself over his marital problems.

In another case a return migrant was murdered in 1982. He was away for many years, and saved enough money to build a house with a small garden in 1967. But while he was away he developed the suspicion that his wife was sleeping with someone else. One villager says that while comming home for one of his August vacations the taxi driver who brought him from the train station started to brag about all the emigrants' wives he was having affairs with. "Two of them live in this parish, and one of them lives right there!" he said, pointing to the emigrant's own house. Whatever the source of the emigrant's suspicions, by the time he retired he was sullen and mean. One of his daughters characterized her father as a "bad man" who used to get drunk a lot and come home and beat up her mother. Village men told me that he had bought a big hunting knife in France, and sometimes in the taverns he would take out the weapon and turn it over in his hand, saying, "Someday I'm going to bury this in my wife's belly."

One night he left the tavern drunk, in an ugly mood, and was found at home the next morning, dead on floor, stabbed with his own blade. His wife confessed to the killing, but their youngest son (age 19) had crossed the Spanish frontier before daybreak and returned to Luxembourg, where he had been working. She served two years in prison, and came home just before I left the field in 1984. Her neighbors were disgusted that she was free, and only a very few of her closest kin would associate with her.

There are other stresses, less dramatic but more common, associated with long-term emigration. Men regret that their children grow up without their father's guidance and children miss their absent father. Husbands and wives miss each other when they are apart, especially since talking by telephone is expensive and virtually impossible, and the low level of literacy prevents some couples from even writing letters.

In France the men tend to work and live with men from their home area, often with kinsmen. One man told of working on a cooling tower for a nuclear power plant, surrounded by men from Penabranca. Even so they feel isolated and alone, especially since the French are starting to resent the presence of foreign workers. Perhaps the dominant feeling these men have is a kind of martyrdom, that they have sacrificed themselves for their families.

Conclusion

Reaching a decision is not always a drawn-out, complicated process. Some choices are the most logical for all household members. This is true for small decisions like when to plant potatoes, and for big decisions like buying a tractor. For a very big decision, like whether to emigrate or not, and if emigrating, whether the whole family should emigrate or just the husband, there is invariably a household decision making process. Yet the observation that people with much land tend not to emigrate, people with no lend tend to emigrate as whole households, and households with some land tend to send off only the husband suggest that material factors strongly influence the decision to emigrate. Cultural values about marriage and divorce help some households to decide to send the husband alone to a foreign country, because the values of marital commitment, economic fidelity, and deferred gratification guarantee to both marriage partners that the money earned in Europe will be saved for the good of the whole household and that household members in Portugal will be largely self-supporting in the husband's absence. This cultural morality which is called into play in the household decision making process creates stress for at least some people, so that violence and informal separation take the place of divorce for a few households, and all households suffer emotionally from the separation.

Acknowledgments

I acknowledge PROCALFER (USAID/Lisbon), the Department of Agricultural Economics of the University of Arizona, and the Tinker Foundation for funding.

The Anthropology Department, University of Arizona, provided space for data processing. The Departamento de Proteccion Vegetal of the Escuela Agricola Panamericana (Honduras) housed me while I wrote, and payed my expenses to the meetings of the American Anthropological Association in Chicago in 1987, where I read an earlier version of this paper. I thank Elizabeth Bentley for reading and commenting on this paper. Much thanks to Richard Wilk, for encouraging me to write this paper, and for a number of stimulating discussions along the way.

References Cited

Bentley, Jeffery W. 1986. "Kinship, Inheritance and Land Fragmentation in the Minho (Portugal)." Presented at the Thirteenth European Congress of Rural Sociology, in Braga, Portugal, April, 1986.

———. 1987. "Technical Change in a Northwest Parish" in Scott R. Pearson et al. (eds.), *Portuguese Agriculture in Transition*. Ithaca: Cornell University Press.

———. 1987a. "Economic and Ecological Approaches to Land Fragmentation: In Defense of a Much-Maligned Phenomenon." *Annual Review of Anthropology*. 16: 32–63.

Blok, Anton. 1981. "Carneiros e Cabrões: Uma Oposião Chave para o Código Mediterrôneo de Honra." Perspectivas sobre o Norte de Portugal. *Estudos Contemporâneos* 2/3: 9–29.

Brettell, Caroline B. 1979. "Emigrar para Voltar: A Portuguese Ideology of Return Migration." *Papers in Anthropology* 20(1): 1–20.

———. 1982. *We Have Already Cried Many Tears: The Stories of Three Portuguese Migrant Women*. Cambridge, Mass.: Schenkman Publishing Co.

———. 1983. "Emigrão, a Igreja e a Festa Religiosa do Norte de Portugal: Estudo de um Caso." Comunidades Rurais: Estudos Interdisciplinares. *Estudos Contemporâneos* 5: 175–204.

Caldas, João Castro. 1981. "Caseiros do Alto Minho: Adaptão e Declinio." A Pequena Agricultura em Portugal. *Revista Crítica de Ciências Sociais* 7/8: 203–216.

Carvalho, Agostinho de, Vítor Coelho Barros and José Ramos Rocha. 1982. *Que Futuro para a Produão Leiteira: Grande ou Pequena Explorão?* Oeiras, Portugal: Instituto Gulbenkian de Cincia.

Davis, Harry L. 1976. "Decision Making within the Household." *Journal of Consumer Research* 2: 241–60.

Dias, Jorge. 1981. *Rio de Onor: Comunitarismo Agro-Pastoril*. (Second Edition). Lisbon: Editorial Presença.

Douglass, William A. 1975. *Echalar and Murelaga: Opportunity and Rural Exodus in Two Spanish Basque Villages*. New York: St. Martin's Press.

Goldey, Patricia. 1981. "Emigrão e Estrutura Familiar—Estudo de um Caso no Minho." Perspectivas sobre o Norte de Portugal. *Estudos Contemporâneos* 2/3: 111–127.

Guerreiro, Manuel Viegas. 1981. *Pitões das Júnias: Esboço de Monografia Etnográfica*. Lisbon: Serviço Nacional de Parques, Reservas e Património Paisagistico.

Guichard, François. 1982. *Atlas Demográfico de Portugal*. Lisbon: Livros Horizonte.

Hymes, Dell. 1974. "Toward Ethnographies of Communication" in *Foundations in Sociolinguistics: Essays by Dell Hymes*. Philadelphia: University of Pennsylvania Press.

Instituto Nacional de Estatística. 1964. *Recenceamento Geral da População (1960)*. Lisbon.

Leach, E. 1968. *Pul Eliya: A Village in Ceylon*. Cambridge: Cambridge University Press.

Lucas, António M. Rolo. 1983. "O Lugar da Palhaça e a Feira dos Quatro Caminhos." *Comunidades Rurais: Estudos Interdisciplinares. Estudos Contemporâneos* 5: 151–73.

Monke, Eric. 1987. "Agricultural Factor Markets" in Pearson et al. (eds.), *Portuguese Agriculture in Transition*. Ithaca: Cornell University Press.

Netting, Robert McC. 1974. "Agrarian Ecology." *Annual Review of Anthropology* 3: 21–56.

———. 1981. *Balancing on an Alp: Ecological Change and Continuity in a Swiss Mountain Community*. New York: Cambridge University Press.

———. 1988. "Small holders, Householders, Freeholders: Why the Family Farm Works Well Worldwide." Scott-Hawkins Lecture, Southern Methodist University. September 22, 1988.

O'Neill, Brian Juan. 1981. "Proprietários, Jornaleiros e Criados numa Aldeia Transmontana desde 1886." Perspectivas sobre o Norte de Portugal. *Estudos Contemporâneos* 2/3: 31–73.

———. 1984. *Proprietários, Lavradores, e Jornaleiras: Desigualdade Social numa Aldeia Transmontana, 1870–1978*. Lisbon: Publicações Dom Quixote.

———. 1987. *Social Inequality in a Portuguese Hamlet: Land, Late Marriage and Bastardy, 1870–1987*. Cambridge: Cambridge University Press.

Park, C. Whan. 1982. "Joint Decisions in Home Purchasing: A Muddling-Through Process." *Journal of Consumer Research* 9: 151–162.

Pearson, Scott R., Francisco Avillez, Jeffery W. Bentley, Timothy J. Finan, Roger Fox, Timothy Josling, Mark Langworthy, Eric Monke, and Stefan Tangermann. 1987. *Portuguese Agriculture in Transition*. Ithaca: Cornell University Press.

Portela, José. 1981. "Fragueiro: Notas sobre a Agricultura Local. A Pequena Agricultura em Portugal." *Revista Crítica de Ciências Sociais* 78: 217–46.

Rhoades, R.E. and S.I. Thompson. 1976. "Adaptive Strategies in Alpine Environments: Beyond Ecological Particularism." *American Ethnologist* 2: 535–51.

Rodrigo, Isabel. 1981. "Uma Forma Associativa de Produção numa Aldeia da Serra Algarvia." *Revista Crítica de Ciências Sociais* 78: 401–19.

Rowland, Robert. 1986. "Sistemas Matrimoniales en la Península Ibérica (Siglos XVI–XIX): Una Perspectiva Regional" in V. Perez Moreda and D. S. Reher (eds.), *La Demografía Histórica de la Península Ibérica*. (Actas de las I Jornadas de Demografía Histórica, Madrid, Diciembre 1983). Madrid: Editorial Tecnos.

Serrão, Joel. 1982. *A Emigração Portuguesa: Sondagem Histórica*. Lisbon: Livros Horizonte.

Silva, Rosa Fernanda Moreira da. 1983. "Contraste e Mutações na Paisagem Agrária das Planícies e Colinas Minhotas," Comunidades Rurais, Estudos Interdisciplinares. *Estudos Contemporâneos*. 5: 9–115.

Spiro, Rosann L. 1983. "Persuasion in Family Decision-Making." *Journal of Consumer Research* 9: 393–402.

Stanislawski, Dan. 1959. *The Individuality of Portugal: A Study in Historical-Political Geography*. Austin: University of Texas Press.

Wilk, Richard. 1988. "Consumer Goods as Dialogue about Development." Paper presented at the 87th Meetings of the American Anthropological Association. Phoenix, AZ November 16–20, 1988.

Willems, Emilio. 1962. "On Portuguese Family Structure." *International Journal of Comparative Sociology* 3: 65–79.

6

Separation Between Trading and Home for Asante Women in Kumasi Central Market, Ghana

Gracia Clark

Along with other West African market traders and craft workers, the predominantly female and Asante traders in the Central Market of Kumasi, Ghana's second largest city, present a strong contrast to larger enterprises following Western corporate or civil service models in the same city and in more industrialized countries. They show all the characteristics essential to the definitions of petty commodity or simple commodity economic activity, or the informal sector (Moser 1978; C. Smith 1984; Hart 1973). The scale of operations and capital investment of the vast majority of traders is extremely small. Only a handful employ wage labor, and the most common source of supplementary labor is daughters. Their profits go primarily towards the subsistence needs of their families, rather than capital accumulation. Even though some sell imported and manufactured goods made in formal or corporate firms, they are not directly dependent on those firms through, for example, subcontracting or credit sales (Bromley and Gerry 1979; Babb 1988).

This chapter questions the usefulness of analyzing the market trading enterprises of these Asante women as household enterprises. Direct links between trading and household membership or resources are few, weak and brittle. Traders cannot freely draw on labor and other resources of all household members, nor can non-traders draw freely on resources generated by trading, making models of household redistributive exchange hard to defend. Trading survival and success depends on the further insulation of Asante women traders from demands on their time and money from domestic tasks and budgets, rather than on pooling. Decision making and resource allocation among spouses, close kin and co-residents follow patterns very different from the European peasants who inspired

the ideal types of the simple commodity and domestic modes of production.

The concept of the family or household business, like that of the
family farm or farm household, addresses the contrast between contemporary Third World economic activities and their industrial equivalents
by classifying them with practices considered typical of the precapitalist
economic relations of Europe. Household members not only reside in a
single house, but pool their labor and capital resources to support their
various economic and non-economic activities. Central management of
these resources aims at ensuring the long-term security of the unit, rather
than profit maximization, as in capitalism. The household remains the
dominant economic unit even while sending some individuals out to
work for wages in non-household enterprises, if the decision is taken at
the household level and the wages shared (Davin 1984).

In household production, the goal of mutual survival, rather than
individual profit, dominates resource allocation. Sahlins developed this
goal contrast into his concept of a domestic mode of production based
on the household unit by building on Chayanov's model of Russian
peasant farmers and Polanyi's model of barbaric empires. These included
psychological assertions about precapitalist economic actors motivated
towards redistribution, rather than profit (Sahlins 1972; Chayanov 1966;
Polanyi 1957).

All three argue that the family context of work relations in precapitalist
production systems holds down technically possible production levels.
Sahlins argues that household survival places limited demands on household workers, in most cases. Decisions about resource use aim to benefit
the group as a whole, rather than to run specific activities as efficiently
as possible. More labor may be employed on a task than necessary, if
persons cannot be more productively employed elsewhere. Conversely,
less labor may be employed than available, if subsistence needs are already
met. Hyden draws very similar conclusions about the socially determined
inability of contemporary African farmers and urbanites to accumulate
capital or generate technological progress (Hyden 1980).

Current efforts to produce a cross-culturally valid definition of the
household have emphasized the more abstract criteria of joint decision-
making and pooling of resources in the process of backing off from
Eurocentric assumptions about kinship, marriage and co-residence (Friedman 1986; Netting, Wilk and Arnould 1984). The influential review
articles of Yanagisako (1979) and Wilk and Netting (1984) follow critical
analyses of the variation of household composition and functions between
and within societies by returning to resource sharing as the common
denominator of the household. In fact, Asante decision-making and
resource allocation processes are fragmented enough to raise serious

questions whether the urban Asante household functions as a significant economic unit for either production or consumption, let alone dominates other units of cooperation.

Asantes and Households

Several characteristics of Asante residence and marital patterns contradict conventional household models of co-residence and pooling directly (as in Laslett 1972). The high frequency of duolocal marriage and its high social value, together with an expectation of virtually complete separation between personal budgets of husbands and wives, keeps conjugal relations from becoming the focus of either a nuclear or extended household in the majority of cases. Nor is this a result of atomization of a lineage society under contemporary urban pressures. Loyalty to matrilineal kin, individually and in general, remains strong for both men and women in the city. Rural and precolonial kinship relations accommodate and encourage individual ambition.[1] Long-standing commercialization gives cash transfers, as well as labor or in-kind transfers, a hallowed place in defining and confirming kin and marital relations.

Flexibility and negotiability in Asantes' relations with kin, non-kin and spouses result in a wide range of combinations of co-residence, labor, income and expense sharing, joint decision-making, and their absence in specific cases. The full acceptance of individual options and variations frustrates typification of role content in terms of unconditional rights and duties. Fortes, drawing on research in small Asante towns in the 1930s, concludes clearly that resources are not pooled, but exchanged by request, or mutual agreement.

> The dwelling group does not, as a rule, have a common food supply nor do its members pool their incomes for the common support. But the norm is for the dwelling group to consist of a single household in the social sense, that is, a group in which the rule holds that food and assistance are freely asked and given between members. (1949a: 64)

Exchanges Between Spouses

In Asante duolocal marriage, both spouses retain separate dwelling places, either with kin or independently. Young people who marry within the same town or village can both remain living in their natal houses. A wife sends the evening meal daily to her husband, and visits his room to spend the night with him. If a man marries additional wives, they take turns cooking his evening meal and sleeping in his room. In middle age, women often cease visiting their husbands and spend more time on their own lineage affairs. Such women have essentially retired from marriage, not requiring a divorce since they do not intend to remarry.

Children belong to the mother's lineage, but have close personal ties to both parents. They live in their mother's room, whether in lineage or commercial property. Fathers maintain strong bonds despite duolocal marriage, since children can visit or even eat daily in their father's house. They often carry their father his meals, for example, and remain to share the leftovers and collect the dishes. A father takes responsibility for his children's moral and vocational education, especially for his sons, and contributes to their financial support. The mother also contributes substantially to the children's expenses by providing food from her farms, or from her income from trading or other work. A husband provides cash or other resources for food to his wife in return for her domestic services, but does not give her directly any other access to his income (see Clark 1989). Each spouse depends on the other to fulfill their part in supporting the children, but most decisions on working or spending are made individually, or in consultation with lineage kin. Divorce need not rupture either maternal or paternal contact, since neither partner changes residence. Ideally, even in death the father's successor, a member of his own lineage, takes over his paternal responsibilities.

The strength of lineage identification by both husband and wife ensures separation of economic activities and property even in a long lasting marriage marked by strong affection. Although a sound choice of marriage partner shows good character, and maintains the purity and prestige of the lineage, too much attention to romantic relations by either men or women draws censure for lack of seriousness and irresponsibility towards kin. In farming areas, each spouse farms on lineage land, as before marriage. Each cooperates strongly with matrilineage kin, exchanging labor and capital for investment. Important decisions are discussed with them, and gifts of cash, food and labor are expected to kin in need. The husband can call on his wife for farm labor without reciprocating, and expects her to cook the meals for his hired farm laborers. Women living away from their kin have less access to their own land and kin cooperation, but may travel back to establish farms during the farming season.

Duolocal residence further reduces pooling of incomes and shared decision-making between spouses. In discussions of the relative advantages of living with and apart from their husbands, traders remarked themselves that they could claim support for their children more effectively from co-resident husbands because they would be present as expenses arose. Co-residence would give their husbands even greater access on their own time and resources, however, since a wife should defer to her husband.

Many women would rather forgo some support than allow these reciprocal claims.

Migration away from the natal or lineage house reduces the incidence of duolocal marriage, but does not eliminate it. Rural towns founded by relatively recent migration had lower, but still substantial, rates of separate residence. In the farming towns studied by Fortes (1949) and Beckett (1944), married couples lived separately as often as together. Couples who migrate together more often live together, as they may not have resident kin. Interviews in one declining cocoa center in 1979 revealed that siblings who migrated to more remote rural locations for better cocoa land often left as married couples, but some had migrated as brother-sister pairs. Small town informants also reported a tendency for newly married couples to stay in nearby farm hamlets during the farming season, for increased intimacy. Both long and short-term migrants often reported staying in their respective lineage houses on return visits.

Asante traders in Kumasi, the second largest city in Ghana and the historic capital of the Asante people, could and did exercise both joint and duolocal marital options. A survey of Asante market women in Kumasi Central Market revealed that 59% of the currently married traders lived with their husbands.[2] Most traders reported towns of family origin (called "hometowns" in English) outside the Kumasi area, so that they could not presently be living in their true lineage houses. However, a majority of traders grew up in Kumasi, so that they had their childhood homes there. In addition, the numbers of long-established Asante urbanites meant that most traders had relatives in the city who could find them places in housing built or at least rented by family members. Shared conjugal residence avoided extra expense and search (because of a local housing shortage), but the positive desire for separate accommodation led even some recent migrant couples without kin in Kumasi to rent separate rooms.

Discussions with men and women traders revealed both an expectation of divergent interests for spouses and a positive value on separate decisions. Those strongly preferring separation included some who claimed to have excellent relations with their husbands. They argued that separate residence prevented quarrels. According to them, couples living together would be more aware of each other's income, expenditures and daily schedule of going out and coming back. Besides the temptations to mutual jealousy, they were bound to have differences of opinion about the best way to spend time and money. Informants assumed decision-making would remain separate even with joint residence.

Asante women were particularly reluctant to depend on a husband's income. Personal dignity requires that an adult woman be able to dispose of her own income without explanation or permission from others. Most husbands expect their wives to have independent incomes, because they are not prepared to support the family entirely alone. Only rarely, in elite circles, does the disproportionate income of the husband permit a woman to consider relying on his support. Even then, the traders' ideal is for the wife to take advantage of his connections or his generous support of the children to build up a substantial business of her own. Of course, those who had chosen dependency would not have appeared in the ranks of Kumasi Central Market traders, but ethnographic and literary sources confirm the rarity of inactive wives (for example see Aidoo 1970; Oppong 1974; Rattray 1923).

Asante women considered work in joint enterprises with their husbands even less attractive. Because of the husband's higher status, any joint enterprise was presumed to be under his control. With separate budgets, this income would be his personal property, not their joint property. In rural farming villages, for example, women went to considerable trouble and expense to make their own farms, with hired labor if necessary, in addition to the farms belonging to their husbands. Land cleared by the husband was considered his farm, regardless of how much labor the wife expended in planting, weeding and harvesting. This created little conflict as long as the foodstuffs or cash sales went towards feeding the children, but each woman also wanted her own discretionary income, as men did.

Asante women very frequently mention the need to protect themselves against the constant possibility of divorce or widowhood when discussing their attitudes to marriage. This concern apparently inhibits both economic and emotional commitment to marriage. Financial support usually drops sharply when a husband marries a new wife, or divorces an old one. Retirement also brings support to an end for many waged workers, regardless of the age of the children. Incapacitating illness or death can strike the most devoted father, with his maternal relatives inheriting whatever property he possesses. While heirs recognize their responsibility to keep his children from starvation, a mother's independent income is essential for adequate clothing, school fees, and other sponsorship (Clark 1989).

Asante lineage ideology and cosmology gives priority to the lineage tie, represented as eternal and inalienable, over the marital tie, represented as transient and idiosyncratic. The proverb "you can get a new husband (or wife), but not a new brother (sister)," was quoted both by men and women. Supporting the spouse at the expense of the lineage is considered immoral by these standards. Partners expect relatively immediate reciprocity from spouses, but they will support lineage members to avoid future trouble or enable the recipient to help others in future. While Asante women's commitment to their lineages is reinforced by their central position by virtue of matrilineality, this attitude has also been reported in patrilineal and bilateral West African societies with high divorce rates (Schildkrout 1982 and Goody 1973).

Extensive interviewing turned up only a few cases of apparent long term reciprocity or free sharing with no expectation of return between spouses. These seemed to be a sign of special trust between these individuals, rather than an expectation from married status. The supportive spouses in these two cases stressed that they were reciprocating past favors. One elderly woman explained that she now fed her very elderly husband, who lived with her, from her trading earnings, because he had been very generous in support of the family before his retirement. Another legal clerk in his late thirties justified using his cherished savings for law school to buy family food when his wife's cloth trade collapsed, during price control, by saying she had contributed a great deal earlier. In both cases, they seemed more embarrassed than proud of their actions, speaking rarely, softly, and privately of them, while those voicing their independence or even complaining of neglect spoke loudly and openly.

Exchanges with Siblings

Duolocal residence often results in adult brothers and sisters living together. This presents the possibility of a sibling-based household, with siblings pooling resources, as in the duolocal area of Japan described by Befu (1968). Unlike those household members, however, Asante siblings maintain a high level of individual property and decision-making. Inheritance is not restricted to the eldest, nor do the others acknowledge his free access to their labor or earnings, even if they live in the original lineage house. Asante brothers and sisters are much more likely to cooperate financially and in decision making than husband and wife, but their relationship still seems to fall far short of pooled resources.

Assistance between Asante siblings rarely continues beyond the short term without definite reciprocation, although not necessarily of the same kind given. Sisters living in the same house, for example, normally cook separate meals and then share the cooked food freely with each other and other neighbors. Many were seen to exchange help on an ad hoc basis with domestic tasks, watching each others' boiling pots and children as needed. There was no careful accounting of who did what, but each returned the same kind of aid when requested.

When one sister takes over long-term domestic responsibilities for the other, the reciprocity is spelled out in terms of paying for food, school fees, or a maid. For example, one adult woman acted as a kind of "housewife" for two co-resident sisters who ran two distinct trading operations. She supervised the children and cooking at home, while they contributed money for food, supported a young maid to assist her, and helped support all the children from their trading profits.

Women welcome economic support from their brothers, but do not seem to expect it very often. Women farmers, for example, mentioned the desirability of a brother clearing a farm for them, but remarked that it was a rare brother who did it. Such a farm would belong to the sister outright, unlike the one her husband cleared for her, they explained, so the clearing would be a free gift of labor. The sister's children are the immediate heirs to her brother's property. If they all live in the same house, he has daily interaction with them, activating his moral authority. Maternal uncles are natural figures to ask for school fees or other significant sponsorship when needed, but when the uncle complies the children then show him extra reverence, showing this help is not taken for granted.

Exchanges between brothers and sisters seem to be negotiated voluntarily between the individuals involved, on the basis of mutual trust and proven reliability, rather than extended automatically because of the blood relationship. Cooperation is also extended for limited, specific purposes. For example, traders mention the appropriateness of giving siblings money for safekeeping, or borrowing or lending them money, in contrast to spouses. No cases appeared of women farming or trading jointly with their brothers, although some traders volunteered that they would sooner do so with a brother than a husband. Pairs of same-sex siblings trade together more often, but not full or nearly full sibling groups.

Siblings are considered the most intimate of blood relatives, and so their level of entitlement to each others' assistance is highly significant. The 1978–80 research period was rich in commercial and public crises that provided examples of traders needing and seeking help of various kinds. Siblings, especially of the same sex, did tend to be the first asked for help or advice. They found it hard, though by no means impossible, to turn down the request of a brother or sister, and did provide valuable help.

Still, asking and even frequently receiving help from individual siblings differs from pooling resources and acting as a household-type unit. Siblings are a natural pool of potential partners, but their help cannot be compelled or assumed on a routine basis. One certainly cannot dispose of their resources as one's own. A person should assist brothers or sisters, if only to prevent them from needing future help, but need not help them when or in the way they are asking. Unreliable or incompetent siblings cannot be totally disavowed, but they can be gradually excluded from all but the lowest level of subsistence support. The kinship tie means that reciprocity can be delayed for long periods, but it is expected eventually, even if indirectly through helping another relative. High rates of migration break up most sibling groups geographically, making consistent pooling of resources impractical. Persons with small, absent, or unhelpful sibling sets tend to cultivate closer ties with more distant relatives who live nearby and show interest.

Exchanges Between Parent and Child

Resources are shared more freely between parent and child than in any other relationship in Asante, but even here considerations of past or probable reciprocity give the exchanges some degree of negotiability. Adult children refer to unconditional pooling of food in asserting the priority of their tie to their mothers. The statement "she would not eat if I was hungry," both defines and distinguishes the maternal bond so clearly for Asantes that one suspects it need not hold true for other close relatives. Men as well as women work hard to provide for their children's subsistence and advancement, but men acknowledge other goals more openly as well. The fact that both parents know they will depend on well-established children for their future security does not reduce this support to economic calculation.

Decision-making authority is neither restricted to the parent-child unit or absolute within it. Other kin's opinion on matters affecting the children carries considerable weight, whether co-resident or not. The child's preferences, actions and aptitudes also play a strong part in education, employment and residence decisions. While children should not openly defy their parents, they can and do express strong opinions before and refuse to cooperate after a decision. Normal filial obedience clearly does not extend, for example, to working in parental enterprises on demand. Many adolescent children interviewed had never worked with their parents, and others had quit against their parents' wishes while still living at home.

A child automatically has some economic separation from each parent because of its relation to the other. Both pay individually for children's expenses and gifts. Fathers often give money, clothes and other goods directly to their children, rather than to the mother, so she has little opportunity for redistribution. Half siblings therefore may get quite different levels of support.

It is in allocating support and property transfers above the survival level that parental, like sibling, relations become more conditional. Although parents would like to offer maximum support to all their children, actual resources are always limited. Disparities in treatment between full siblings are linked to the quality of the specific parent-child relation, as well as the changing fortunes of a given family over time.

Children's work histories affect short-term benefits they receive, including food. Dutiful children who run errands and pound *fufu* cheerfully get extra food as well as praise. Chronically absent children get fewer gifts and handouts, and sometimes are threatened with no dinner. In one family, each daughter in turn gained weight markedly as she took charge of the family cooking. A child working in a parent's business receives extra clothes and money from its profits, compared to siblings not working there.

Children's outside earnings may compensate for weaker parental exchanges. Errands or unpaid help for a neighbor, distant relative or teacher earn a child immediate snacks and tips, and also demonstrate suitability for long term sponsorship. Parents encourage these helpful activities when the potential patron seems to offer more advantages than they can. Outside relations like these can free up the parents' own resources for their other children.

Major capital outlays on children range from fees for secondary and further schooling, through provision of apprenticeships and trading capital, depending on parental income. Perceptions of an individual child's ability to profit from such support and likelihood of reciprocating it in the long run are freely discussed when decisions are made about which child to educate, or what training to finance. These opinions of the child's character and intelligence are based primarily on their short-term reciprocity through work. In combination with good grades, conspicuous obedience and helpfulness identify school children less likely to run away or get pregnant.

Childrens' work also establishes differential rights to inherit property, a key household activity in Wilk and Netting's model (1984: 5). When rural men establish cocoa farms with the help of their wives and children, the work contributed is used to justify giving or bequeathing them part of the farm, away from the lineage heir (Hill 1963 and Okali 1983). An adult daughter who moved into her father's house to care for him in old age was pointed out as earning lifetime residence rights in that house not shared by his other children. The daughter who spends years working in her mother's business is most likely to inherit it at her mother's death, or receive the capital earlier in massive transfers, because of both her service and her proved competence to preserve its value.

If unusual devotion reaps unusual rewards, filial duty can also be minimized or diluted under some circumstances. In a few cases, conspicuous parental neglect or long loss of contact made adult children feel justified in evading or rejecting parental requests for financial or other help. Fostering children with kin does not break the birth parent's emotional bond or decision-making authority, but foster parents and siblings deserve loyalty and assistance in their own right. Asantes consider reinforcing such lineage ties through co-residence a good argument for fostering. Foster parents may even take emotional precedence if the co-residence was long, especially in cases involving orphans or childless women.

Exchanges on the Lineage Level

An Asante lineage, or *abusua*, does control and allocate significant resources, but not to the degree usually associated with a household unit.[3] It does not function as a primary production or consumption unit. Residential mobility is high in Asante, with migration common both to cities like Kumasi and to other rural areas with available land. Only a small minority of the minimal lineage members, descended from one grandmother, live together or even in the same town or village at one time. Children and young people move between relatives and friends' houses for education and fostering. Kumasi residents maintain strong loyalties to their rural lineages and hometowns for generations and return frequently for ceremonies and visits. The original lineage house remains their home, a refuge in old age or bankruptcy. Migrant members seek relatives' advice, help and consent on major decisions, but distance weakens lineage participation in day-to-day affairs.

Decision-making authority within the lineage rests primarily with the *abusua panin*, or lineage head. Normally a man of the senior living generation, he consults with other elderly men and women, including the *obaa panin*, or senior woman, in deciding land allocation and inheritance cases, finding caretakers for elderly relatives, and representing lineage members in disputes and community affairs. Funds for lawsuits, school fees and farm or business expansion may also come from lineage resources. Elders' opposition in marriage or other important life decisions can be defied, but only at the cost of future lineage support. Inherited land, houses or money, as opposed to self-acquired property, should be used for the general benefit.

Moral guidelines leave abundant room within Asante lineages for the continual negotiation and redefinition of relations and exchanges typical of most Asante relationships. Lineage members recognize mutual responsibility for long-term survival, but there are few binding claims beyond that level. Any wealthy lineage member is fair game for requests to support the destitute or sponsor the deserving. The person is definitely approached because of the lineage tie, and the assistance requested by reference to it, but the relation itself does not establish access to the resources needed. Other people with needed resources are similarly approached through links traced through shared residence, hometown or occupation.

Although a person ought and usually wishes to show generosity to kin, he or she has considerable leeway as to which requests to honor.

Examples of self-sacrifice for kin coexist with evasions and open refusals. Legitimate considerations include the recipient's ability to profit from and reciprocate the assistance, as well as need. These conditionalities apply to virtually every kind of support, both material and non-material, immediate and promised.

The distinguishing feature of exchanges with lineage kin is the possibility (not the presumption) of long term, rather than immediate, returns. Asantes confirm the contrast identified by Bloch (1973) in their ideas and their practice. The eternal, undeniable aspect of lineage ties makes non-specific reciprocity more plausible between kin than between spouses or neighbors. Kin who receive help will be accessible through family networks in a later time of need. At the very least, these successful relatives will absorb some of the requests for assistance from needy ones in the future, who might otherwise approach the donor.

Such exchanges, when established, resemble those classified by Sahlins (1972) as generalized reciprocity, except that they are here optional rather than compulsory between close kin. Not all kin are considered reliable long-term partners and accepted as such. On the other hand, neighbors and friends also build such long-term exchange relations as each proves reliable in shorter-term exchanges.

The delayed but unlimited returns expected by kin for labor and capital contributions have both advantages and disadvantages recognized by traders. Long-term "borrowing" on social credit speeds capital accumulation for traders with access to family resources. Help without immediate cost was vital to the survival of many families and enterprises during the continuing Ghanaian economic crisis, particularly acute during fieldwork between 1979 and 1984. In contrast, some traders said they avoided mixing kinship and business because they feared the open-ended nature of the claims made later. Precisely by not soliciting kin assistance, they could successfully avoid later claims on their trading income and capital.

In general, however, the desire for independent resources is reinforced rather than inhibited by expectations and desires to receive and give large amounts of help from a variety of kin and others. Personal income establishes each individual as a free agent in asking, offering, refusing and negotiating these exchanges, within culturally-accepted limits or beyond them. Asantes with independent incomes from farming, trading or other enterprises nonetheless frequently count on substantial access to labor, goods and money from spouses, kin and neighbors. Working children, for example, take over more of their personal expenses without renouncing access to the resources of either parent. In fact, higher personal income makes the person a more desirable exchange partner, attracting assistance from others eager to create future obligations. Extensive and long-lasting reciprocity networks are desired, respected and expected, both in reinforcing lineage and community solidarity and demonstrating personal power.

Independent income is an important aspect of personhood in Asante for women and children as well as adult men. Women speak of valuing the ability to make personal decisions about how to spend their money, however little, rather than having to justify their needs to others. The ability to assist kin, contribute to funerals, travel, and support children is necessary to become a full social adult in the lineage and community.

Small children take pride in their first earnings and receive lavish praise for them, but they also accept the other side of independence. One eight-year-old on her first day at work was told by her mother to buy her own lunch. If family finances allow, they are encouraged to save and accumulate from their earnings and casual gifts. Child traders can make sizable incomes relative to their consumption levels. Many traders reported such savings as their major source of initial trading capital. Children with no family support spend all they earn on their own food.

Exchanges Within the House

The standards of co-residence or commensality habitually used for household boundaries clearly do not define a set of persons with complete or virtual pooling of resources, even when they coincide. Closeness of genealogical relationship and co-residence intensify exchanges of cooked food, labor and money, but appear not to define them absolutely. The degree of automatic access or joint decision making implied by the term pooling cannot be linked definitively to either kinship, coresidence or commensality, although the idea of pooling is certainly invoked vigorously by Asantes in negotiations or quarrels over access to resources.

While not absolute socioeconomic units, houses and their residents and "holders" remain highly significant to urban Asantes. If residence were irrelevant or trivial, they would have no reason to move near relatives, invite children to live with them, or consider whether or not to live with their spouses. One of the first questions asked of an arriving traveler from another town is *efie te sen?*, or *fiefoo ho te sen?* (literally, How is the house? How are the people of the house?). Asantes focus so much of their considerable economic energy on building houses, in Kumasi or their hometowns, because of the lasting identification of a house and its inhabitants with its builder and each other, not just because housing is a lucrative investment. Repairing the *abusua fie* or original lineage house is a strong obligation for solvent lineage members, because of its importance to lineage identity (Mikell 1987).

The accessibility of co-residents makes them a natural set of persons on whom to draw for exchanges of labor, loans, and other forms of cooperation, but one set among many. Sanjek establishes this point convincingly in his discussion of households in the Adabraka neighborhood of Accra, Ghana as ". . . staging areas of social life." (Sanjek 1982) Some aspects of identity focus on the house, but many also focus elsewhere. Awusabo-Asare discusses the cooperation between *fiefoo* in his interesting critique of census concepts such as the household (Awusabo-Asare 1988). He translates it as "people of the house," but points out that it usually includes several distinct households not eating together or sharing rooms.

As potential sources of assistance, house neighbors are already a valuable resource to preserve and augment. Concrete relations of cooperation will have also been established with many of them at any given time, most likely with those sharing some reinforcing links such as kinship, marriage, occupation, age or sex. Individual circumstances, negotiations and acknowledged conflicts of interest affect access to others' resources sharply within the house. Personal interests and unequal access distinguish even full siblings in their relations to parents, let alone to more distant kin and non-kin. Husbands and wives and parents and children living together or nearby usually eat from the same cooking pot and have considerable access to each other's resources.

Trading and Households

With this degree of negotiability and individualization of the most intimate ties of kinship and affinity in Asante families, it is not surprising to find that structures of labor recruitment and capital rights in trading enterprises also show flexibility and independence from household control. Traders recruit their helpers and their capital most often from among close kin, but just as often work without helpers, loans or kin sponsorship.[4] Household heads or other members not active in the enterprise do not participate in decision making about trading strategies or spending income or capital. Traders consult various relatives or friends for advice, and face demands on their income and capital for non-trading purposes from their own children and other kin. But they clearly do not work as extensions of a household unit, for the benefit and with the resources of the whole unit, according to the usual definition of a household enterprise.

Family Capital and Labor

Market trading businesses are founded and operated by individuals with family relations, not by family groups, as indicated by the sample survey. Almost half of the Asante women traders (46 percent) work alone, and a further 35 percent have only one helper. While most of these assistants are kin, especially daughters, a large number of equivalent kin normally exist who do not work in the enterprise. It is much more common for market traders to use available kin and non-kin helpers for cooking and child care at home, rather than in the market.

This situation clearly contrasts with a business which draws freely on the entire labor resources of the household. Smart describes a Hong Kong shop, for example, where the entire family took turns helping in the shop, in between schoolwork, housework, and other duties (Smart 1988). The only way these adult, professional children could resist such labor demands was to convince their parents to close the shop. In Asante, more indirect family support through supplier credit or clientship is also rare. A majority of Kumasi traders surveyed (62 percent) do not even have relatives in the same line of trade. Family trading connections seem rather to be the rule among the Hausa in Nigeria, and the overseas Chinese in Java and the Philippines (Cohen 1969; Dewey 1962; Davis 1973).

Historical descriptions by older traders and old Kumasi residents suggest that conditions may have been more favorable to large family enterprises or business networks previously. Descriptions of vegetable trading patterns in the 1920s and 1930s mention well-known family networks of traders with "agents" in several towns and cities, although it was not possible to determine how integrated these networks were. Traders in all commodities mention that current erratic economic conditions create a high-risk environment in which having assistants, for whose debts one is responsible, is less desirable than attracting clients. A trader uses her capital to sell goods on credit to buyer clients, or advance money to supplier clients to buy for her, but only shares their losses to the extent of that credit.

One multi-location family network in non-perishables that had been established on the agency model in the previous generation still existed in theory, but it operated only irregularly because of unreliable supplies. Jointly purchased goods were accepted when available, but in effect these siblings now operated as a client network. Each "agent" managed one local stall or store and arranged for most supplies from a variety of sources.

Patterns of kinship within market trading enterprises confirm that they are not operated by a kin group, but by activation of dyadic ties with individual kin of the same sex. Women traders not working alone almost always worked in teams of a mother and one daughter. Given normal family size and high female activity rates, other daughters would have found unrelated work. Sisters frequently retained independent finances even when they shared the same market stall. Men most often sold with or alongside equal-status brothers or friends, rather than accept daily subordination to fathers or other elder kin. Many market men were craftsmen, who recruited mainly unrelated assistants through apprenticeships.[5]

As already mentioned, husband-wife partnerships were especially rare and such enterprises would be assumed to be the husband's. The survey curiously revealed more husbands claiming wives' assistance than women who admitted working with husbands. The few women contacted made a point of explaining their work status as the result of serious illness or another misfortune that put them out of business. Several stressed their plans to start trading independently as soon as possible.

The only woman expressing satisfaction with a joint operation had induced her husband to join in the provisions business originally started by her own mother. They split profits strictly down the middle, rather than pooling, in a formal agreement she referred to as a "company." It is hard to imagine a woman receiving, in effect, half ownership in the parallel situation, after joining a business started by her husband's father.

Economic constraints prevent enterprises from including all eligible family members, or from being restricted to the closest kin. A woman trader rarely has the capital to gainfully employ more than one of her daughters, so that the others must find other occupations. In many cases, a trader cannot employ even one. Poorer market women place their own daughters as assistants with more prosperous market neighbors or clients, and hometown or urban neighbors may also locate suitable opportunities and vouch for the girl's character.

Very successful traders, who might conceivably have enough capital to employ all or most of their daughters or collateral relatives, are discouraged from doing so by two considerations. The unstable economy already mentioned makes it safer to diversify into several distinct operations, rather than to expand a large family firm. Wealthy market women expand into transport, farming and real estate, in addition to clientship. This diversity makes it difficult to employ the whole family in a systematic way, although such entrepreneurs may still recruit workers from among their kin and neighbors.

These relatively rare wealthy women also want to educate their daughters, as well as their sons, with the aim of preparing them for professional or civil service employment, not market trade. Although reflecting larger power relations in the nation, this strategy also serves as further diversification. In such cases, rural or otherwise disadvantaged relatives are brought in for trading assistance as well as domestic help. These assistants are groomed to take over the market stall or inherit it, although income and capital have been continually bled out for non-trading assistance to the trader's own children. Even limited school attendance, to which most

Kumasi families aspire, restricts the number of years daughters are available as full-time assistants. If an assistant is urgently needed, the mother may need to look elsewhere.[6]

Even for women whose aspirations for their daughters include trading, the short generation interval for women makes direct mother-daughter succession problematical. Many mothers are just entering their most active trading years when a daughter is ready for independence. In one of the larger extended family networks, a woman's eldest daughter had been placed for training with the grandmother and the next daughter with an older aunt because the mother's trading could not yet support a full-time assistant. The youngest daughter assisted her own mother, and is taking over gradually as she retires. The ability and inclination of specific children also influences their career paths, some girls proving useless at trading or disliking it.

Market leadership positions are rarely handed down directly from mother to daughter for the same reasons. These leaders are elected by commodity groups from among a council of elders. They perform functions of dispute settlement and external representation for members. They are rarely the wealthiest traders in the group, so that not all of them manage to educate their daughters out of the market. When their daughters do follow them into trade in the same commodity, however, the daughters either lack the experience in the council of elders to make viable candidates when their mothers die, or lack the patience to wait in a secondary position. In one case, the daughter of a commodity queen migrated to another city to become the leader there. The granddaughter remained as assistant to the leader in Kumasi, and performed her grandmother's official duties when she became an invalid, as heir apparent.

Trading and Domestic Life

Traders in Kumasi do not seem to expect their trading assistants to live with them and do domestic chores. Daughters still living with their mothers were the most common assistants, but trading reduced, rather than confirming, their domestic roles. The daughter who was primary trading assistant did not usually also have primary responsibility for domestic chores; another daughter took that role. Other assistants were not expected to even help out at the trader's home unless they also lived there as foster children.

Assistants not living with the trader were not considered exceptional. For example, some collateral kin assistants lived with their own mothers or other kin within Kumasi, but up to ten miles away from the trader. They reported for work daily, were fed on the job, and were given spending money which took into account their need for bus fares and snacks. Daughters also moved out on marriage or for other reasons and continued working with their mothers.

Conversely, maids and fostered relatives who helped with domestic duties lived with a trader, but rarely helped in the market stall. They might sell something near the house for a few hours daily, but this was not necessarily part of the trader's primary business. Domestic helpers had their own standards of remuneration, considerably lower than trading assistants. One craft worker, a baker, hired two categories of young girls she called "maids." One group did her housework and the other, which she also called her "apprentices," hawked her bread in the market and streets and gradually learned to bake at the ovens behind her house.

Indirect Household Support

Kumasi trading enterprises are not linked tightly enough to any stable unit of kinship and residence to be considered household enterprises, but that does not mean that kinship, marriage and residence are irrelevant relations for business survival and success. The contributions made by spouses, children, co-resident kin and maids are nonetheless essential when they do not participate directly in the trading enterprise. Their contributions in labor and money at home enable the trader to insulate herself and her business at least partly from the financial and labor demands of childrearing and marital life. In contrasting cases where family unity seems necessary to free capital for entrepreneurial activity, as in Wilks (1984), family members apparently find it difficult to invest productively on their own accounts.

If compatibility with domestic tasks fully determined women's work, the huge urban markets of West Africa could hardly be predominantly female. Trading operations in a large, urban market, such as Kumasi Central Market, are not amenable to part-time work or to simultaneous child care or cooking, as Brown seems to assume (Brown 1970).[7] Asante women, far from restricting their trading during peak childbearing years, trade most actively at those ages (25–34 and 15–24) because of the financial demands of motherhood (Clark 1984). Instead, they confirm the hypothesis that domestic surrogates can effectively release women for incompatible tasks (Pasternak, Ember and Ember 1976; Reyna 1977).

Since Asante women retain primary responsibility for domestic tasks, traders need someone to substitute for them who is under their control. Adult kin only occasionally provide this assistance. It is non-trading older daughters, foster children and maids who enable women to keep long, consistent market hours to avoid loss of capital and to rise to the more lucrative trading roles that accumulate capital. Wholesaling, for example, requires either flexibility to travel as a buyer or long uninterrupted hours in the market to attract and retain clients. The smallest traders, without capital reserves, go bankrupt at the slightest public or private crisis.

A husband can also give his wife indirect support in her business by consistently paying his share of family expenses. Constant urgent demands on her trading profits for school fees, clothing, medical care, and other items, supposedly a father's responsibility, erode many mothers' capital or prevent accumulation. A wife who can rely on regular child support can commit more of her own money to her trading. With the income from this higher capital, she can support extra dependents or keep an older children at home to take over domestic chores. This paradoxically detaches her even more from the house, and makes her less rather than more identified with a household-type unit.

Pooling Within the Enterprise

Another indication of special links between traders' businesses and their household units would be sharp distinctions between the conditions of work of assistants and clients who are and are not kin or co-residents with the trader. The issues most central to household membership would be decision-making and control over capital, including eventual inheritance. A close comparison of cases on these issues reveals more similarities than differences in treatment of unrelated helpers, but the small number of the latter makes the conclusion tentative.

The range of variation in conditions of work and remuneration is substantial for both kin and unrelated associates. It stretches from closely-supervised and trusted partner/helpers through subordinates who work autonomously for limited, definite returns (such as commissions), ending with totally independent clients. The amount of remuneration, degree of joint decision-making and eventual capital participation of co-workers who are close kin and/or live together do tend to be higher and more reliable than for purely economic associates, but the separation is not very sharp.

Even small children can be found working on terms that encourage independent decision-making and finances. Kumasi market helpers often sold alongside their mothers only during the noonday rush. The rest of the day they hawked the same goods without direct supervision, selling small amounts from head trays while walking around. After rudimentary training or testing on change making and arithmetic, children as young as eight are let loose as hawkers, to learn by trial and error. They use their mother's capital, and she covers their losses, but they do not work under very different conditions from the many children the same age who hawk on their own accounts. Independent child hawkers can become steady clients of their suppliers and gain access to some of the supplier's

capital by selling goods taken on credit in addition to those they buy for cash.

Few young trading assistants have a formally agreed level of cash remuneration resembling a wage, and none of these were kin. Nonwage workers expect full or complete subsistence, substantial gifts out of profits, and eventual access to capital. These general principles were applied in cases representing own children, collateral kin and non-kin, and co-residents and non-residents. Assistants' expectations are not always fulfilled, since they depend on both the good faith and solvency of the employer. Kin ties help to enforce the former, but do not guarantee it. Several women reported leaving their mother's businesses as teenagers because they felt their mothers were not giving them enough money. Reciprocity can be delayed, but not indefinitely.

On the other hand, enterprise heads do not always achieve the complete control of profits and trading decisions they expect by using young assistants. Loose supervision enables clever children working for others to make private incomes on the side. One young girl hawked second-hand children's clothes for her father's sister. The aunt told her their sale prices, but she usually managed to sell them for more and pocket the difference. The girl reported her aunt was more than satisfied, thinking that she had sold all the items at the full price. The girl received cash bonuses and gifts of clothing her size, and was even pressed to come and live with this aunt. The girl bought cloth and household items with the money she saved, as a hedge against inflation, and stored them in a neighbor's house to conceal them from her father, with whom she lived.

These supposedly dependent assistants operate with a degree of de facto independence and concealed profits typical of relations between unrelated clients. In another example, an adult daughter not living with her mother worked as her assistant, traveling to buy yams for her with a substantial proportion of the family capital. She gave an oral account of her transactions, but could easily conceal the exact price paid for the yams if she bargained well. Unrelated clients given capital advances for the same purpose by her mother were supposed to divide the profits in half, but calculated those profits themselves. As long as both parties profit sufficiently, neither looks too closely at the accounts.

Traders' opinions varied on whether kin and household ties increased the effective degree of authority over subordinates. Some traders said they preferred kin assistants because they were more reliable and obedient. Others avoided kin as assistants or even as clients, because it was more difficult to break the relationship if kin acted badly. Apparently the distinction in standards of behavior was not sharp enough to be unmistakable.

The degree of open sharing of control of capital, both in terms of commercial decisions and of consumption, becomes significant when the assistant approaches adolescence. One girl of 12 or 13 managed her mother's small town market stall while her mother sold wholesale and traveled to get supplies. When the girl came home one day bragging of selling more fish than many adults in the market, her mother not only praised her, but remarked publicly that she was setting aside substantial amounts of the profits for the daughter's future use. This girl's unusual skill level not only earned her extra income, but made it possible for her mother to do business on the wholesale level. In return, the young girl had effective control over much more capital than she could hope to accumulate independently for many years. Other girls become independent traders at this skill level, with or without their mothers' blessings.

When daughters remain trading with their mothers well after adulthood, maternal authority blurs almost imperceptibly into joint decision-making. The daughter gradually assumes more independence with the growing portion of capital entrusted to her. She may add to it money she has managed to save for herself, just as a supplier client buying with borrowed capital will also trade with her own on the same trip. Since long-standing clients also commonly consult each other on trading strategy, it can be difficult to tell if a given daughter should be considered a partner or a client. The testing and manipulation of deference amounts to unspoken negotiations resembling those in the gradual separation of Andean households described by Weismantel (this volume).

Inheritance can be as gradual a process as independence, unless hastened by unexpected death. Many daughter assistants eventually become independent traders in the same commodity. They incorporate some of their mothers' capital, which can be considered as a pre-mortem inheritance, perpetual credit or recompense for their years of assistance. When the mother or other older relative is getting ready to retire or reduce her level of activity, she gradually turns over decision-making authority to the young woman assisting her at that time, along with effective control over the remaining capital. This creates a strong tendency to ultimogeniture. Very elderly women either become a kind of elder statesmen, consulted on delicate points of trading strategy, or become virtual assistants to their more active successors.

Some of these processes are duplicated by unrelated apprentices and helpers. After several years of service, they also expect assistance in setting up their independent businesses, if on a reduced scale, as a kind of muted inheritance. Apprentices often receive supplier credit from former masters, and sometimes loans of capital or equipment. Even if their former employer is less than supportive, they have become well known to those doing business with her and earned a useful reputation.

After all, these intangible resources are the only ones most impoverished mothers have to pass on to their daughters.

Inheritance rights are one of the main distinctions between kin and unrelated helpers. Only occasionally does a nonkin apprentice or helper take over a business, in the absence of any designated kin heir. The cases encountered all related to the expulsion of non-Ghanaian traders in 1969. The expectation of eventually taking over a thriving business keeps a daughter working with her mother beyond the point when she could set up on her own. Nonkin assistants would try to work on their own account at this point, if only on credit. Asante inheritance is a function of the lineage, rather than a basic household function, as in so many peasant societies (Wilk and Netting 1984). Even this distinction therefore does not identify the business strongly with a household.

In fact, effective transfer of business capital and clients is only possible to someone familiar with the skills and personal relations needed to keep the specific enterprise going, namely a current assistant. This puts some pressure on older traders to select a young kinswoman as an assistant for training. When a trader dies suddenly without training a successor, lineage elders name an heir, but such an heir inherits much less. She hardly knows what debts to collect, in the absence of written records, so much of the capital is lost. She inherits mainly the market location itself and some goodwill from the dead trader's friends and neighbors there. Only someone with trading experience can take full advantage of these resources, and so the closest lineal relative may be passed over. Inheritance depends on a combination of kinship status with work performance, and so is partly a reward for the work.

Trading, Family, and Household

This degree of individuation of interests and actions within the group of persons who would be candidates for household status makes plausible abandoning the idea of the household altogether in favor of overlapping single-function groups or networks (Verdun 1980; Wong 1984). Stack used the network approach fruitfully with US Black families (Stack 1974).

Grappling with African examples including the Asante, Carter remarks, "In these cases, it may be difficult to imagine that any particular variety of household has much significance, and the household concept in general therefore may not be regarded as of much use." (Carter 1984: 52) He next admits that the European assumptions underlying the household model create part of the conflict. "The problem with the West African material is not that there are not task-oriented units, or even that there are so many as to render the household concept meaningless, but rather that the rights and duties of male and female household members are quite unlike those found in Eurasian households." (loc. cit.)

The consanguineal household allows different gender roles without negating the principle of the household as pooling unit. Clarke and Gonzalez describe strong solidarity within Caribbean households organized around very different gender, sibling and marital roles (Clarke 1957; Gonzalez 1969). Befu describes certain Japanese areas in which large households were recruited primarily through duolocal marriage and matrifiliation (except for the patrilocal household heads) precisely in order to preserve the advantages of a larger production and consumption pool (Befu 1968). Vaughan and Poewe describe matrilineal systems in southern Africa that generate sets of sisters, with one brother as head, functioning as fairly tight units of residence, production and consumption (Vaughan 1985; Poewe 1981). Saul describes the vestiges of a matrilineal production unit, in which matrilineal groups of women produce shea butter and bring it to an elder, who redistributes it for joint sale, consumption and private sale, in this volume. Neither rural or urban areas visited in Asante revealed cases of true joint production or consumption by either consanguineal households or lineal groups.

More sophisticated conceptualization of the household has accommodated both incomplete pooling within and sharing between households. Discussions have moved beyond the naive "black box" stage, when households could be analyzed as indivisible units whose joint decision-making (whether authoritarian or consensual) and redistribution of resources for production and consumption (whether equal or unequal) demonstrated their economic solidarity. Counter-examples and critiques, many based on African material, have revealed the significance of divisions within and cooperation between residential households.[8] Lockwood analyses an excellent example of significant independent production by married women, but on a much smaller scale than production at the household level because of the prior claims of the household head on their labor, in this volume.

While accepting some intra- and inter-household allocation, however, household analysis continues to define the household as the most important level of resource control. In this volume, for example, Rutz defines urban Fijian households by their pooling of income and non-wage labor, although detailing the reservations of junior members and subgroups. Hammel (1980) refers to "the smallest grouping with the maximum corporate function." He later states categorically "The household in any society, I suggest, is that social group larger than the individual that does not fail to control for its members all those resources that any (adult) member could expect to control for himself." (Hammel 1984: 41) Wallerstein (1984) draws his conclusions on the household's functions in the world economy precisely on its income-pooling nature and joint management (see also Wilk 1984 and Rutz this volume).

Households also continue to be defined as inherently the most important group for social identity and action. Netting, Wilk and Arnould consider households ". . . the primary arena for the expression of age and sex roles, kinship, socialization and economic cooperation," and emphasize the many decisions made and activities carried out in these "task-oriented residence groups," that involve the "pooling and sharing of resources" (Netting, Wilk and Arnould 1984: xxii–iii). Hackenberg, Murphy and Selby speak of ". . . the household as the unit of decisionmaking," though accepting census residential criteria for membership (Hackenberg, Murphy and Selby 1984: 187). Wilk and Netting (1984) refer to the relative density of acts of production, distribution, transmission, reproduction and co-residence within the household as important in identifying its culturally-specific boundaries. If these definitions are taken as given, then clearly few households exist in urban Asante, or in the other southern Ghanaian ethnic groups discussed by Sanjek (1982).

The pattern of relations constructed by these urban market women is individualized, but not atomized or individualistic. They actively engage in multiplex exchanges and recognize mutual obligations with as many kin and friends as they can manage. Indeed, like other Asantes they partly measure their personal strength and reputation by the number and range of such contacts they can sustain. Their marital, residence and kin statuses include norms and duties that significantly constrain as well as motivate these activities, but their participation is individually constructed, not defined by any single dominant unit membership or role.

The number of traders using labor or credit supplied by kin and co-residents under conditions of indefinite reciprocity creates a kind of illusion of household enterprises. Taking the next step of specifying household/trading links, however, immediately reveals the immense difficulties of identifying the membership or boundaries of such a pooling unit. The extremely complex patterns of residence, food sharing and labor recruitment found arise from the high rate of duolocal marriage and fostering of kin and fictive kin among Asante, but also from the very strength of lineage and hometown loyalties. Asantes claim and recognize the rights as more distant kin and neighbors often enough to undermine the validity of a more limited idea of the household as a unit either privileged or dominant in this kind of resource sharing.

It could be argued that this autonomy of action is atypical of Asantes or urban Africans, and an aberration of traders linked to their occupation. It is certainly true that women living as dependents on either husbands or kin would hardly show up among traders. Of course, in cities where up to 80 percent of the women trade, traders can hardly be dismissed as atypical (Robertson 1984). But the elements that comprise this pattern are so widespread and so widely accepted among both urban and rural Asantes that it seems misleading to link their autonomy too tightly to their trading. More precisely, the fluidity of relations of kinship, marriage and residence in Asante society, which seems almost to positively avoid rigidly defined units at the household level, enables Kumasi market women to construct enterprises in this way without substantial conflict with established family and marriage norms.

Notes

1. Discussions of Asante kinship, family relations and individualism in the pre-colonial and early colonial periods appear in the classic ethnographic works of Rattray (1923) and Fortes (1949) and in historical research by Wilks (1975) and many others. More recent ethnography by Bleek (1975), Okali (1975) and Mikell (1987) reveals substantial continuity on these points.
2. The survey of Kumasi Central Market was conducted in July 1979. A 1/20 sample of all non-transient areas yielded 618 cases, with 3 refusals. For the figures used in this paper, Asante traders were separated from non-Asantes and craft workers, and men from women. Details of the procedures and questionnaire are available in Clark (1984), which includes tables on these and other variables.
3. For convenience of typography, the brief Twi phrases used in this article are not printed with the correct phonetic letters.
4. For exact figures and additional tables, see Clark (1984: 110).
5. For tables on these variables and a fuller discussion of craft workers, see Clark (1984: 114, 167–8).
6. Robertson (1984) discusses the influence of education and wage work on commercial training with primary reference to Accra, where wage work is more important.
7. Domestic labor processes and conflicts are discussed in more detail in Clark (1989).
8. See Bennholdt-Thomson 1981; Guyer 1981, 1986; Jones 1986; Sanjek 1982; Vaughan 1985; Poats, Feldstein and Rocheleau, this volume, among many others.

References Cited

Aidoo, Ama Ata. 1970. *No Sweetness Here*. London: Longmans.
Awusabo-Asare, Kofi. 1988. "Interpretations of Demographic Concepts: the Case of Ghana." Paper presented at British Society for Population Studies conference, Nottingham, September 1988.
Babb, Florence. 1988. "Marketers as Producers: The Labor Process and Proletarianization of Peruvian Marketwomen," in David Hakken and Hanna Lessinger (eds.), *Perspectives in U.S. Marxist Anthropology*. Boulder: Westview Press.

Beckett, W.. 1944. *Akokoaso: A Survey of a Gold Coast Village.* London: Percy Lund, Humphries and Co.

Befu, Harumi. 1968. "Origin of Large Households and Duolocal Residence in Central Japan." *American Anthropologist* 70: 309–19.

Bennholdt-Thomson, Veronika. 1981. "Subsistence production and extended reproduction," in Kate Young, Carol Wolkowitz and Roslyn McCullagh (eds.), *Of Marriage and the Market.* London: CSE Books.

Bleek, Wolf. 1975. *Marriage, Inheritance and Witchcraft.* Leiden: Afrikastudiescentrum.

Bloch, M. 1973. "The Long Term and the Short Term: the Economic and Political Significance of the Morality of Kinship," in J. Goody (ed.), *The Character of Kinship.* Cambridge: Cambridge University Press.

Bromley, Ray and Chris Gerry. 1979. "Who are the casual poor?" in Ray Bromley and Chris Gerry, (eds.), *Casual Work and Poverty.* New York: John Wiley.

Brown, Judith K. 1970. "A Note on the Division of Labor by Sex." *American Anthropologist* 72: 1073.

Carter, Anthony. 1984. "Household Histories," in Netting, Robert, R. Wilk and E. Arnould (eds.), *Households: Comparative and Historical Studies of the Domestic Group.* Berkeley: University of California Press.

Chayanov, A.V. 1966. *The Theory of Peasant Economy.* Homewood, Illinois: Irwin, Inc.

Clark, Gracia. 1989. "Money, Sex and Cooking: Manipulation of the Paid/ Unpaid Boundary by Asante Market Women," in Benjamin Orlove and Henry Rutz (eds.), *The Social Economy of Consumption.* Lanham: University Press of America.

———. 1984. *The Position of Asante Women Traders in Kumasi Central Market, Ghana.* PhD thesis, Dept. Social Anthropology, U. of Cambridge.

Clarke, Edith. 1957. *My Mother Who Fathered Me.* London: Ruskin.

Cohen, Abner. 1969. *Custom and Politics in Urban Africa.* Berkeley: University of California Press.

Davin, Anna. 1984. "Working or Helping? London Working-Class Children in the Domestic Economy," in Smith, Joan, Immanuel Wallerstein and Hans-Dieter Evers (eds.), *Households and the World Economy.* Beverly Hills: Sage Publications.

Davis, William. 1973. *Social Relations in a Philippine Market.* Berkeley: University of California Press.

Dewey, Alice. 1962. *Peasant Marketing in Java.* Glencoe: Free Press.

Elwert, Georg. 1984. "Conflicts Inside and Outside the Household: A West African Case Study," in Smith, Joan, Immanuel Wallerstein and Hans-Dieter Evers (eds.), *Households and the World Economy.* Beverly Hills: Sage Publications.

Fortes, Meyer. 1949. "Time and Social Structure: an Ashanti Case Study," in Fred Eggan and Meyer Fortes (eds.), *Social Structure.* London: Oxford University Press.

Friedman, Kathie. 1984. "Households as Income-Pooling Units," in Smith, Joan, Immanuel Wallerstein and Hans-Dieter Evers (eds.), *Households and the World Economy.* Beverly Hills: Sage Publications.

Gonzalez, Nancie. 1969. *Black Carib Household Structure.* Seattle: University of Washington Press.

Goody, E.. 1973. *Contexts of Kinship.* Cambridge: Cambridge University Press.

Guyer, Jane. 1981. "Household and Community in African Studies." *African Studies Review* 24: 87–137.

———. 1986 "Intra-Household Processes and Farming Systems Research: Perspectives from Anthropology," in Joyce Moock (ed.), *Understanding Africa's Rural Households and Farming Systems.* Boulder: Westview Press.

Hackenberg, Robert, A. Murphy and H. Selby. 1984. "The Urban Household in Dependent Development," in Netting, Robert, R. Wilk and E. Arnould (eds.), *Households: Comparative and Historical Studies of the Domestic Group.* Berkeley: University of California Press.

Hammel, E. A. 1980. "Household Structure in Fourteenth-Century Macedonia." *Journal of Family History* 5: 242–73.

———. 1984. "On the *** of Studying Household Form and Function," in Netting, Robert, R. Wilk and E. Arnould (eds.), *Households: Comparative and Historical Studies of the Domestic Group.* Berkeley: University of California Press.

Hart, J. Keith. 1973. "Informal Income Opportunities and Urban Development in Ghana." *Journal of Modern African Studies* 11: 61.

Hill, Polly. 1963. *Migrant Cocoa Farmers of Southern Ghana.* London: Clarendon.

Hyden, Goran. 1980. *Beyond Ujamaa in Tanzania: Underdevelopment and the Uncaptured Peasantry.* London: Heinemann.

Jones, Christine. 1986. "Intra-Household Bargaining in Response to the Introduction of New Crops: A Case Study from North Cameroon," in Joyce Moock (ed.), *Understanding Africa's Rural Households and Farming Systems.* Boulder: Westview Press.

Laslett, Peter. 1972. ed. and intro., *Household and Family in Past Time.* Cambridge: Cambridge University Press.

Mikell, Gwendolyn. 1987. "Theory Vs. Reality in Contemporary African Kinship Dynamics: The Akan of Ghana." Paper presented at African Studies Association meetings, Denver, Colorado, November, 1987.

Moser, Caroline. 1978. "Informal Sector or Petty Commodity Production: Dualism or Dependence in Urban Development?" *World Development* 6: Sept/Oct.

Netting, Robert, R. Wilk and E. Arnould (eds.). 1984 *Households: Comparative and Historical Studies of the Domestic Group.* Berkeley: University of California Press.

Okali, C. 1983. *Cocoa and Kinship in Ghana: The Matrilineal Akan of Ghana.* London: Kegan Paul.

Oppong, Christine. 1974. *Marriage Among a Matrilineal Elite.* Cambridge: Cambridge University Press.

Pasternak, Burton, C. Ember and M. Ember. 1976. "On the Conditions Favoring Extended Family Households." *Journal of Anthropological Research* 32: 109–24.

Poewe, Karla. 1981. *Matrilineal Ideology: Male-Female Dynamics in Luapula, Zambia.* London: Academic Press.

Polanyi, Karl. 1957. "The Economy as Instituted Process," in K. Polanyi, C. Arensburg and H. Pearson (eds.), *Trade and Markets in the Early Empires*. New York: Aldine.

Rattray, R. S. 1923. *Ashanti*. Oxford: Clarendon Press.

Reyna, S. 1977. "Marriage Payments, Household Structure, and Domestic Labor-supply among the Barma of Chad." *Africa* 47: 81–88.

Robertson, Claire. 1984. *Sharing the Same Bowl*. Bloomington: Indiana University Press.

Sahlins, Marshall. 1972. *Stone Age Economics*. New York: Aldine.

Sanjek, Roger. 1982. "The Organization of Households in Adabraka: Toward a Wider Comparative Perspective." *Comparative Studies in Society and History* 24: 57–103.

Schildkrout, Enid. 1982. "Dependence and Autonomy: The Economic Activities of Secluded Hausa Women in Kano, Nigeria," in Edna Bay (ed.), *Women and Work in Africa*. Boulder: Westview Press.

Smart, Alan. 1988. "Resistance to Relocation by Shopkeepers in a Hong Kong Squatter Area," in Gracia Clark (ed.), *Traders Versus the State: Anthropological Approaches to Unofficial Economies*. Boulder: Westview Press.

Smith, Carol A. 1984. "Forms of Production in Practice: fresh Approaches to Simple Commodity Production." *Journal of Peasant Studies* 11: 201–21.

Smith, Joan, Immanuel Wallerstein and Hans-Dieter Evers (eds.). 1984. *Households and the World Economy*. Beverly Hills: Sage Publications.

Stack, Carol. 1974. *All Our Kin*. New York: Harper.

Verdun, Michael. 1980. "Shaking off the Domestic Yoke, or the Sociological Significance of Residence." *Comparative Studies in Society and History* 22: 109.

Wilk, Richard. 1984. "Households in Process: Agricultural Change and Domestic Transformation among the Kekchi Maya of Belize," in Netting, Robert, R. Wilk and E. Arnould (eds.), *Households: Comparative and Historical Studies of the Domestic Group*. Berkeley: University of California Press.

Wilk, Richard and R. Netting. 1984. "Households: Changing Forms and Functions," in Netting, Robert, R. Wilk and E. Arnould (eds.), *Households: Comparative and Historical Studies of the Domestic Group*. Berkeley: University of California Press.

Wilks, Ivor. 1975. *Asante in the Nineteenth Century*. Cambridge: Cambridge University Press.

Wong, Diana. 1984. "The Limits of Using the Household as a Unit of Analysis," in Smith, Joan, Immanuel Wallerstein and Hans-Dieter Evers (eds.), *Households and the World Economy*. Beverly Hills: Sage Publications.

Yanagisako, Sylvia. 1979. "Family and Household: The Analysis of Domestic Groups." *Annual Review of Anthropology* 8: 161–205.

7

Fijian Household Practices and the Reproduction of Class

Henry J. Rutz

Unfortunately what is liberty for one man is often the negation of liberty for another. In a developed society a man's property is not merely something which he controls and enjoys, which he can make the basis of his labour and the scene of his ordered activities, but something whereby he can control another man and make it the basis of that man's labour and the scene of activities ordered by himself.

—L.T. Hobhouse 1913

The World-Economy Hypothesis About Households

World-economy theorists have come to view the household as the locus for analyzing labor-force formation in the capitalist world-economy. Taking the interests of capitalists as their point of departure, these theorists hypothesize that the household is an institution of optimal labor-force formation. It allows for variable labor inputs over time, it is mobile across space, and—most importantly for capitalist interest in the rate of profit—wage labor is reproduced by the household at a cost below its value. In other words, the household is *the* institution with the right combination of malleability and continuity that can reproduce short term market labor while ensuring stability over time. And it does so not on its own terms or by its own design but on variable terms dictated by capitalist requirements.

In Wallerstein's (1984: 18ff) view, the household in our historical epoch is an institution created out of the requirements of capital accumulation on a world scale. In contrast to those who would argue that the household is a vestige of precapitalist modes of production, destined for the dustbin of history by the contradictions it poses for the advance of capitalist relations, Wallerstein argues that household transformations are generated by capitalism, for capitalism (Smith, Wallerstein, Evers 1984: 8). Household variability is explained by the historically specific conditions of uneven capitalist development between core and periphery. The appeal of this bold and assertive hypothesis is obvious; if true, it would help to organize a diverse literature on households within a single logic of recent world history.

The purpose of this chapter is a sympathetic critique of the world-economy hypothesis in the light of an analysis of urban middle class Fijian household structure and processes. The world-economy approach has much to recommend it. Historical, empirical, and processual—it provides a compelling alternative on a grand scale to the now discredited ahistorical, normative, and typological perspective of modernization theory that it set out to replace. But the Fijian case illuminates, in a concrete way, methodological and conceptual problems that are not likely to be overcome, given the objectives of the world-economy approach. There are at least two drawbacks to the world-economy perspective on household structure and processes. The first is a methodology of economic reductionism that, once understood, weakens the apparent claim to explain structure.

The second is a conceptual vagueness about processes that all but vitiates the further claim that most of what goes on inside the household can be understood in terms primarily of labor markets. Because the critique of the world-economy hypothesis on grounds of reductionism and oversimplification is separable from, and more general than, the application of the hypothesis to the Fijian case, it will be useful to review its underlying postulates that lead to a definition of the household.

Reductionism and Oversimplification

The world-economy hypothesis is premised on an apparent paradox, an observation, and a conclusion. The apparent paradox is that, while wage labor has increased in the capitalist world-economy, a substantial part of labor power is generated by nonmarket relationships and processes (Smith, Wallerstein, and Evers 1984: 8). The observation is that, especially in the periphery of the world-economy, wages tend to be low relative to the market costs of reproducing labor. The conclusion is that two postulates take as their conceptual locus the interests of capital.

First, it is in the interests of capital to create and to maintain an institution that will combine wage and non-wage labor as a means to replenish labor power at wage rates below the cost of its reproduction (cf. Meillassoux 1981). The 'household' *by definition* is such an institution: "With the increasing commodification of everyday life has gone a decline in co-residentiality and kinship as determinative of the boundaries (of households). The end point of this secular pressure is not . . .'the individual' or the 'nuclear family' but a unit whose cohesiveness is increasing (sic) predicated on the income-pooling function it performs." (Wallerstein 1984: 21) Friedman (1984: 46) develops this theme and defines the household as a set of relationships between people that impose sharing obligations. It is clear from the context that she means pooling wage and non-wage labor. The household, so defined, is a useful instrument of labor-force formation precisely because it is "intermediate" (Wallerstein 1984: 22) between a proletariat stripped of its connections to community (presumably, this would be a costly labor force to maintain and perhaps would be economically unreliable and politically untenable) and a labor force enmeshed in kinship, territory and coresidentiality (presumably, this would be a labor force immobilized by its multi-dimensional social connectedness and unresponsive to signals from the wage market).

Second, especially in the periphery of the world-economy, the intermediate household satisfies another interest of capital. Wages are low relative to the income necessary to sustain and reproduce the labor force over long periods (Friedman 1984: 45). Household processes not only pool wage and non-wage labor, they pool the meagre money incomes of wage earners and thereby satisfy the interests of capital in the continuity of labor power.

The conditions that must be satisfied in order for the world-economy hypothesis to be supported are twofold: people establish (unspecified) relationships of pooling incomes and sharing consumption, i.e. they have households; they do so in (unspecified) ways that replenish labor power for capitalist accumulation, i.e. they daily and continuously supply labor for capitalist profit. If households persist and capitalist labor power is replenished, the hypothesis is supported. In effect, householding—the practices that would tell us how wage earners and non-wage earners find each other, what social interactions and communicative acts constitute the hypothesized relationships, and what ideological and cultural constructs underlie 'sharing obligations' and the *social* 'reproduction of labor'—remains a black box.

The world-economy hypothesis is a tautology based on a double economic reduction. Exogenous factors shaping the household and its members' activities are reduced to the impersonal "forces" of labor markets. Endogenous practices such as social interactions and communicative acts that establish and maintain norms of sharing and consumption, or disputes over principles of equitable distribution and rights to a share of household income, are reduced to the mechanical processes of swapping variable combinations of wage and non-wage labor. The hypothesis is conceptually vague because, although it links labor markets to household reproduction of labor, it explores causality in one direction

only. The interests of a class of capitalists in households is specified but
the interests of other classes in the market is ignored. World-economy
theorists examine labor markets in minute detail but relegate the practice
of householding to a typological stasis. The counter-thesis would be that
household practices *not* generated by the market direct the flow of labor
to it in ways that help explain why the interests of capital can be frustrated
by the interests of other classes.

Capitalist Labor Power and "Intermediate" Households: The Urban Fijian Middle Class

The political economy of Fiji underwent a major transformation during
the two decades that straddled independence from Britain in 1970.
Government policies reflected a shift of ideology from economic gradualism
to development. Major private and public investment programs, financed
by foreign investment, became the driving force behind successive five
year development plans. These political and economic changes resulted
in the rapid emergence of an urban Fijian middle class whose political
stake was in nationalism and whose economic base resided in the civil
service. However, one of the most striking aspects of the new Fijian
middle class, related to its telescoped history, was its retention of what
in Fijian is termed *vaka i taukei* (Fijian custom), or what has come to
be known in English as "traditionalism"—the active construction of a
Fijian way of life during a century of colonial administration.[1]

The locus of tension or conflict between the moral economy of the
Fijian way of life and the market economy that underwrites the emergence
of class culture is the urban household. The daily practice of household
members is an encounter with established temporal rhythms of hospitality
or social rituals juxtaposed to an accepted work-discipline that comes
with industrial capitalism and the bureaucratic apparatus of a new nation-
state (cf. Hareven 1982). The vulnerability of a Fijian household to
"obligatory requests" and to continual gift-giving is juxtaposed to its
necessity to budget income in the interests of own members welfare.
Expenses include mortgage payments, taxes, utility bills, education fees,
and new consumption goods of a middle class that has made irrevocable
commitments to wage labor, private property, education, and an urbanized
and commodified use of time. The universals of formal education, which
are the key to occupations and incomes that reproduce the new Fijian
middle class, come into conflict with strong values of authority, hierarchy,
and inequality that suffuse the Fijian way of life.

The intersection of these political, economic, moral, and cultural
tensions and conflicts emanating from the larger society are difficult to
disentangle in any discussion of household processes of pooling income

and sharing consumption. Urban middle class Fijians themselves find it difficult to reconcile the many conflicting bases for household allocation and distribution, instead falling back on a coherent ideology of kinship and chiefship whose practice fits their own conditions of existence only imperfectly and, on occasion, not at all. These tensions and conflicts, which are often represented in consciousness as confusion, are the material out of which urban middle class Fijians construct their daily household life. In order to see the value of their own constructs and practice for understanding household structure and processes, and how these might influence the reproduction of their labor, it is useful first to return briefly to the world-economy hypothesis and its application to urban middle class Fijians.

Does the world-economy hypothesis account for urban middle class Fijian household structure and processes? "Intermediate" households are postulated as sets of relationship that combine the labor of wage and non-wage workers for the pooling of income and sharing of consumption in ways that satisfy two conditions: the reproduction of household labor and the replenishment of labor power for the market economy, both on a daily basis and in the long term. Additional postulates pertain to the malleability of households over time and across space in response to shifts in labor markets. The following account is based on a small sample of fifteen households from the oldest and most established Fijian middle class residential area in the capital of Suva, the industrial, commercial and administrative center of the nation.[2]

It would be surprising if urban middle class Fijian households did *not* satisfy all of the postulates and conditions of the world-economy hypothesis. Certainly, the very existence of the urban Fijian middle class is predicated on the labor market for civil servants. There was no Fijian middle class until it was created by a government policy of localization as a prelude to independence in 1970. As Fisk (1970: 27) observed, "as an employer, the public service is important both for the number of its employees and for the proportion in higher income levels." The size of the civil service, while remaining a constant proportion of the growing number reported in manual employment, grew by 55.7 percent from 1961 to 1968. Fiji's *Seventh Development Plan* (1975: 22) projected the growth of employment in government services between 1976–80 at more than 4.5 percent, second only to the building and construction sector during a period of rapid growth in tourist development. By 1979, 42.5 percent of all professional and technical workers, and 32.4 percent of all clerical and related workers, were Fijian. And half the total wage earners in the country resided in the capital of Suva.

The picture of a Fijian middle class rooted in civil service employment and supported by public revenue fits my sample of households (Tables

Table 1. Household Size and Composition
by Wage and Non-wage Workers
in a Sample of Urban Middle Class Fijian Households

HH	Wage workers			Non-wage workers			Wage/Non-wage workers		HH size	
	(1) M	(2) F	(3) T	(4) M	(5) F	(6) T	(7)	(8) M	(9) F	(10) T
Type I--Nuclear										
A	1	0	1	0	1	1	1:1	3	3	6
B	6	2	8	0	1	1	8:1	9	6	15
C	1	0	1	0	1	1	1:1	4	2	6
Type IA--Nuclear plus										
D	1	1	2	0	1	1	2:1	2	3	5
E	2	0	2	0	1	1	2:1	2	3	5
F	1	2	3	0	0	0	3:0	1	2	3
G	0	3	3	0	2	2	3:2	1	9	10
H	2	0	2	0	4	4	2:4	3	6	9
Type II--Stem										
I	3	1	4	0	1	1	4:1	3	2	5
J	3	1	4	0	2	2	4:2	7	3	10
K	1	1	2	0	2	2	2:2	2	4	6
Type IIA--Extended										
L	2	1	3	1	1	2	3:2	5	7	12
M	3	3	6	0	2	2	6:2	5	11	16
N	1	2	3	0	2	2	3:2	3	10	13
O	2	1	3	0	2	2	3:2	3	5	8
Tot	29	18	47	1	23	24	47:24	53	76	129

Source: Suva Fijian Study Area Survey (SFSAS), January to April,
1982 (cf. Gounis and Rutz 1986).

1 and 2). A quarter of all Fijians who are employed can be found in
occupations classified as professional, technical, and clerical. Nearly two-
thirds of wage workers in my sample are civil servants employed in these
occupations (Table 3). With two exceptions, every middle class household
has at least one wage worker in government employment. Two-thirds
have managed to secure public employment for at least two household
members. Conversely, seven households maintain the socially necessary
consumption of the middle class (see below) with no members employed
in the private sector.

Fijians in private sector employment tend to earn much less than
those in the public sector. This, together with the greater numbers of
workers employed in the public sector, accounts for the disproportionately

Table 2. Socially Necessary Consumption and Reproduction of Labor
(all figures in 1982 Fijian dollars)

HH	Total HH Expenditure per month (1)	HH Head Net Income per month (2)	Total HH Net Income per month (3)	Total HH net surplus per month (4)	Net Surplus surplus/income per month (5)
I	396.99	660.00	1428.91	1031.92	.72
B	784.14	604.00	2256.00	1551.86	.69
F	131.49	200.00	316.00	184.51	.58
D	470.84	708.00	1044.00	573.16	.55
K	288.82	376.00	624.00	335.18	.54
M	758.43	612.00	1561.50	803.07	.51
G	425.71	312.00	852.00	426.29	.50
C	241.07	464.00	464.00	222.93	.48
J	281.01	192.00	336.00	134.99	.40
L	507.21	280.00	848.00	340.79	.40
O	436.18	380.00	752.00	295.82	.39
A	502.76	688.00	688.00	185.24	.27
N	1018.09	392.00	1172.00	153.91	.13
H	293.98	160.00	320.00	34.02	.11
E	374.00	362.00	362.00	-12.00	-.03
Tot	6910.72	6390.00	13024.41	6261.69	.48

Sources: Suva Fijian Study Area Survey (SFSAS); Household
Budgets-Lami Subdivision

Notes: (1) figures for total household expenditures per month are
            estimates from answers to survey questions;
       (2) recorded savings are added to expenditures and
            subtracted from net income to arrive at a figure for
            "surplus";
       (3) the exchange rate in April 1982 was $1.00US=$.88F.

Table 3. Sectoral Employment of Wage Earners
in Middle Class Fijian Households

Sector					Households (numbers of workers)										
	B	G	I	D	E	H	J	K	M	O	A	C	N	F	L	Total
Public	5	3	3	2	2	2	2	2	2	2	1	1	1	0	1	29
Private	3	0	1	0	0	0	2	0	4	1	0	0	2	3	2	18
Total	8	3	4	2	2	2	4	2	6	3	1	1	3	3	3	47

Source: Suva Fijian Study Area Survey (SFSAS)

Table 4. Source of Income in Urban Middle Class Fijian Households:
Private and Public Sector Employment

						Households								
A	B	C	D	E	F	G	H	I	J	K	L	M	N	O

Sector

Public

A	B	C	D	E	F	G	H	I	J	K	L	M	N	O
688	1636	464	1044	312	0	852	320	1268	0	624	488	1241	740	120

Private

A	B	C	D	E	F	G	H	I	J	K	L	M	N	O
0	620	0	0	0	316	0	0	160	336	0	360	320	432	632

Total HH Net Income per Month

A	B	C	D	E	F	G	H	I	J	K	L	M	N	O
688	2256	464	1044	362	316	852	320	1428	336	624	848	1561	1172	752

Ratio of Private Sector Net Income to Total Net Household Income

A	B	C	D	E	F	G	H	I	J	K	L	M	N	O
0	.27	0	0	0	1.0	0	0	.11	0	0	.42	.20	.37	.84

Ratio of Public Sector Net Income to Total Net Household Income

A	B	C	D	E	F	G	H	I	J	K	L	M	N	O
1.0	.73	1.0	1.0	1.0	0	1.0	1.0	.89	1.0	1.0	.58	.80	.63	.16

Source: Suva Fijian Study Area Survey (SFSAS)

large share of total household net income contributed by household members with steady full-time work in the civil service (Table 4). The average contribution of public sector employment is 78 percent of total household net income. Private sector workers contribute the lion's share of household income in only two cases.

The conditions of civil service employment are as important as wage levels for the establishment and maintenance of an urban Fijian middle class. Education is a prerequisite. Civil service employment requires at least secondary or technical/vocational training past primary school. English is the common language of bureaucracy, and most Fijians with only primary school education speak English poorly. There is a high positive correlation between income, occupation and attained level of education in the economically active population of Fiji (Gounis and Rutz 1986: 71, Table 11). While 22.4 percent of the economically active population has attained a level of education above primary school, in my sample this figure is 50.7 percent. The implication is clear: to reproduce household labor, education fees are a part of socially necessary consumption for the middle class.

Another condition of the labor market for public service that affects the reproduction of the Fijian middle class is security of employment. The prospect of lifetime employment assures households of permanent income as long as the earner stays in the household. The expectation of permanent income allows households to rationalize their economic and social behavior in ways not possible for working class and rural village households. Civil servants benefit more from the national pension scheme than other workers, loosening the tie of kinship insurance between generations without eliminating it entirely. A household with a predictable income from week to week also can rationalize the welfare of its own members and loosen its dependence on relationships outside the household. Permanent and predictable incomes over time have obvious implications for the continuity of households and the supply of labor power to the market, a point not considered by Smith et. al. (1984).

A relatively high permanent income allows middle class households to qualify for mortgages, consumer credit, market insurance, and personal bank loans. This, in turn, encourages class definitions of consumption (Rutz 1989), especially in the acquisition of housing in the capitalist real estate market. Urban middle class Fijians aspire to owning multiple room stucco houses on large private lots in subdivisions with European style landscaping. Subdivisions have sewers, paved roads, electricity, garbage collection, mail delivery, telephone lines, and all the amenities associated with middle class culture, especially indoor plumbing for toilet and shower. The interior of these homes is arranged according to universal middle class notions of privacy and comfort.

The commodified household of the urban Fijian middle class, in part the result of the labor market for civil servants, has implications for the reproduction of labor for that market. Household reproduction *as a class* must take into account a middle class interest in household accumulation. If labor is reproduced in terms of socially necessary consumption, what is socially necessary is escalating, a phenomenom that may or may not serve the interests of capital.

The data also lend *some* support to the thesis that capitalist labor markets are *one* important determinant of household structure and processes. With regard to the economic structure of the household, all but one combine wage and non-wage workers in their composition (Table 1, col. 1–6). Furthermore, all but two households have multiple wage earners (Table 1, col. 3). Wages do tend to be low relative to the cost of reproducing the household, but on this score there is significant variability. If total household expenditures are used to measure the socially necessary consumption that reproduces household labor *as a class*, i.e. the reproduction of middle class labor, then the largest single income in nine of fifteen households is below the minimum necessary to meet current consumption (Table 2, col. 3). All nine households have "solved" this problem with multiple incomes.

However, the more interesting fact is that all but one household show a "surplus" over what is required to reproduce household labor; in most cases the "surplus" over socially necessary consumption is surprisingly large and would compare with the middle classes anywhere (Table 2, col. 5). If household structure is primarily a response to the conditions of labor markets and their replenishment, it might be expected that households would "solve" the problem of low wages with combinations of multiple incomes that satisfied more efficiently their socially necessary consumption. Clearly, by any standard of middleclassness, urban Fijians are themselves accumulators. We need to view household practices not only from the standpoint of the interest of capital but also from that of privileged labor, and not only from the standpoint of production but also distribution and consumption.

Even when household structure is reduced to its economic base, the case of urban middle class Fijians raises more questions than the world-economy hypothesis answers. A predominance of "intermediate" households and the presence of multiple wage earners characterizes, in part, the new Fijian middle class, whose emergence can be traced to capitalist development and a newly independent nation-state. But questions remain. There is a long tradition in anthropology of viewing needs as socially determined. The question is, are the new needs *also* a part of the capitalist world system? At present, the prevalence of women as non-wage workers cannot be deduced from the structure of labor markets (Table 1, col. 5). And the ratio of wage to non-wage workers varies more than would be expected on the hypothesis that labor markets determine this relationship (Table 1, col. 7).

Most importantly, the 'reproduction of labor' has little meaning apart from a determination of 'socially necessary consumption'. This contention is not really surprising, since social interactions in any household are centered around issues of equity and rights in the distribution of the product for consumption at least as much as a division of labor and its allocation to production. The urban Fijian middle class is new, created in two short decades out of the requirements of an independent nation-state. Viewed from the perspective of the interests of the new middle classes, (not the capitalist class), the household is a unit that must satisfy "traditionalism" as well as the wage market. The urban middle class Fijian household is a locus of the intersection of wage and non-wage labor, of two different modes of production and consumption. But it is more than this intersection and cannot be reduced to them. In order to understand its structure and processes, we need to turn to the political and discursive practices of its members.

The Politics and Discourse of Authoritative Allocation

Notwithstanding the implications of labor markets for householding, the world-economy hypothesis is silent on which of a number of possible alternative social relationships is most likely to occur, and why. The folk model of authoritative allocation, whose origin lies in a thousand rural villages scattered throughout the hinterland, is practiced in urban middle class households to a surprising extent.

When Fijians talk about householding, they pursue two lines of thought. One they term *sala vakailavo*, or the "money way," which they often characterize as foreign to their way of thinking (even when the speaker is the graduate of a university and conversant with wage income, mortgage rates, bank savings accounts, and budget practices). Their description of householding often includes an account of low wages and rising prices, of the costs of educating children, and of the high expense of living in Suva compared to the village. The village is often romanticized as a place where "food is free, people will build a house for you, and there is no need for money." One's time is one's own, to be passed telling stories around the kava bowl, sleeping and eating. One needn't work every day: only when one wants to. This romantic illusion, one might say delusion, is important not for its description of village life but for what it tells us about urban middle class commitment to capitalist culture at the historical moment of its domination in Fijian society. At best, this commitment is acknowledged more than accepted. Uneasiness about capitalist culture surfaces in a joking and playful attitude about the "money way." A person will say to a group gathered around the kava bowl, "Fijians don't know business; it isn't ours. If you give a Fijian money, he will just spend it or give it away, or someone will come and ask him for it. Fijians aren't careful and don't think about tomorrow. You won't see a Fijian plan. We don't know how to save. Fijians are bad with money." Such talk draws assenting nods and some laughter from the audience familiar with the refrain. It expresses a double message about a degree of resentment toward a capitalist culture to which Fijians are committed and an affirmation of the social superiority of their own, despite the inevitable conflict engendered by a conscious attempt to constitute their own culture of capitalism.[3]

The second line of thought about householding is referred to as *sala vakavanua*, or literally "the way after the manner of the land." A folk model of Fijian households can be summarized in a straightforward and unambiguous way, though its implications for the practice of householding are both subtle and complex. The household is a construct delineated by Fijian language. As a nexus of relationships, Fijians have little trouble demarcating the household as a category different from, but related to, clan or community. As a unit for the continuous allocation of members' resources to production and consumption, and for the periodic allocation of resources to clan or community, the household has a definite function. And conceived as a bundle of property rights, the household is a locus of everyday distribution and equity.

Provisionally, the folk model is most easily explicated in a rural village setting. The reasons are not fortuitous: most Fijians continue to reside in villages. Also, the majority of urban working and middle class Fijians retain strong ties to their villages of origin. There is an important paradox in the practice of urban householding, one that has implications for labor markets. As their material conditions of existence have become dominated by the market, Fijians have embraced with greater tenacity the apparently timeless virtues of their folk model.[4]

There is little problem in locating households in Fijian language or behavior. There are terms for "housesite," "house," "household," "household members," and "head of household." Housesites are claimed on grounds of ancestral occupation and rights extend intergenerationally. Houses have "owners." Senior males are privileged over their juniors, males are privileged over females, and senior females are privileged over their juniors. Oldest sons have the greatest claims to property, loyalty, and the service of other household members. As heirs of the headship they also have the generalized responsibility for the well-being of everyone.

A household, whatever its composition, is set off from other households but shares with them definite obligations to contribute to the affairs of respective kin groups and villages. These affairs are termed *na i tovo vakavanua;* literally, "duties after the manner of the land." They constitute the richest, most rewarding, but also the most burdensome activities undertaken by households. Considerable activity of a household is directed at "its preparations" to meet some socially defined share of kin group and community welfare. An ideal household is one with a leader who can pool the labor of members to meet its obligations when an official call comes from clan or community leaders. A household can be located from the standpoint of how its head relates to clan and community leaders and from the standpoint of how clan or community relate to it. A household *qua* household is able to provision itself in terms of socially necessary consumption, normatively defined by the community. In return, the community provides the household with its house, an essential item of property which the household members should *not* build themselves (Rutz 1984).

The structure of a Fijian household is hierarchical and based on relations of inequality. While households need not consist of persons related by kinship, the folk model conceives of the structure in terms of close genealogical kin relations and co-residency. Starting from the bottom of the structure, older siblings have authority over younger ones, brothers have authority over sisters, husbands have authority over wives, and fathers have authority over their sons. These relations are practiced daily in language habits (the use of a complex system of pronouns to express rank and status; the use of teknonymy), in spatial arrangements for the social partition of the house and movements of its members (Sahlins 1976: 32–36), in the sexual division of labor for domestic production, and in various activities such as eating meals or receiving and entertaining visitors. In the folk model, equity is conceived to result from the proper practice of hierarchy and inequality embodied in the respect accorded to an elder head by household members. He is judged by members for his generosity and by non-members for how well he prepares the household to meet onerous social commitments. A Durkheimian moral glue of mutual trust percolates through the hierarchy and ensures repetition at each rank.

In the folk model, there is no contradiction between his privilege as head, his authoritative allocation in the interests of clan and/or community, and his responsibility toward the well-being of individual household members. To understand the Fijian variant of benign patriarchy, it is necessary to place authoritative allocation within a matrix of a given sexual division of domestic labor, a highly developed system of rank and status with its privileges and prerogatives, and a powerful ideology of mutual help and respect that accompanies the pooling of resources and sharing of consumption. Household processes, then, consist of norms, conventions, and cultural practices—including a mode of discourse— which constitute whatever arrangements are observed for pooling income and sharing consumption.

The lynchpin of authoritative allocation is the construct of the chiefdom. The chiefdom is the most important single construct in Fijian society, evoking powerful sentiments of respect, duty, loyalty, and service. When describing the "strength" of the Fijian way of life (including the household), when a Fijian wants to explore "in depth" what it means to be Fijian, at those times he/she falls back on images of chief and chieftainship. Chiefdoms and households differ in structure and origin. They no doubt have different histories and different political ends. What they share is a common imagery of authority and the correct behavior of superordinates and subordinates. They differ in the specific form in which chief-like authority is practiced.

The chief *is* the people (Sahlins 1983). His well-being is their well-being. The fertility of the land and people are represented in the health of the chief. The chief conquers but does not exploit. A chief receives by right but gives out of generosity. His relations with people are built upon fundamental reciprocities of sentiment: "mutual respect," "mutual help," "mutual service," and "mutual love." The chiefs hold the wisdom and it is the people's duty to follow, not to question. To question is to challenge mutual trust. If everyone works for the chief, then all benefit. The ideal is for everyone "to go together." These and similar statements are repeated endlessly as a part of the formulaic speeches and presentations of gifts made on innumerable public occasions over which chiefs preside. Strict rank and precedence operate on such occasions, where everyone has a place and that place is acknowledged in proportion to its social distance from the chief. All benefit when each knows his place and performs his duty.

The cultural construct of the Fijian chiefdom intensified during a century of British colonial rule even as the actual structure was transformed into a modern bureaucratic-administrative organization. The validity of the nation-state has come to rest upon the legitimacy of the chiefdom and has influenced recent national politics. It should not be surprising, therefore, to discover that the partriarchal household modelled on the authority of the chief remains vital among working and middle class urban Fijians. His authority derives from an analogy to that of chiefs in the larger polity. Just as the chief is accorded respect and given service by commoners, the head of household is accorded respect and given service. But just as the chief has the interests of his people uppermost in his mind and demonstrates this by virtue of his generosity, the head of household cares for others and is generous toward them within the framework of equity based on hierarchy. The head receives in order to give by organizing the pooling of resources for the sharing of benefits.

A model of authoritative allocation can address some questions left unanswered by the world systems approach. One question has to do with recruitment. How members are recruited has obvious implications for the structure of social relations and the composition of urban Fijian middle class households. The model of authoritative allocation posits a male head, a sexual division of labor, close genealogical ties among members, and rank according to sex and age seniority. Eleven of fifteen sample households have a male head. The four households with a female head are anomalous in the same way: their husbands have died within the year and eldest sons are not yet in a position or of an age to assume the headship. Moreover, kinship based on close genealogical ties forms the social basis for the practice of "mutual respect," "mutual service," "mutual help," and "mutual love." Nearly every person in my sample stands in a relationship to other members of her/his household as one or more of a limited set that Fijians classify as "close" as opposed to "distant": (real) "father," (real) "mother," "husband," "wife," (real) "son," (real) "daughter," (real) "brother," (real) "sister."

The important point that follows is that urban middle class Fijians continue to reproduce the structure and composition of rural households under urban market conditions for labor. Given the necessity of having multiple wage earners to reproduce market labor *as a class,* authoritative allocation is only one of many possible solutions. In fact, it is not at all the most obvious solution in the interests of capital. The single exception to recruitment by means of close kinship helps to make the point. In one house, the head has recruited a nuclear family unrelated by kinship through common employment with its head in the same government department. Of the many possible solutions to the problem of recruiting multiple wage earners, one of the most elegant from the standpoint of the market would be for recruitment to occur in the workplace. Urban Fijians *do*, in fact, form associations on the basis of "classmates," "workmates," and other strictly urban bases of sociability. But these function largely as ephemeral drinking groups and changing networks for small personal loans of cash, not as the basis for recruiting members of households.

Why not? Perhaps the answer lies in the recruitment of non-wage workers to urban Fijian middle class households. Here the sexual division of labor in the model of authoritative allocation comes into play. Fijian women are used to working. They have primary responsibility for most domestic tasks and, in some regions of Fiji, women also do many agricultural and foraging activities. Fijian men never resisted the idea of women entering the urban wage labor market. Quite the opposite: women are educated and actively seek employment in wage labor markets, many of which are sex-segregated in Fiji because of the culture of western capitalism. But, although men have begun to do some domestic tasks, there is a substitution of non-wage female labor for tasks formerly done by women who now work. Unmarried daughters, or sisters of wives, are major sources of supply of household labor. Kinship is an effective way in which to recruit nonwage labor to the intermediate household, but it is the culturally established relationship between the Fijian sexual division of household labor and the western sexual division of market labor, and not the interests of capital, *per se,* that account for the composition of households.

The size of urban middle class Fijian households also is informed as much by the folk model of authoritative allocation as by the conditions of labor markets. Beyond the purely technical question of why combinations of wage and non-wage labor balance income and expenditure, the world-economy hypothesis stops short of a more compelling question about why particular combinations of wage and non-wage earners should vary. But in the Fijian case there are wide disparities in household income, the number of wage earners per household, the ratio of wage to non-wage labor, and the number of children that "reproduce" labor in the next generation (Tables 1 and 2). Every chief or head of household is esteemed for the number of followers or members who are a part of his retinue. A crowded, busy, complex household brings esteem to its head. His ability to preside over such a unit is a source of pride and will be commented upon publicly. Small, nuclear households are viewed as socially isolated and impoverished, unable to muster the labor necessary to meet the total set of obligations that now define socially necessary consumption. The notion of social well-being—by which is meant many visitors, much food, and plenty of labor to serve those ascendant in the hierarchy—is paramount in the Fijian view of what makes life worth living. The commodification of life is a fact of urban living. But household accumulation has an uneasy co-existence with kinship reciprocities, and both characterize the consciousness of the urban Fijian middle class. In fact, mere wealth has no social value and confers little status among urban Fijians. Taking care of a large retinue of dependents, working for the improvement of clan or community, unselfish generosity toward specific others—these beliefs, when put into practice, bring esteem to all. Next to the social esteem derived from raising one's whole group, class status markers such as competence on the job, personal achievement in education, success in career, or capacity to generate income, in and of themselves, are unrewarded.

The size of urban Fijian middle class households, therefore, tends to be large by any standard of comparison (Table 1, col. 10). Six of fifteen sample households have ten or more members, and five households have between six and nine members. The largest household has sixteen members, all "recruited" by means of close genealogical connections. The average size of middle class households is larger than either their working class counterparts in the city or their rural kinsmen in villages.

Fundamentally, households are about equity, not equality. However they are defined, the pooling of labor and sharing of consumption links unequal contributions of labor, income, or service to unequal shares in product or benefit. The fundamental inequality of householding suggests some practical value to kinship, whatever the ultimate cause of its altruism. The resilience of kinship goes beyond the reduction of its practice to mere ideology, as some world-economy theorists would have it (Smith, Wallerstein, and Evers 1984: 8). Chiefship lends to authoritative allocation the legitimacy required to relate acts of production to acts of consumption through distribution rules other than "equal rewards for equal work." It is necessarily otherwise in households, and the Fijian model provides a powerful historical paradigm for reproducing a new urban middle class under emergent market conditions. The cost, however, is that issues of equity have come to the fore. This is most evident in the politics and discourse of household members' claims about property rights.

Authoritative allocation is practiced, in the last analysis, as acts of pooling and sharing, whatever form these take under specific conditions of daily existence. These conditions are neither strictly nor primarily material. Allocation is a rational activity based on claims about property rights that reside in some notion of mutual trust. Without trust, grounded in a chiefly legitimacy, the Fijian edifice of householding collapses easily into petty jealousies, cheating, and even violent physical fights between husband and wife or siblings. Communicative acts are crucial to the practice of authoritative allocation. Norms of Fijian discourse are part and parcel of the message of chiefly behavior. Consider, for example, the communication of authority, property rights, and underlying norms in the following exchange during a visit of my research assistant and I to the elderly head of a house in our sample. Other household members are present, and the speaker is taking advantage of our visit to send a message.

> Jone: I am the "chief of the house." The "household members" are "respectful" toward me. I tell them things like "All right, five dollars from you for food [pointing to his wage earning adult daughter], five dollars from you [pointing to his adult wage earning son]. . . ." In Keteira, Moala, where I come from, several houses go together as one. They all know "their duties" toward "the preparation" of the "household." *Eratou e lako e muri na nodra i liuliu.* (They follow their leader.) *E dodonu.* (It is correct.) . . . I don't have to "request" food or fish. Everyone knows his/her duty. When someone goes fishing, that person brings the fish to my house. When someone goes to the garden, the food comes first to my house. The leader has *lewa*, the right to dispose; the household is *kaukauwa* (strong).

Jone appears to have ended his speech, so his daughter Kuini, the oldest sibling who remains a household member, picks up the speech where Jone has left off.

> Kuini: Our "housesite" (in Keteira, Moala) is *tabu* (sacred) to others. No one will build on it without the permission of the leader.

Jone adds the conclusion, though by now everyone has gotten the point about authoritative household allocation.

> Jone: When I am absent (from Keteira), no one lives at that house. When my young people marry, I direct a house to be built for them and "release" them to go live in it. If I do not release them, they dare not go.

However, Tevita, a friend and teacher who has accompanied us to this house, and who is head of his own household, is moved to speak on such an important topic.

> Tevita: In Fijian households, the head is responsible to see that household members "prepare for the Fijian way of life." The household must be prepared to meet its duties. Others will talk about the leader. A prepared

house is one that can meet its obligations. One can labor hard on one's gardens. But if the leader wants the food, he can take it. It is correct.

Similar authoritative discourse about what it means to be Fijian is a daily event in Fijian houses, whether rural or urban, rich or poor. Many routine events, repeated daily, are commented upon within such a normative framework of discourse. Common social interactions are pronounced to be the way Fijians ought to behave toward each other: they are "correct." An opinion, carefully marked as such by circumlocutions of the speaker, is pronounced "true." The discourse is formulaic and authoritative. That is, its content not only is about authority but it is delivered authoritatively, matter of factly. Norms of everyday discourse fit hand-in-glove with the politics of authoritative allocation, making its practice more a part of everyday life than what otherwise might be true were ideology and the communicative act separated.

The key construct in Fijian discourse is *veitalanoa* (storytelling). The storyteller narrates a story from beginning to end without interruption. Persons in the story commonly are given their own voices. To achieve this narrative effect, the storyteller raises the tone of his/her voice and quickens the tempo of a dialog (often with humorous intent). A storyteller is careful not to speculate or otherwise to comment upon the actions or words attributed by him/her to persons in his/her story. The storyteller neither attributes motives to the actions or thoughts of persons in his/her story, nor does he/she make inferences from the narrative sequence about harmful or beneficial consequences of thoughts and actions. When the story is finished, the listener is in no way obligated to participate in speculation, imputation, inference or analysis. Quite the opposite. Silence, a "thank you very much," a disapproving click of the tongue and shake of the head as if to wonder at the facts—these are the appropriate responses. Voice inflection and animated gestural language accompanying speech, especially if the subject is "weighty," are not the norm. In the rare instance when a listener wishes to ask a question, he/she will circumspectly introduce it cautiously with the phrase, "A question. . . ."

In the context of authoritative allocation, norms of everyday discourse promote the politics of pooling and sharing and reinforce the generalized political norms of mutual respect, duty and service. When speaker and listener are superordinate and subordinate, respectively (father-son, husband-wife, brother-sister, older sibling-younger sibling), the authoritative knowledge of storytelling easily becomes the language of request, command, and obedience. Discourse *is* ideology. A head of household often begins or ends a statement with the notion that the implied action would be correct in the Fijian way of life. He draws implicitly on the legitimacy of the whole chiefly tradition when he makes what appear to be matter-of-fact statements. Authoritative knowledge goes hand-in-hand with authoritative allocation. Norms of discourse assign the assessment of what a speaker says to who the speaker is, i.e. to social hierarchy. In speech, as in behavior, there is structured inequality that is "correct" and "true." It is expected that one's personal thoughts, if they do not conform to the norms, will and ought to go unspoken. (One can disagree, but one ought then to go along with authority and not "spoil" it for those who dutifully follow convention.) On such occasions when personal motive, feelings, or opinions that would offend authority are in the air and sensed by the group, there are quiet but audible cautionary mutterings of the phrase "go slow." This usually is enough to silence the person who would violate the group norms of discourse.

The implications of authoritative allocation and discourse for householding among urban middle class Fijians are several. First, the folk model explains why, out of all the possible relations for sharing obligations of intermediate households, kinship dominates and accounts for the overwhelming majority of household relationships. Second, the folk model explains why most non-wage workers are women even when there is no labor market or cultural restriction on women working for wages. In addition, the folk model is a point of departure for addressing questions about specific points of tension and conflict in the practice of householding that relate to the way the reproduction of middle class household labor affects labor formation in the capitalist market economy. Finally, the folk model provides insight into the continuity of labor beyond its daily reproduction.

Tension and Conflict in Household Practices

Household practices of the Fijian middle class are drifting in cross-currents of material and ideological forces. Middle class households are becoming committed to an urban consumer culture, while the material conditions of their existence favor the retention of pooling and sharing arrangements whose validity rests on precapitalist notions of social reciprocity. The resurgence of Fijian nationalism has reinforced the legitimacy of the politics and discourse of authoritative allocation when household property, income, and consumption have become increasingly individualized (cf. Wilk, this volume, on the link between politics and the household).[5] Tension and conflict that result from commodification and personal well-being on the one hand, and social reciprocity and household welfare on the other, can be illustrated in property rights issues surrounding housing and income.

If the folk model of authoritative allocation lies at the heart of household practices, then a conception of property rights is at the center of authoritative allocation. The approach taken here draws heavily upon Demsetz' (1967) definition of property rights as expectations one may reasonably hold regarding the consent of others to allow one to act in a particular way. In other words, property rights are attributes of society, not the individual. The logic of an allocative process rests on some shared notions of the validity of a distribution of rights over things and persons. As the epigram to this chapter indicates, Hobhouse clearly recognized that rational allocation rests on a political process of exclusion and inclusion, (in the present context) a political economy of the household.

The contention here is that the very stuff of household practices consists of competing claims of members not only to the product of household labor but also to a distribution of rights to the product. The most frequent quarrels in householding are about equity and fairness. The reason is obvious: no matter what the household structure, distribution of reward is incommensurate with effort. All household structures appear to require strong normative systems in which there is both a politics of gifts and a discourse of generosity within a framework of social reciprocity. Property rights ensure indirect access to resources of those who have some direct control by those who otherwise would not. Household welfare is an emergent concept based on compliance, one that is fundamentally different from the concept of personal well-being of individual members.

The idea that things and persons are bundles of property rights allows refinement of middle class Fijian household practices. Authoritative allocation is the basis for tension and conflict among household members as they bargain and negotiate the harmful or beneficial effects on each of the others' actions.

In the folk model, the Fijian house is a bundle of property rights, with members claiming benefits on the basis of differential rights or the same right in varying degrees. A complete folk model of property rights would take into account not only different parts of the house but also different temporal points in daily and weekly cycles. To simplify a complex set of claims, there are, from the standpoint of members, exclusive and inclusive rights to the house, i.e. those which exclude nonmembers and include all members. Exclusive rights can be divided further into those of the owner/head and other household members. The owner/head has strong claims over the house, household things, and persons. All other members have rights, albeit not equal, to expend labor on household production (according to the social division of labor by sex and age) and to share in household consumption, including daily meals, the use of household space for sleeping and socializing (according to social status and rank), and the enjoyment of household goods. In the folk model, these rights are permanent. For example, a younger brother may leave the house for some years, or a sister may get married and depart to her husband's home. But each may return and reassert rights based on original membership.

There also are inclusive rights to a Fijian house. The claims are most clearly evident in the village, where clan and community (i.e. nonmembers) build the house in exchange for work-meals (*oca*) and work-gifts (*veilomani*) provided by household members (Rutz 1984). The rights in the production of the house constitute a material basis for the rights of clan and community to enter a house at their own discretion and to receive hospitality. All they need do is present a *sevusevu* (small gift of kava as welcome) to assert their claims over the space of household members. If the door to an American house is "closed" and rights to enter to use its space are controlled by the owner through "invitation," then the door to a Fijian house is always "open" by rights of access granted clan and community.

One might summarize the bundle of property rights in houses by noting that, in the folk model, they are uncommodified rights. Houses are not bought and sold; they have no market price. Houses have value in use but not in exchange; they are productive assets, but rights in them cannot be converted into instruments for accumulation (cf. Rodman 1985). For these reasons, the blurred distinction in the folk model between ownership and other exclusive rights is not likely to be a point of tension and conflict. Household welfare and personal well-being merge without the necessity to refine the distinction.

In the urban houses of the new Fijian middle class it is otherwise. Specifically, as houses have become marketable assets and the major source of lifetime material accumulation for most people, rights have changed. The most significant shift is toward a more precise definition of members' exclusive rights of members. The inclusive claims of kinship and community, albeit not absent, have weakened relative to those in working class settlements and urban villages, and represent changes in kind from the rights described for rural villages (Rutz 1987). Middle class informants all state that Fijians who can afford private property will purchase it in preference to alternative arrangements.

The market not only offers Fijians an opportunity to rationalize authoritative allocation by forming a boundary around the household in the more exclusive interest of its members, it also strengthens the rights of owners against other members, causing social divisiveness and a debate that opposes personal well-being to household welfare. The middle class house owner holds exclusive leasehold of land, title to house, and legal liability for a mortgage. Houses are built by contractors and paid for at market rates. Private ownership in market terms is the single biggest indicator of the class status of Fijians, implying as it does the negation of all the reciprocal and inclusive rights to the house. Economic conditions in the urban area have been favorable to accumulation over the past two decades: a house which cost $3,000F to build in the early 1960s was selling for $40,000F in the early 1980s.

The most significant means of household material accumulation is in the hands of the owner under urban market conditions. And variable combinations of wage and nonwage labor maintain the productive asset without legal rights to a share in accumulation or market appreciation. Such issues of the fairness of the distribution of rights in the folk model when applied to the conditions of the capitalist market are not lost on household members, especially women and younger sons. As one wage-earning daughter put it, "We know that our parents will give more to our brothers than to us. My oldest brother will get the house. There is nothing we can do about it, so we just learn that this is the way it will be."

Evidence from the Registry of Titles suggests she is right.[6] The folk model is practiced when it comes to middle class ownership of houses. Two of fifteen household heads in the sample are in Suva on short-term postings and simply pay market rent for their housing. Of the remaining thirteen houses, all are owned by registered title to private property in the name of the head and/or his immediate male heir. Neither women (wives or daughters) nor younger sons appear in the Registry. Fijian property law, based on English law, in no way restricts ownership, allowing joint ownership by husband and wife, by the whole family, or by other combinations.

By opting for the patriarchal folk model of house ownership, middle class Fijians have brought the practice of authoritative allocation inside capitalism. And by doing so, they have revealed the tension between household welfare and personal well-being concealed in the precapitalist property rights of all members. Over time, the possibility of differentiating household laborers into those members with an accumulative basis and those without is real. This threat to the reproduction of households as a class has implications for wage labor markets but, more importantly, it has immediate implications for the continuity of the household. There is a heightened awareness among household heads and other members of the danger. Household heads clearly recognize that it is in their interest to reaffirm those exclusive rights of all members established in the folk model. The bargaining strength for such claims comes from nonowning wage-earning members.

The pooling practices familiar in the countryside are a misnomer for middle class households. It would be more accurate to refer to the practice of negotiated contributions, not "pooling," despite the authoritative discourse of the head. The most common practice in the sample of middle class households is for household expenses to be met by individual contributions to particular categories of expenditure, and for there to be some rotation of assignments over time. For example, one wage-earner pays the mortgage, another pays for food, another the utility bill, and so on. Periodically, "gifts" of durable consumer goods are made by individuals to the household. A son might purchase a stereophonic system, a daughter might give a carpet, several wage-earners might purchase a refrigerator, and so on. These practices both reflect and overcome the market practice of paying wages to individual workers.

A household head no longer has direct control of this labor and the authority to expropriate its product, i.e. income. Labor is now controlled by capital or the state, and individual wage-earners control their own product. Most have their own bank accounts. Their exact wages often are not known to each other or to the head. Therefore, the head neither knows the rate of personal savings nor does he know the precise level of expenditure on personal well-being. Male wage-earners, especially, spend large sums on drinking and eating with other men, activities which reaffirm their position within the system of social rank while their consumption goes relatively undetected. The distribution of benefits *de facto* is reorganized by the ability of individuals to hide a part of their various incomes in the interest of enhancing personal well-being at the cost of household welfare. Accusations of cheating are common as a result of the shift in costs and benefits that attach to exclusive household property rights. Complaints about fairness also are common. Household heads complain that members do not meet their assigned contributions, and wage earning members complain that they pay to maintain a house in which they have no legal or market share.

For example, in one household, the head had taken advantage of the norms of authoritative discourse to conceal from members his transfer of sole title and ownership of the house to his oldest son. About to retire from a long career in teaching, he used his rights to relinquish house ownership but to continue to live there with his wife. All other members maintained their exclusive rights and made contributions to household welfare. When a daughter discovered the secret, she was surprised but acknowledged its propriety while insisting on its unfairness. She had to reassert her claims to live there with her three children. The oldest brother never challenged these claims.

To take another example, in several cases household heads had made additions to their houses. The necessary mortgages were repaid by the wage-earning members of the household. This, in fact, is a major way in which authoritative heads resolve the question of ownership and members' exclusive rights. The house grows with expanding families,

authoritative allocation is maintained, and members feel secure about
rights to parts of the house not withstanding absence of a formally
registered title. When it works, the problem of daily reproduction and
reproduction over time is solved, and the practice approximates the rural
ideal. This strategy accounts for the prevalence of stem and extended
family households in urban areas (Table 1). An interview with the male
head of a house to which he has exclusive legal proprietorship reveals
the thinking of many other urban middle class household heads:

> I have five sons. My plan is to extend my house to make five units. When
> complete, my five sons and their families will live here. My oldest son is
> fourteen, my youngest just born. Whether I save or put the money into
> my house, its all the same.

When authoritative heads do have the trust and respect of their members,
conflicts remain under control and everyone can benefit. The household
accumulates wage earners over time and produces a surplus that is
calculated to be well above socially necessary consumption. The problem
of labor continuity is solved because, as members leave school and become
new wage earners, they have secure housing.

Perhaps the most difficult problem faced by the urban middle class
Fijian household is continuity. The problem takes two main forms: what
to do with the retired and elderly, and what to do with youth. Authoritative
heads benefit from the full-blown patriarchal household because it solves
a personal problem of well-being in old age. The folk model, once again,
provides the best guidance on the practice of middle class householding.
Fijians are loathe to rely upon the old age homes they see used by
Europeans and Indians. In the folk model, young people are taught that
they will take care of their parents in old age. Eldest sons who inherit
the house also inherit the position of responsible authoritative allocation,
one aspect of which is to provide for their parents. And one way a
household head whose pension is insufficient for retirement can ensure
himself of care and well-being in old age is to ensure other household
members of their shared and exclusive rights to the house, rights which
the eldest son already is obligated to honor. In this way, the folk model
establishes a basis for recruitment, partially determines the size of
households, and is a means for smoothing over potential tensions and
conflicts that arise from the commodification of houses. When it works,
the urban middle class Fijian household satisfies the condition for intergenerational continuity of wage labor for the capitalist market.

Another source of conflict in household practices arises from the
application of norms of sharing to the fruits of commodified labor. The
conflict is most apparent with female wage earners. In one case, women

are sisters who owe obedience to their brothers. In another, they are daughters-in-law who owe obedience to the authoritative head. In the first case, that of female wage earners who are sisters, their income is a source of benefit to their brothers. There is a tendency for brothers to invoke the folk model by making "requests" of their sisters for money. These transfers frequently are in the context of purchasing kava, beer, or tobacco for men of different households to meet their obligations towards each other to be sociable and drink together. Since these gatherings occur nightly and are a regular form of male sociability, the expenditures can be quite large and debts can accumulate. In the second case, that of female wage earners who are daughters-in-law of the head, their income is a source of benefit to a head and his direct heir, perhaps at the expense of her children and husband if the latter does not stand to benefit from the rule of primogeniture.

A married brother of a woman had accumulated money debts because of his sociability, despite his very good salary earned as a teacher. He wasn't making his contributions to the household, so his sister decided to help him by holding a game called "drinking for money," in which it is understood by guests that they purchase a drink for a named other. She bought four cases of beer, expending her entire income for that week. As she explained, "It was *vakarokoroko* (respect) for an older brother." But before the party, he came to "request" the beer for a party he was giving his cousins. "I should have given it to him" she explained, "But he was drunk and I hid it. I refused him and he called me 'selfish.' Then he sent our 'real cousin' to request it. My parents weren't present, or they would have told me to give it to him because that would be 'correct.' I refused again and went to hide. They were drunk. Later that night, my brother's wife and I wanted some beer, so we drank it. The next morning my brother fought with his wife and me and beat us up. Now I will 'request' someone to give me $20 for my contribution to the water bill."

Wage earning daughters-in-law seem the most reluctant to turn over their earnings to authoritative heads, especially if their husband isn't the eldest son. For example, one young woman seemed very reluctant to participate in a family budget study because she would have to reveal her income and list her expenditures for a week. My female Fijian research assistant knew the family and was certain that she was understating her income to the head in order to increase her own savings. The household head and his oldest son happened to have purchased the house recently and held it under joint ownership. In another case, the daughter-in-law was the single largest wage earner in the household. She felt it was unfair to have to spend her own wages to contribute to the welfare of a household in which she was assigned peripheral status in the folk model.

These examples could be multiplied. Simply put, when personal well-being becomes differentiated from household welfare as labor is commodified, authoritative allocation erodes into various forms of negotiated contributions, hedged by opportunities for cheating. The mutual trust that rational allocation depends upon becomes itself a field for contending claims between a head and household members, and among members themselves.

Authoritative allocation continues to inform the practice of house-holding in the new Fijian middle class. The folk model has enormous sentimental and emotional value that seems to strengthen its appeal under the very conditions of the urban market economy that would appear to undermine its continued existence. Its retention is best explained by an intersection of ideological and practical considerations that cannot easily be reduced to the labor process—at least not without taking into account political and discursive practices of household members as they struggle to reconcile household welfare with personal well-being. The voices of two informants on the dilemma of inclusive and exclusive rights that pull in different directions speak to this point. A woman who held a high civil service position described her obligations:

> A *momo* (mother's brother) came to stay with us two weeks ago from Lau. He just arrived, my husband and I didn't know he was coming. He mentioned once that he might return to Lau for Christmas, but then he changed his mind. Since he is my *momo*, it would be inappropriate for him to speak of a date for his departure. We knew he would need a ticket back, so I knew that I should pay for it without anything being said. I also knew that I would buy gifts and give him money to take back to the village. My husband and I discussed this, and we simply agreed that we would do without Christmas ourselves and give the gifts to my relatives. Relatives visit us all the time, but they don't plan. We Fijians know our duties. When they come, everything is on credit and nothing will be repaid. My parents arrived in Suva this week. They were going for a holiday to visit relatives in Vanuabalavu. The cost of the boat passage would come from me and my husband, since we were told about the holiday and we understood what that meant.

Another civil servant, high up in the Native Lands Trust Board, articulated his personal dilemma along similar lines:

> Fijian households have a double burden. They have to take care of their own members and also to meet many social obligations. Fijian responsibilities create problems of time and money that get in the way of urban life. I am from Gau. Many people in the village have no money to pay the head tax. So we in Suva pay more because we have more. We think we should

pay more. Sometimes I go to three funerals a week. If we hear about them, it is our duty to go. There is no way for me to escape my obligations. There is always the idea in each of us to return to the land. We stay in it for the land. I intend to send several of my children back to the village. That is why I took them back for a *mata ni gone* (presentation of face of the child) to introduce them to their relatives so they would not be strangers and would be welcome. If I didn't do this, there would be trouble. Fiji is not a rich country. The Fiji National Provident Fund is only twelve years old. I've been in it from the beginning, but I won't have sufficient funds to retire. Maybe I will return to the village. You will see very few Fijian households in which savings are sufficient to send a child to the university, yet it is the responsibility of the household. We rely on scholarships or live with the idea that a person cannot go on. If you are a Fijian, either you have nothing and receive gifts or you have much and give everything. There is no in-between in Fijian life.

Conclusion

The world-economy approach to explaining household structure and processes is a conceptual framework erected on the site of the ruins of modernization theory. Both are in the architectural style of the grand tradition, whose foundation rests on impersonal forces that move societies through stages along determinate paths of development. Each is a variant of what, Gellner refers to as "world-growth stories." (1964: 9ff) Both, at bottom, focus on the malleability of the household to the growth and spread of capitalism. Both trivialize other histories. They differ in their moral appeal, which goes far in explaining why a current generation of scholars is willing to overlook the methodological shortcomings of the world-economy approach. How much of their difference is clothed in language only time will tell.

Whether or not commodification of social life in Fiji will result in a decline of kinship and co-residentiality as determinate of the boundaries of households (Wallerstein 1984: 21) seems impossible to say at this point in Fijian history. To say that neither is necessary to household relationships, but that kinship may play an ideological role in their constitution (Smith, Wallerstein, and Evers 1984: 8), is to sacrifice the practice of Fijian householding to several tautologies of economic reductionism. We then would have to conclude that the theory was a success but the case failed. The evidence in the Fijian case points to a more modest conclusion. In middle class households, where commodification has proceeded farthest, kinship and chieftainship have crawled, as it were, inside class formation and curled up for what appears to be an extended stay. To date, authoritative allocation dominates alternative householding arrangements despite changes in objective conditions for its existence, including commodification of property rights and household labor.

Nevertheless, tension and conflict among household members sow the seeds for possible transformation. But to predict that the transformation implies the demise of authoritative allocation would be premature. It survives and even prospers under current political and economic conditions in Fiji. Without denying, indeed by asserting, the importance of labor markets for household relationships, it is worthwhile to ponder the effect of authoritative allocation (which, after all, is not the only possible set of relationships for reproducing labor power for Fijian capitalism) on labor force formation in Fiji. While middle class Fijians have embraced formal education as their entrance ticket to capitalism, and while they have accommodated themselves to the work-discipline of an ameliorated variety of industrial capitalism, they continue to hold both in some contempt and approach them with deep suspicion. There is a record of poor school performance of Fijians in competition with Indians. In interviews for work histories, Fijians express only weak interest in definitions of work that incorporate capitalist notions of "career advancement." Expertise and specialization are weaker among Fijians despite numerous opportunities to embrace the western concepts of modern work. In the civil service, which Fijians control, efficient, competent, and hard-working bureaucrats have always been in short supply. In private enterprise there is genuine confusion about capitalist culture when there is not outright contempt shown toward it. It is hard to reconcile these facts with assertions that Fijian household structure and processes can be explained by the interests of capitalism. In Fiji, at least, there is much about capitalism that can be explained by the practice of authoritative allocation.

Acknowledgments

Field research was supported by NSF grant no. BNS-8120354. An early draft of this chapter was presented at the 1987 American Anthropological Association meetings in a session organized by Richard Wilk entitled "Householding—Process, Decision-making, Allocation and Conflict Inside the Household." In addition to Wilk and discussants Peggy Barlett and Donald Donham, the following have provided comments incorporated in the final draft: Hy Van Luong, M. Estellie Smith, David Gray, Jeremy Beckett, and Victoria Bernal.

Notes

1. On the invention of tradition in Fiji, see Belshaw (1965) and France (1969). On the preservation of Fijian culture as an aspect of the politics of a

bipolar ethnic state, see the articles in Lal (1986). In 1986 Fijians were 46 percent and Indians 49 percent of a total population of about 700,000.

2. The small sample (n=15) was drawn from a larger sample (n=36) of middle class households in Lami subdivision who, along with samples (n=38, n=20, respectively) of households from Naivi working class settlement and Suvavou urban village (total N=94), participated in a socioeconomic survey conducted in 1981–82 (Suva Fijian Study Area Survey). For further information on the survey, see Gounis and Rutz (1986). Data for this paper are drawn from survey questions on the SFSAS, family budgets, interviews with household heads and some members, tax records, a registry of titles, and the author's daily journal (based on participant observation). These data were used as the basis for constructing a household profile for each household in the small sample.

3. The ambivalence of Fijians toward market enterprise is not independent of Indian domination of commerce and British colonial administrators' disdainful attitude toward Indian and ex-patriate businessmen. Fijians were encouraged, by word and law, to remain on the periphery of capitalist development in Fiji and to enter the market only sporadically, either to pay head tax or to satisfy "subsistence" needs.

4. Compare with Gellner's (1964: 162–163) perceptive comment that "The connection between nationalism and the situation in which fully human men can only be made by educational systems, not by families and villages, underlines an amusing fact—the inverse relationship between ideology and the reality of nationalism."

5. A military coup d'etat in May of 1987 had the objective of restoring Fiji to the chiefs, the land, and the Lord (Dean 1988: 14–15). Anti-capitalist and anti-liberal sentiments were apparent in events following the coup.

6. Data on title, liens and mortgages was researched by Konstantinos Gounis.

References Cited

Belshaw, Cyril. 1965. "The Effects of Limited Anthropological Theory on Problems of Fijian Administration," in Roland W. Force (ed.), *Induced Political Change in the Pacific.* Honolulu: Bishop Museum Press.

Becker, Gary S. 1974. "A Theory of Social Interactions." *Journal of Political Economy* 82: 1063–1091.

Dean, Eddie with Stan Ritova. 1988. *Rabuka, No Other Way.* Suva, Fiji: Oceania Printers Ltd.

Demsetz, Harold. 1967. "Toward a Theory of Property Rights." *American Economic Review Papers and Proceeding of the 79th Annual Meeting of the American Economic Association.* Vol. 557: 347–59. May 1967.

Fiji Central Planning Office. 1975. *Fiji's Seventh Development Plan 1976–80.* Suva: Government Printer.

Fisk, E.K. 1970. *The Political Economy of Independent Fiji.* Canberra: Australian National University Press.

France, Peter. 1969. *The Charter of the Land.* Melbourne: Oxford University Press.

Friedman, Kathie. 1984. "Households as Income-pooling Units," in Joan Smith, Immanuel Wallerstein, and Hans-Dieter Evers (eds.), *Households and the World-Economy*. Beverly Hills: Sage Publications.

Gellner, Ernest. 1964. *Thought and Change*. Chicago: The University of Chicago Press.

Gounis, Konstantinos and Henry J. Rutz. 1986. "Urban Fijians and the Problem of Unemployment," in Christopher Griffin and Michael Davis (eds.), *Fijians in Town*. Suva: Institute of Pacific Studies and University of the South Pacific.

Hareven, Tamara. 1982. *Family Time and Industrial Time. The Relationship Between the Family and Work in a New England Industrial Community*. Cambridge and New York: Cambridge University Press.

Lal, Brij. Editor. 1986. *Politics in Fiji*. Honolulu: University of Hawaii Press.

Meillassoux, Claude. 1981. *Maidens, Meal and Money: Capitalism and the Domestic Community*. Cambridge: Cambridge University Press.

Rodman, Margaret. 1985. "Moving Houses: Residential Mobility and the Mobility of Residences in Longana, Vanuatu." *American Anthropologist* 87(1): 56–72.

Rutz, Henry J. 1984. "Material Affluence and Social Time in Village Fiji," in Richard F. Salisbury and Elisabeth Tooker (eds.), *Affluence and Cultural Survival*. Washington, D.C.: American Ethnological Society

———. 1987. "Capitalizing on Culture: Moral Ironies in Urban Fiji." *Comparative Studies in Society and History* 29(3): 533–557.

———. 1988. "Culture, Class and Consumer Choice," in Henry J. Rutz and Benjamin S. Orlove (eds.), *The Social Economy of Consumption* Lanham, Maryland: University Press of America.

Sahlins, Marshall. 1976. *Culture and Practical Reason*. Chicago: The University of Chicago Press.

———. 1983. "Other Times, Other Customs." *American Anthropologist* 85(3): 517–544.

Smith, Joan, Immanuel Wallerstein and Hans-Dieter Evers. 1984. "Introduction," in Joan Smith, Immanuel Wallerstein, and Hans-Dieter Evers (eds.), *Households and the World-Economy*. Beverly Hills: Sage Publications.

Wallerstein, Immanuel. 1984. "Household Structures and Labor-Force Formation in the Capitalist World-Economy," in Joan Smith, Immanuel Wallerstein, and Hans-Dieter Evers (eds.), *Households and the World-Economy*. Beverly Hills: Sage Publications.

8

Authority and Conflict in Slavonian Households: The Effect of Social Environment on Intra-Household Processes[1]

M.K.G. Olsen

Introduction

This is an essay about the effects of environmental conditions on household boundaries and activities. It is about the ways in which social and economic changes have produced selective changes in households, particularly in relations of authority and in patterns of conflict and sharing. It is also about the ways in which households have not been affected by changes in the social environment, particularly the division of labor in domestic work.

Domestic work is an activity, or a set of activities which, in many societies, is carried out by household groups. This is an essay about the sharing of domestic work by women who are related as mother and daughter, or mother-in-law and daughter-in-law, and who may or may not also share a residence. There are three main points to be made.

First, this chapter shares with others in this volume a concern with activities carried out by households. In the case to be described, some of the activities which households perform are shared across what would have traditionally been regarded as household boundaries (older definitions of households assume that common residence is a condition of household membership). This essay does not seek to define households, but rather to illustrate the dynamic quality of households, and the permeability of their boundaries (Guyer 1981).

Second, it is often assumed that changes in a society's economic system produce changes in other aspects of life. When a household economy gives way to a state economy, one would expect activities and relationships within households to change. The changes that are produced, however, are not always what are expected or planned. Ideas people have sometimes affect the ways in which they perceive and react to changes; sometimes change is selective.

Third, communities can enforce social pressure on household members and groups to conform to certain normative patterns of behavior. In the situation described below, the community, particularly the community of women, plays an important role in reinforcing a traditional division of labor within households, in spite of changes in the society at large which might lead us to expect a shift away from such a division of labor.

Households as Activity Groups

Families and households were once spoken of in the ethnographic literature as loose categories. It was taken for granted that, as members of such groups, we all knew what they were. British social anthropologists, interested in social rules and institutions and how they worked (as opposed to how they often fail to work) focused their inquires on the ways in which domestic group organization and behavior were the products of those rules (Fortes 1962; Goody 1962). This mode of analysis is no longer favored because it is based on a high level of abstraction or generalization, and does not tell us about real households (Bailey 1960, 1971a; Spiro 1977; Wilk 1988; Wilk and Netting 1984; Yanagisako 1979).

More recently households are viewed as activity groups which are able to adapt to changes in the environment and economy (Arnould and Netting 1982; Wilk and Netting 1984). Recognition has been made of the interplay between customs or ideas, and practical concerns (Yanagisako 1979). But most researchers still tend to focus either on the ways in which environment and economy affect households, or the ways in which customs (rules of residence, for example) shape household form and function. Few anthropologists have examined what actually goes on in households, and the mechanisms by which they adapt to changing social environments.

In order to better understand the variables that shape households, we need to better understand what households do, and how they respond to circumstances outside their own control. If households are activity groups, what kinds of activities concern them, and how are these carried out? How do people define their relationships with and obligations to each other, as members of household groups? Are there any patterns or trends in the behaviors we observe?

While people respond to economic and other social changes by adapting household relations and activities to fit new circumstances, the ways in which they perceive those changes depends not only on objective assessment of the situation, but also, to some extent, on past experiences, and on ideas about the way things should be done. Cognitive and affective variables can influence the ways in which people perceive alternatives available to them, and what behavioral changes they regard as acceptable. They can explain why people respond in one way rather than another, and of course, at an individual level, why variations in behavior are found within social groups. Household activities cannot be understood without taking into account cultural and psychological as well as social and ecological variables (Gilliland 1986).

The Research Area[2]

The research for this paper was carried out in 1983 in Milograd, a town in the Croatian Republic of Yugoslavia, about halfway between Zagreb and Beograd, on the border of Croatia and Bosnia.[3] Milograd has a population of 50,000, and an economy based on one large factory which employs nearly 14,000 workers. The town lies within a region known as Slavonia, in a large fertile agricultural basin, the Pannonian Plain. Slavonia was in the past an agricultural region, characterized by small peasant farms (twenty-five hectares average size).[4]

Prior to 1945, 70 percent of all Slavonians lived in rural communities, while only 30 percent lived in towns and cities. This ratio flip-flopped after World War II, with the establishment of a socialist government in Yugoslavia, and planned industrial and urban growth. Sociologists and anthropologists in Yugoslavia and in the West have been interested in the effects on families and households of these planned changes (Burić 1976; Halpern 1963, 1965; Simić 1982). Of particular interest to feminist scholars has been the impact of planned changes on women's roles and of working women on family and household life (Denich 1977; First-Dilić 1973; Mihovilović 1975).

Studies of Yugoslav households are dominated by concern with household size and structure, rather than process and relationships within households. For example, a number of anthropologists have assumed that smaller residential groups mean smaller households. They treat households as uniform structures, and do not investigate actual household relations or activities. (Biconić 1965; Tomasić 1948). While residential groups today are smaller, it is not clear that households are. In order to determine this, we must look at activities, not just rules and patterns of residence.

Defining the activities of Slavonian households, and to some extent household boundaries is somewhat easier for the pre-industrial period. Prior to industrialization households were the primary social units in society; economic activities, care for the young and the old, education such as it was, and recreation were carried out within household groups. Contemporary households are more difficult to define, if only because many aspects of life once governed by the household are now taken care of by highly specialized institutions outside the home, such as kindergartens, schools, hospitals and old age homes. The most significant change is that people no longer work directly for the household, under the authority of senior household members. People are no longer dependent for a living on property held in common by the household, or for care in old age, for medical insurance, and so on. Even housing, in many cases, is provided for families by their places of employment. Statuses and roles in the work place are not directly relevant to those at home.

In this essay I discuss the consequences of social engineering for household organization, activities and relations, particularly the distribution of authority within families and households, and the division of labor.[5] The changes that have been put into place since World War II have affected members of households asymmetrically; that is, the changes in the economy have had greater positive consequences for relationships among men within households than for women. There have been changes in patterns of residence, and in patterns of household formation and activities. The reasons for this are complex.

Briefly, I explain relations of authority and the distribution of domestic work in terms of the following variables: (1) social changes which have lessened, but not eliminated economic dependence of adult children on parents, and of aged parents on adult children; (2) socialization of children by grandparents; (3) persistent attachment to ideas regarding the desirability of family self-sufficiency, and a separation of men's and women's activities; (4) the power of social pressure in small, close-knit communities. This analysis looks at the ways in which the economy, culture and social behavior interact in the formation of patterns in household behavior. It is not only about the ways in which households and cultures change; it is also about the ways in which they sometimes, unpredictably, do not change, or do so in limited ways.

The Argument in Brief

Changing circumstances in Yugoslavia, and particularly in Slavonia, have affected the activities, roles and relationships within households there, and have made household boundaries very fuzzy (if they were not already so in the past, a point difficult to ascertain from historical and ethnographic records).

Policies prescribing equal opportunities for women in jobs, education and social services have, to some degree, affected the division of labor in the work place. Perhaps it was assumed that these policies would also affect gender roles and relations within households. Perhaps those making the policies, being members of their own culture, did not perceive gender roles within households as something which needed to be changed. Roles and relations within households do seem to have changed, but the result is not sexual equality, or an equal division of domestic labor. Planned social changes have largely failed to penetrate domestic walls.

Changes have been primarily in the following dyads: father/son, mother-in-law/daughter-in-law and mother/daughter. The husband/wife relationship has been affected in some cases, but not in others. For example, women with higher education and incomes that approximate their husbands' generally report greater sharing of domestic jobs and of decision-making, and greater satisfaction with their marriages (First-Dilić 1973; Mihovilović 1975). I focus here on changes in the other dyads, which are unexpected.

First, I will describe historical events, and especially economic changes, which seem to have affected not only household composition but relations of authority within households. Second, I will discuss a recent change in patterns of sharing domestic work.

Prior to World War II, it was the custom for married couples to reside with the husband's parents, at least at the start of their marriages. Mothers-in-law and daughters-in-law shared most domestic work—cooking, cleaning, sewing and child care. Today about an equal number of young couples in the neighborhood where I worked seem to live with the husband's parents, with the wife's parents and neolocally.[6] Roughly two-thirds of young married women cooperate with their mothers, not their mothers-in-law, in carrying out domestic work. This has had two consequences. First, it gives young women more authority regarding domestic matters. Second, it means that men are still not required in many cases to help with housework and child care. This new alliance of mothers and daughters makes women's lives easier in some ways (eliminates conflicts which commonly arose between mothers-in-law and daughters-in-law, conflicts which were overtly about cooking and child care, but probably also about authority and autonomy), but perpetuates the segregation of men's and women's work and the double burden women bear.

Finally, the neighborhood, or local community, plays an important part in perpetuating the segregation of men's and women's roles, and reinforces the notion that domestic work is properly women's work.

Households in Historical Perspective

Large, extended family households known as *zadrugas* were found throughout the Southern Slav territories and what is now Bulgaria and

Albania, up through the modern era (Mosely 1940, 1976). According to Hammel, who surveyed census material from medieval Serbian monasteries, about 50 percent of Serbian households in the fifteenth century were zadrugas, or extended households. He surmises from available data that the developmental cycle of the fifteenth century zadruga was similar to that of the sixteenth, nineteenth and early twentieth centuries; that is, brothers do not stay together long after their own children are born (Hammel 1980).

In Slavonia the situation was different. From 1700 till 1850 Slavonia was under Austro-Hungarian rule, and was included within a territory known as the Croatian Military Frontier. Land to the south, modern-day Bosnia, was held by the Ottoman Turks. Slavonian men were conscripted into the Austro-Hungarian army, and peasant households in the region were regarded by the Austro-Hungarian government as military units (Guldescu 1970; Rubić 1953; Rihtman-Augustin 1982). Erlich (1966) reports that households were forbidden by law to divide, except by appeal to a military court. The government required households to stay intact because in this way enough men were available both to serve in the army and to provide labor needed to maintain self-sufficient peasant farms. Larger households were more efficient, and could produce a greater variety of food and other subsistence goods for their own use. Smaller households would feel the loss of a few men more than would larger households.

According to Erlich (1966), Lovretić (1896) and Lukić (1919), households were internally stratified by gender and by age. This follows the pattern noted by Bailey (1971), Michaelson and Goldschmidt (1971), Shanin (1971), Wolf (1966) and others who have studied European peasant households. In the zadruga, a male head of household (*domaćin*) had authority over all other men, and organized work in the fields and other chores designated as men's work. A female head of household (*domaćica*) was in charge of organizing the women for domestic labor. For example, each week one woman was in charge of the kitchen, while another was put in charge of mending clothes, and still others were sent to the fields to hoe. Old women would mind the babies and children too small to lend a hand in work (Erlich 1966; Byrnes 1976).

Although the *domaćin* was officially in charge, decisions affecting the welfare of the group were made democratically. All adult (married) men had a vote; in some matters the *idomaćica* was also allowed to vote (Erlich 1966).[7]

This way of life came to an end in the late 1800's, when the Austro-Hungarian war with the Turks also ended. Slavonian peasants were no longer required to maintain large households, and according to Lukić and Lovretić they began to break into smaller extended family groups.

Still, Lukić and Lovretić both refer to extended family households as zadrugas; they write that zadrugas began to disintegrate internally, and to diminish in size and frequency of distribution as a result of other changes that came about between about 1850 and 1910 (Lovretić 1889; Lukić 1919).

Households in Transition: Before World War I

Significant changes took place at the end of the nineteenth century which broadened the social environment in which Slavonian peasant households existed. First, the Austro-Hungarian government wanted to establish a modern government. Heavy taxes were imposed on Slavonian peasants. No longer could they pay in kind as they had done in the past; they were now required to pay in cash. Second, in order to get the cash they were forced to sell their produce. Prior to this time, most of these peasants had very little to do with markets; they had been primarily subsistence farmers. Other changes came about at this time. Railroads and steamships were invented, and a railway from Zagreb to Beograd passed through Milograd, increasing market activities. Several large industrial plants were built in and around Milograd, and the town was chosen as the site for a factory which manufactured railway cars and other heavy equipment (Rubić 1953). These changes, it is argued, are responsible, at least in part, for what is perceived as increased conflict within and fragmentation of households (Erlich 1966; Gilliland 1986; Lukić 1919, 1924; Rubić 1953).

The advent of industry and especially new forms of transportation was linked with a pan-European agrarian crisis. Cheap grain produced primarily in America (where the railroad also facilitated westward expansion and the start of industrial agriculture in that country) was transported to Europe, competing with European peasants who were forced to sell their own grain at lower prices. At the same time prices for manufactured goods, which peasants began to see as necessities were steadily increasing. Taxes also were rising. Peasants needed cash for taxes and for manufactured goods, and began to sell not only produce, but land.

Large, self-sufficient groups who lived and worked together, and who shared most property in common, were once the Slavonian peasant's insurance against poverty (Erlich 1966). But this new and radically different economic situation spelled the end of such groups, as many found themselves impoverished and embroiled in conflicts about who had the right to sell produce and land, and how cash and manufactured goods would be distributed within household groups. In Slavonia the agrarian crisis was exacerbated by the dramatic increase in population between 1880 and 1890, due to the control of epidemic disease, the end of the war with the Turks, and the growth of cities (Bičanić 1937; Erlich 1966: 48–50; Rubić 1953).

The causal relationship between authority relations within households and economic and social changes outside of households is not entirely clear. Did the breakdown of authority within zadrugas render households vulnerable to outside pressures, or did the outside pressures affect household structure and relations? Lovretić, Lukić and Rubić claim that although the very large zadrugas of the Military March quickly gave way to smaller zadrugas when they were once again allowed to partition, qualitative changes within households, that is increased conflict and changes in authority relations, arose in response to new pressures from the outside. An increase in monetary transactions—selling land, paying taxes, buying manufactured goods—seems to have been the single most disruptive influence in the domestic life of Slavonian peasants. It is fair to say, however, that whatever provided the impetus for changes in households—whether it was the breakdown in authority which came first or second—more than a single variable was involved.

Increased conflict and fragmentation within households seem to correspond to changes in the social environment, but those changes within households were not as far-reaching as the changes in the larger social context. For example, ideas such as self-determination and romantic love, which were growing in popularity throughout Europe at the time, began to affect choices people made, and especially the desire of many young people to choose a husband or wife whom they loved, and to strike out on their own, apart from their families (Erlich 1966; Lukić 1924). But people could not yet be entirely independent of their families. Old age pensions did not yet exist; aged parents depended on their adult children for support and care (Adamić 1934). Although men could go to work in factories, it was not yet common or accepted for women to work outside the home. Women were still dependent on fathers and husbands. Men also still generally depended on their fathers for an economic start in life; they would have liked the situation to be different, and some young men behaved as if it were. Erlich describes a family which had nine acres and nine sons. The eldest son greedily took his acre, and broke with his father and brothers only to discover he could not make a living on so small a piece of land (Erlich 1966).

Changes certainly occured. Households began to partition every generation. Some peasants gave up farming altogether, and moved to towns and cities to work for wages. Conflicts were increasingly common within households, and in general, social life was disrupted in comparison with life in the zadruga (Lukić 1919, 1924).

Perhaps, however, Lukić was remembering the large zadrugas as the golden past. Perhaps the conflicts he recorded then were not so different from conflicts in the days of the zadruga. With industry, people had some new opportunities, and with increased taxes and low prices for farm produce, the peasant's life was made difficult in a new way. For 70 percent of the population, however, daily life went on fairly much as it had before industrialization began. The social environment had changed in grand ways, but the opportunities available to peasants were still very limited, and so their lives were affected, but also in a limited sort of way.

Contemporary Households

After World War II, the population of Slavonia shifted from a predominantly rural to predominantly urban distribution. Cities impose different limitations on domestic groups than villages and family farms. Few dwellings in urban centers can accommodate a large residential group, nor can city households even approximate the degree of self-sufficiency found among village families. Wage labor changes relationships within families, at least to some degree. In Yugoslavia today, sons can make a living even if they do not inherit property from their fathers. Socialism in Yugoslavia has meant additional changes in family and household life. Single women with children receive help from the state, and although their lives are not easy, they can support themselves and their dependent children. (Gilliland 1986). This was not true for peasant women living in villages prior to World War II, or even for most urban women before socialism. Unmarried women can earn a living and remain single if they so choose. This also was not possible in the past. Old people receive pensions, and again, although they cannot easily support themselves, they are no longer the economic burden on their children that they once were. Day care facilities, schools and hospitals further reduce the responsibilities that family members, and co-residents must bear.

From the end of the nineteenth century through World War II, Slavonian men and women struggled with their conflicting desires for autonomy and for familial attachment and support. They struggled likewise with their desires for economic independence, and the reality that most households faced—larger households could produce more and live better. This struggle has not disappeared altogether in contemporary Yugoslavia, although it has been modified.

Theoretically socialism guarantees jobs for all, but in practice unemployment is a problem and young people often wait for a year or more for a job after completing school or university. They usually live at home and depend on their parents for financial support during this waiting period. Housing is also a problem. Apartments are provided by factories and work organizations, but the waiting lists are long, up to eight years in some cases, and there are not enough apartments to go around. Private apartments are expensive and many consider them a waste of money. Families encourage adult children to live at home instead of renting private apartments. In this way money can be saved and put towards construction of a new apartment or house, a better investment of resources. A government apartment usually costs about one-tenth of a family's monthly income, while a private apartment may cost as much as half a family's monthly earnings, and usually is less private and less comfortable.[8]

Finally child care and housekeeping are problems. In spite of the fact that most women now work outside the house, women still bear the burden of housework and child care alone, creating a double work day for women (Denich 1977). Young couples with small children cannot always afford day care, even though it is subsidized by the state. Those couples who have a grandmother in residence, or nearby, benefit financially. The wife's life is made easier by a mother or mother-in-law's help with shopping, cooking and other household chores. Most people prefer to have a grandmother care for their children; they believe it is better for the child (Gilliland 1986).

Women, Family, and Community[9]

Power refers to the ability to effect the outcome of a situation. It can be achieved in any number of ways. Authority is legitimate power; that is the individual making a decision is acknowledged as having a right to do so. It has been argued by many anthropologists that women often gain power indirectly, through manipulation of men, and through gossip in the women's community (Bailey 1971b; Saunders 1981). In traditional Slavonian zadrugas, however, it seems women also had some authority in domestic matters. The *domaćica* legitimately gave orders to other women, organized household affairs, and voted with the men on household matters. There was still a difference, however, in the kinds of authority that men and women had.

Authority is sometimes acquired automatically along with a social position or status. Alternatively, it is sometimes the case that an individual who occupies a certain position has the right to earn authority, but must still prove his or her worth.

Slavonian men at marriage automatically gained authority over their wives. They had to earn authority over other men, with age and hard work. When a woman married, however, she did not gain authority as a consequence. Women could earn authority, over time, but within a more limited sphere than men. Mothers had authority over their children, but even that was not absolute. A husband or mother-in-law or brother-in-law could override her decisions regarding her children. Older women eventually had daughters-in-law, over whom they did gain automatic authority. A woman's authority was usually confined to the kitchen—to decisions regarding domestic work and child care. Men had control over work outside the house, and the disposition of communal property. Women did not have authority over men, unless they were too young, or too old, or too sick to be involved in productive activities. They did not have control of resources, unless they were widowed, and without grown sons.

In pre-industrial households, a young married man had authority over his own wife, although he was still subject himself to the authority of his father and older men in the group. Older men retained control over younger men in a household because they also controlled the means of production and the household purse. In the zadruga, young adult men could voice an opinion, and vote, but the *domaćin* reportedly had the final say.

According to Erlich, quarrels between fathers and adult sons became increasingly common from the end of the nineteenth century till World War II. Sons wanted to move out on their own, take their inheritance, and not continue to work under a father or elder brother's domination into their adult years. Because there were limited resources, and because both fathers and sons wanted to control them, these were turbulent times (Erlich 1966; Lukić 1924).

These quarrels apparently began to diminish after World War II, as economic policies and growth began to take effect. According to Erlich, conflict gave way once again to easier relations, at least in economic matters, because fathers and sons did not have to compete for limited resources. Today it is common for a father and his married son to live together. Both have jobs (or pensions), and their own incomes. While conflict may still erupt between fathers and sons, whether they are living together or not, the main cause of friction seems to have been eliminated. Sons no longer have to challenge their fathers to gain access to resources, nor do fathers have reason to fear being displaced by their adult sons.

We might expect a similar change for women who work and bring money into the household, in their relationships with their husbands, and with their mothers-in-law, but the outcome of economic and social changes so far is qualitatively different for women and men. After World War II, women entered the work force in large numbers, and found more opportunities to obtain an education or training for skilled jobs. They were encouraged by the state to work. Families did not oppose wage labor for women; women had always worked on the farm, so the idea of women working was not new. The economy demanded that families have more than one income, partly because salaries were, and still are, generally low. In spite of changing roles for women outside the home, certain traditional attitudes persisted, particularly those regarding gender roles and relations within the domestic circle. This is generally due to patterns of socialization, which do not reflect ideas about the equality of men and women. Members of the community reinforce expectations that women perform domestic work, without the help of their husbands.

There is still an expectation that, other things being equal, the husband's rather than the wife's natal household is the place where married life should begin. In cases where this occurs, the mother-in-law and daughter-in-law find themselves in a situation which was always considered difficult. Women today are used to greater autonomy before marriage. Many attend college or hold jobs before they are married. They are used to greater freedom of movement and managing their money. Although young people are taught to respect elders, they are less willing to submit to their wishes and demands than were young men and women in the days of the zadruga.

At the same time, young women generally accept the assignment of domestic chores to women. They challenge their mother-in-law's authority, but not that of their husbands. In most cases men do not tell their wives to do the cooking or housework or care for the children; men and women both accept that this is the way things should be.

Although the political and social position of women has officially changed, and although they contribute to the family purse (many families could not manage without the wife's income), they do not in practice have increased authority.[10] Few women are able to participate in public life beyond working in an office or factory (Denich 1974; 1977).

Many of my young and middle-aged female informants said they are proud of their jobs and the money they earn. Older women, also, even those who have never worked for wages, often support the idea of women working. The grandmother in the family with whom I lived is not alone in her opinion that men are not reliable, and therefore women must be able to support themselves should their husbands leave them.

Unlike men, women who have jobs must also run a house. They have no time for outside activities. Furthermore, this means that many women still choose to have jobs, but not careers. Fewer women than men go to college. Women are more likely than men to decline a promotion at work which would mean increased responsibility that they cannot manage if they are also juggling domestic responsibilities and child care.

At marriage, women enter a community of adult women, and are still judged, to some extent, by traditional standards. A woman may be a doctor or a lawyer but unless she is married, has children and is judged a good housekeeper and a thrifty wife, she will not be respected by other women in the community. This often is a matter of self-respect as well. Women who are not married feel they have failed. For many marriage is more important than achieving a position of importance at work (Denich 1977; Gilliland 1986).

Young women want to establish themselves as a *domaćica* (and this word is still used for a woman who runs a house). Older women, however, even those who have worked for wages and have themselves rebelled against a domineering mother-in-law, feel they have put in their time and deserve the respect and often, subservience of a resident daughter-in-law, and are therefore reluctant to relinquish the domestic authority they have worked so hard to gain. In the best situations, of course, mothers-in-law and daughters-in-law work together at home, but as often as not, conflict between the two erupts.

Young women challenge their mothers-in-law but not the entire system. Those who succeed in establishing a separate residence with their husbands must still earn their reputations within the community as worthy women.[11] This means they must carry out domestic work, and do it well, generally without the help of a spouse.

This system is enforced implicitly by men and explicitly by women. Women commonly greet each other "Neighbor, are you virtuous?" or to translate less literally, "Neighbor, are you working hard?"[12] Housewives who meet for morning coffee inevitably recite to one another a list of their activities that day—preparing breakfast, going to the market and the butcher shop, preparing dinner, doing laundry, cleaning house. The list varies little from one woman to the next. By ten o'clock a hard-working woman has accomplished all these things, and feels she can take time out for a visit with her friends, if only to reaffirm her virtue and reputation in her own eyes and in theirs.

It is the women in a neighborhood who keep track of the activities of other women, and who can destroy a reputation with their sharp tongues. All my female neighbors knew that Alma, a housewife who lived with her family in a rented room, never got to the market before nine o'clock in the morning, often too late to buy staples like milk, bread and meat. Alma's neighbors were willing to help her, but they did not respect her or include her in their social gatherings. My landlady recalled that as a bride she won the admiration of her neighbors because she got up at four o'clock each morning to do the family laundry and hang it on the line before she left for work at six o'clock.

Women's housekeeping jobs are labor intensive. Marketing, laundry and many other jobs have to be done daily. Many jobs, like laundry, are still done by hand.[13] Women also are responsible for maintaining stores of food to feed their families and entertain unexpected guests. Because shortages are common, most women like to store enough basic foods to last an entire season (three months). Women worked hard to keep chickens, pigs, gardens, and cupboards full of hams, sausages, bottled fruits, pickles and jams. Women in town spent much of their free time cultivating and maintaining relationships with friends and relatives in villages, from whom they could buy flour, eggs, corn and other staple foods (Gilliland 1985).[14]

The basic separation of men and women and their respective roles remains largely unchallenged. A young wife who lives alone with her husband and children may find she has escaped the domination of her mother-in-law only to find herself saddled with more work than she can manage alone. Still, men are not expected to help in the house or with children. Men who cook or wash dishes are not real men, and it reflects negatively on a woman's reputation if she asks or allows her husband to do these things.[15] These attitudes are beginning to change among young professional men and women, but even so, the reality of men and women sharing housekeeping responsibilities is still far away (First-Dilić 1973; Mihovilović 1975).[16]

Women who find themselves in the situation of trying to run a house and hold a job without a resident mother-in-law often turn to their own mothers for help. Although people told me it was the husband's mother who took care of children, more than half the grandmothers in my neighborhood who cared for children were maternal, not paternal grandmothers. In several cases, the grandmothers also cooked dinner for her daughter and son-in-law. Interestingly, the mothers of sons sometimes objected to this.[17]

The alliance of mothers and daughters was described as cooperative in comparison with the competitive and often hostile relationship between mothers-in-law and daughters-in-law. Mothers try to make their married daughters' lives easier, people say. But this new alliance, in the end, serves to reinforce the separation of men and women in the larger social context. It means that it is women who are responsible for all domestic work, even when they work for wages. Because of these onerous responsibilities, women are discouraged from taking positions of authority at work, and from pursuing political and other outside interests. Many women work outside the house, but do not have authority in the public domain to the extent that men do. Finally, children continue to be socialized to segregated roles at home.

In Slavonia, men still represent their families in the public domain and have authority there; women's activities take place primarily in the domestic or private domain. Within the domestic domain, women at best share authority and decision-making with men; at worst, they are still under the authority of their husbands, and cannot even spend money they themselves earn without their husbands' consent.

Segregated Conjugal Roles, Social Networks, and Historical Experience

Bott carried out a study of conjugal roles among families in East London in the 1950's. Most of these families were working class. Bott analyzed the degree of jointness or separateness in conjugal roles and found that segregated conjugal roles (a strict division of labor and other activities on the basis of sex alone) were most common in families which were not spatially mobile, and whose networks were close knit (that is, most of the people they knew, also knew each other). Women in these families associated largely with other women. As they married and had children, their primary bonds were with their mothers, sisters and other female relatives. This contrasted with the tendency of men to socialize with co-workers and neighborhood friends rather than with brothers or members of their own families of orientation. This behavior was reinforced particularly by close social networks; because networks were close, they functioned well as social censors and promoted conformity to approved behaviors (Bott 1971).

Girls helped with housework at an early age, and stayed close to their mothers, forming strong bonds with their mothers, sisters and mothers' relatives. Boys were encouraged to play outside the house. It was "natural" (i.e. cultural) that when they married, they would be closer to their wives' families than to their own (Bott 1971). This situation is like that of families in Milograd today.

The shift towards association with the wife's rather than the husband's natal household, and sometimes the combination of the two families into a single household, seems to be increasing in Milograd. Economic changes mean, among other things, that a man is not dependent on his father for a livelihood, thus patrilocality is not any longer a necessity (although some people still feel it is "better" for young couples to live with the husband's family, even if it is not economically necessary). At the same time, men's and women's roles are still segregated. Women are encouraged to rely on their daughters for help, and to form close bonds with them, and with other female relatives, especially mothers and sisters.

The first condition is an economic one. The second has more to do with culture than with economics. It is economically necessary for women to work outside the home, but economic necessity is not a factor in determining who works in the home. A low degree of spatial mobility including the tendency for young people to marry and settle near their parents, means that communities are very close-knit, and are effective in exerting social pressure on individuals and household groups to conform to behavior expectations.

Young couples now have a choice about where they will live. Those who live with the husband's parents or with the wife's parents tend to cooperate in household tasks with that particular set of parents. Those who live neolocally most often cooperate with the wife's parents rather than the husband's. When given a choice, women seem to prefer to leave their children with their own mothers, and to share other domestic work with their mothers. Husbands rarely interfere with this kind of decision. Because they are not involved in housework or child care, they rarely think about how it will get done. Yugoslavs explain the choice in terms of the "natural closeness" of mothers and daughters. A mother-in-law and daughter-in-law may also be close, they say, but it more likely that they will compete and disagree about how things are to be done. When families live near by, it is easier (because culturally accepted) for women to ask female relatives to help them, than to ask their husband's to help with jobs considered women's work.

Historically Yugoslavs depended on the family and household for economic aid. Today they continue to do so. Rather than use day care facilities, families prefer to leave their children with a grandparent. It is cheaper and more reliable. Furthermore, the older people expect to take care of grandchildren, and both they and their adult children are conscious that this gives them a purpose and an important position within family groups.

Most grandmothers today remember World War II. Some were alive during World War I. Many of these women lived in villages as children and as brides. They tend to explicitly teach their grandchildren roles and values more in keeping with a peasant economy. These ideas include the segregation of men's and women's roles.

The persistence of a traditional emphasis on household (economic) self-sufficiency is also relevant to the persistence of segregated domestic roles (Gilliland 1986). In peasant households the ability to remain economically self-sufficient was some guarantee of survival and security. Household integrity was promoted and labor organized through rules of respect and avoidance, and a distribution of authority and division of labor.

Older people who have lived through two world wars have seen governments collapse, economies fail and people starve. They do not take the current economic situation lightly.[18] They trust neither the present government or the economy. They have taught their children, and often their grandchildren (today's young adults) to depend on the family and the household, and to value self-sufficiency. Along with these ideas, they have also passed on ideas about what they consider proper relations of authority and a proper division of labor at home (Gilliland 1986).

This is not to say that all children or grandchildren obey their parents or grandparents, or even that all members of the older generation are this conservative, but there is considerable agreement in these views among my adult informants, young and old. The roles that grandparents play in childrearing, and in family life in general, and their past experiences and attitudes towards household life are not insignificant, and contribute towards patterns in household behavior.

Conclusions

This essay addresses one area of household life; housework and child care, and the division of labor at home. I have argued that economic changes have allowed individuals to form a variety of residential groups. These same economic changes have allowed greater choice in matters of cooperation, particularly regarding domestic work and child care. Ideas people have about men's and women's work, however, prevent the sharing of domestic work by married couples. In the past housework and child care was carried out by female members of co-resident household groups. Residence was generally patrilocal or virilocal. Today it is increasingly common for young couples to live with the wife's parents instead of the husband's parents, and even more common for them to reside neolocally, but to share certain household activities with the wife's parents.

Economic factors do not entirely explain the patterns I have described. Past experience, socialization of children by grandparents, and tight-knit communities all contribute to ideas people have about proper behavior.

In our quest for better understanding of what households do we must keep in mind that when households adapt to changing environmental and economic circumstances they often do so in ways that are in keeping with their (culturally-prescribed) perceptions of the world. Furthermore, other social groups, like neighborhoods, or communities, can affect behavior at the level of the household. Culture and historical experience are important factors in the interpretation of economic and social conditions by members of a society, and affect the ways in which societies and cultures change.

Notes

1. I argue in this paper that households are not only affected by their physical environment, but by the total social context in which they exist. For this reason I specifically use the term "social environment."

2. Milograd is a pseudonym used to protect the privacy of my informants.

3. I am grateful to the International Research and Exchange Board (IREX) who funded this research.

4. Slavonia is still a rich agricultural region. Both collective farms and small farms (up to ten hectares) owned and operated by families are found there.

5. I follow a convention used by many anthropologists to distinguish different types of power. Power is a term which refers to the ability to effect the outcome of situations or decisions. Authority is power which is reckoned to be legitimate. Authority contrasts with power gained by coercion or force, or by manipulation. I discuss this later in the article.

6. Although only one-third of all couples practice matrilocal or uxorilocal residence, these and most couples residing neolocally share many household activities with the wife's parents (particularly the wife's mother).

7. The actual frequency of voting among women in these households is unknown.

8. The term "private apartment" means that it is privately owned. Most private accommodations are rooms in someone else's house. At best one must go through a common courtyard to get to an apartment added to a house. People joke that most private flats come complete with a prying landlord or landlady. Like many jokes, this one seemed to often hold true.

9. For a good ethnographic description of the influence of the women's community on women's behavior within households, see Wolf (1972).

10. Legislation was passed shortly after World War II which mandated equality for women in jobs, education and in political office. This was the result of female participation in the partisan army, and in the early years of the new socialist government. As in the case of many policies, behavior falls short of the ideals. Policies do not address the position of women in the family or the home.

11. Worthy is a literal translation of the Serbo-Croatian *vrijedna*. Virtuous or valuable are also possible translations.

12. "Komšenica, je'l ti vrijedna?"

13. My landlady, for example, had a washing machine, as did many of my neighbors. Even those who owned these machines were reluctant to use them. They were not durable enough to wash heavy fabrics. People were unwilling to take a chance because replacement parts were difficult to obtain. Most women felt that the machine did not really clean their clothes, and they preferred to do white laundry especially in a pot of boiling water on the stove. In general, there was strong feeling that things done by hand were better.

14. This behavior was not economically necessary, but fits with the mistrust of the government and the economy, and a desire on the part of most household members to maintain a self-sufficient household.

15. The grandmother in my household called her own grandson *pisda*, slang for vagina, when he expressed an interest in cooking. "I wouldn't have such a man in my house," she said.

16. My neighbor, who has married since I left Yugoslavia, writes to me that her husband helps her at home. He dresses their son in the mornings and makes the coffee. He also goes to the market on occasion.

17. I heard several mothers whose married sons did not live with them complain that if the wife wanted to live separately, then she should do the housework and the cooking, not her mother.

18. The economic crisis in Yugoslavia is more acute now in 1989 than it was in 1983. The inflation rate has soared to over 200 percent. Housing is even more expensive and in shorter supply. According to friends from whom I receive letters regularly, more families are squeezing into tighter quarters. Even government apartments, which usually have one or two bedrooms, are now sometimes shared by parents and their married children.

References Cited

Adamić, L. 1934. *The Native's Return*. New York and London: Harper and Brothers.

Arnould, E. and R. Netting. 1982. "Households: Changing Form and Function." *Current Anthropology* 23: 571–575.

Bailey, F.G.. 1960. *Tribe, Caste and Nation*. Manchester: University Press.

———. 1971a. "Changing Communities," in F.G. Bailey (ed.), *Gifts and Poison: The Politics of Reputation*. Great Britain: Basil Blackwell. Pp. 1–15.

———. 1971b. "The Peasant View of the Bad Life," in T. Shanin (ed.), *Peasants and Peasant Societies*. Great Britain: Penguin Books. Pp. 299–321.

Bićanić, R.. 1965. "Attitudes to the Zadruga," in D. Warriner (ed.), *Contrasts in Emerging Societies: Readings in the Social and Economic History of South-Eastern Europe in the Nineteenth Century*. Bloomington: Indiana University Press. Pp. 341–344.

Bott, E. 1971. *Family and Social Network*. New York: The Free Press.

Burić, O. 1976. "The Zadruga and the Contemporary Family in Yugoslavia," in R.F. Byrnes (ed.), *Communal Families in the Balkans: The Zadruga*. Indiana: University of Notre Dame Press. Pp. 117–138.

Byrnes, R.F. (ed.). 1976. *Communal Families in the Balkans: The Zadruga*. Indiana: University of Notre Dame Press.

Denich, B.S. 1974. "Sex and Power in the Balkans," in M. Rosaldo and L. Lamphere (eds.), *Woman, Culture and Society*. Stanford: Stanford University Press. Pp. 243–262.

———. 1977. "Women, Work and Power in Modern Yugoslavia," in A. Schlegel (ed.), *Sexual Stratification*. New York: Columbia University Press. Pp. 215–244.

Erlich, V. 1966. *Family in Transition: A Study of 300 Yugoslav Villages*. Princeton: Princeton University Press.

First-Dilić, R. 1973. "Struktura moći u porodici zaposlene žene." *Sociologija* Beograd. br. 1, str. 79–102.

Fortes, M. 1962. "Introduction," in J. Goody (ed.), *The Developmental Cycle in Domestic Groups*. Cambridge: Cambridge University Press. Pp. 1–14.

Gilliland, M.K. 1985. "Commercial Exchange and Prestation in Slavonian Weddings." Paper presented at the 84th Annual Meeting of the American Anthropological Association, Washington, D.C.

168 M.K.G. Olsen

_____. 1986. *The Maintenance of Family Values in a Yugoslav Town.* University of California, San Diego. Unpublished Ph.D. Dissertation.

Goody, J. (ed.). 1962. *The Developmental Cycle in Domestic Groups.* Cambridge: Cambridge University Press.

Guldescu, S. 1970. *The Croatian-Slavonian Kingdom 1526-1792.* The Hague: Mouton and Company.

Guyer, J.I. 1981. "Household and Community in African Studies." *African Studies Review* 24: 87-137.

Halpern, J.M. 1963. "Yugoslav Peasant Society in Transition—Stability in Change." *Anthropological Quarterly* 36: 156-182.

_____. 1965. "Peasant Culture and Urbanization in Yugoslavia." *Human Organization* 24: 162-174.

Hammel, E.A. 1980. "Sensitivity Analysis of Household Structure in Medieval Serbian Censuses." *Historical Methods* 13: 105-118.

Lovretić, J. 1896, 1897, 1889/99 Otok. *Zbornik za narodni život i običaje južnih slavena.* Jugoslavenska akademija znanosti i umjetnosti. Zagreb. god. 1-4.

Lukić, L. 1919, 1924. Varoš. *Zbornik za narodni život i običaja južnih slavena* Jugoslavenska akademija znanosti i umjetnosti. Zagreb. god. 24-25.

Michaelson, E. and W. Goldschmidt. 1971. "Female Roles and Male Dominance Among Peasants." *Southwestern Journal of Anthropology* 27: 330-352.

Mihovilović, M.A. (ed.). 1975. *Žena izmedju rada i porodica.* Zagreb: Institut za društvena istraživanja.

Mosely, P.E. 1940. "The Peasant Family: The Zadruga, or Communal Joint-Family in the Balkans and its Recent Evolution," in C.F. Ware (ed.), *The Cultural Approach to History.* New York: Columbia University Press. pp 95-108.

_____. 1976. "The Distribution of the Zadruga Within Southeastern Europe," in R.F. Byrnes (ed.), *Communal Families in the Balkans: The Zadruga.* Indiana: University of Notre Dame Press. Pp. 58-69.

Rihtman-Augustin, D. (ed.). 1982. "Žena u seoskoj kulturi Panonije." *Etnološka tribina.* posebno izdanje. Zagreb.

Rubić, I. 1953. "Slavonski i Bosanski Brod." *Zbornik za narodni život i običaje južnih slavena.* Jugoslavenska akademija znanosti i umjetnosti. Zagreb. god. 36.

Saunders, G. 1981. "Men and Women in Southern Europe: A Review of Some Aspects of Cultural Complexity." *Journal of Psychoanalytic Anthropology* 4(4): 435-466.

Shanin, T. 1971. "A Russian Peasant Household at the Turn of the Century," in T. Shanin (ed.), *Peasants and Peasant Societies.* Great Britain: Penguin Books.

Simić, A. 1982. "Urbanization and Modernization in Yugoslavia: Adaptive and Maladaptive Aspects of Traditional Culture," in M. Kenny and D. Kertzer (eds.), *Urban Life in Mediterranean Europe.* Urbana: University of Illinois Press. Pp. 203-224.

Spiro, M.E. 1977. *Kinship and Marriage in Burma.* Berkeley: University of California Press.

Tomasić, D. 1948. *Personality and Culture in Eastern European Politics.* New York: George W. Steward, Publisher.

Wilk, R. 1988. "Maya Household Organization: Evidence and Analogies," in R. Wilk and W. Ashmore (eds.), *Household and Community in the Mesoamerican Past.* Albuquerque: University of New Mexico Press.

Wilk R. and R. Netting. 1984. "Households: Changing Forms and Functions," in R. Netting, R. Wilk and E. Arnould (eds.), *Households.* Berkeley: University of California Press. Pp. 1–28.

Wolf, E.R. 1966. *Peasants.* New Jersey: Prentice-Hall.

Wolf, M. 1972. *Women and the Family in Rural Taiwan.* Stanford: Stanford University Press.

Yanagisako, S. 1979. "Family and Household: The analysis of Domestic Groups." *Annual Review of Anthropology* 8: 161–205.

9

Separateness and Relation:
Autonomous Income and Negotiation
Among Rural Bobo Women

Mahir Şaul

Classical political economy often draws a contrast between household production and other types of production which involve antagonistic class relations. In peasant households, it is postulated, consumption and the net product are structurally identical. "There are no separate groups to struggle over the division of the product into 'wages' for personal consumption and 'profit' for expansion." Investment is achieved by subtracting "from the single sum potentially available for personal consumption." (Friedmann 1978: 562) Provided one is not distracted from possible flows of surplus value between peasant households, this formulation perhaps has merits for conceptualizing European history. When it comes to West Africa, however, it can become incapacitating, because it conflates critically distinct social relations into one decision-making unit.

It has long been recognized that African conjugal partners and co-residents do not necessarily form joint decision units (Paulme 1963: 4–5). The most dramatic evidence for this comes from matrilineal societies, but the theme has validity in a much wider area. In the Ashanti survey Fortes made his pioneering observation that women had the free use of self-earned income guaranteed on the same terms as a man, and concluded that since each adult earns his or her living, in the large variety of domestic groupings there is no "community of production." (Fortes et al. 1947: 163, 168) Later Dupire showed that in Adioukrou the separation of goods between marriage partners is almost complete, that there are formal rules for sharing the returns to activities they undertake jointly, and that spouses are keen to defend their economic independence against each other (Dupire 1956: 277). The Ashanti perhaps still provide the archetype for our understanding of this situation (see Abu 1983 and the other exciting papers in the same volume by Oppong; see also Clark in this volume). But similar observations have been reported from as far as Nigeria (Sudarkasa 1973) and Sierra Leone (McCormack 1982).

The contractual basis of West African households makes it possible to see them as a locus of conflict, even one analogous to the labor-capital relationship. What about, for example, the struggle among members over the level of consumption? When interests within the production unit diverge, the input of dependent members to the joint projects can be seen as generating a flow akin to "surplus" to the head of the unit. In fact, some of the resulting tension is expressed in the desire of dependent members to withhold part of their labor power from joint production projects, in order to devote it to autonomous personal production or to collaboration with other kinsmen. The returns to personal effort can be used not only to ameliorate immediate consumption, but also to expand the sphere of personal autonomy by means of investment.

The implications of the relative autonomy of spouses have been overlooked in another body of literature that deals with linkages between farming and social organization. That African women contribute significantly to agricultural production, more so than on any other continent, seems now to be well established (eg. Burton and White 1986). Yet the focus in much research has been on task specialization by sex and the aggregate number of work hours contributed by each gender category. The distribution of proceeds, the structure of decision-making, and the organization of management have been neglected as topics relevant to the "contribution of women." This neglect is consonant with another European intellectual tradition, one that sees women's participation on an extensive scale in production as a condition for their emancipation (see for example Beauvoir 1968: 121; Sanday 1973: 1685). Of course, the source of this tenet lies in the historical experience of bourgeois women within the context of Euro-American capitalism, but the limits of the principle informing it become immediately apparent when one turns to the study of working classes in the same societies, or to other societies such as the ones in Africa.

Access to resources and to the returns of one's labor (or we could simply say, to one's labor) are universally subject to social regulation and negotiation. It is Meillassoux who reminded us that women may occupy a dominant place in agriculture as well as domestic labor and not be granted the status of producers (Meillassoux 1981: 77). Even in cases in which women are assigned their own plots on which they make management decisions, the dispensing of food from the supplies harvested and stored may be controlled by men, a pattern one frequently finds in the "female farming" areas of the forest belt (e.g. McCall 1961: 286–7). "Female contribution" has to be unpacked to take account of the degree to which women have autonomous producer status versus being workers. Most West African women are both producers (however small) in their own account as well as workers in household fields, for relatives, or elsewhere. The relative weight of each capacity, however, is different from one society to another, and from one woman to another within the same society. The failure to explore questions of individual autonomy has led to the neglect of factors influencing this balance.[1]

A general outline of production relations within West African farming units can be culled from ethnographic descriptions provided by several generations of workers. Pollet and Winter give a lucid summary of this collective effort as an introduction to their work on the Soninke (1968). Individuals related by kinship go through successive stages of increasing autonomy during their lifetime. Young dependent members of the household spend a great deal of time working on fields managed by their seniors, but are also often allowed a small plot to manage personally. In time the size of this plot increases, but the right to freely dispose of its harvest is again acquired only when one reaches a certain social status. Spouses productive activities constitute distinct spheres, and women possess management and disposal prerogatives, even though frequently on a smaller scale than their husbands. During the largest part of their productive life most people are bound vis-à-vis their guardians and elders by certain obligations which put constraints on their personal activities.

Production groups are often "nested." A field managed by an elderly segment head is farmed with the collaboration of a large number of his juniors. Thus, it constitutes the most inclusive production group. The harvest of such a field is distributed to an equally large group of people either as cooked meals or as uncooked grain. Depending on how much time the junior contributors spend working on it and how much of their consumption they derive from it, such a field may constitute the most important level of economic organization, or alternatively it may serve simply as a marker of loyalty to kinship structures with little economic significance. People contributing labor on this field may come from different residence units, or they may constitute one large unit of coresidence, the "compound" of the West African literature.

In either case, the married men of this most inclusive unit usually also have separate fields that they manage themselves with labor provided by their wife(ves), children, and other more junior people who are directly dependent on them. This constitutes an intermediate level production group. In many parts of the West African savanna such intermediate level groups, which are frequently headed by polygynously married men, are the most critical units in the provision of food and income. Nevertheless, the larger more inclusive units also crystallize occasionally, at least in periodical harvesting parties.

An even narrower production unit emerges in the activities undertaken independently by adult bachelor men and the women within the intermediate farming groups. These consist of small personal parcels and odd non-farming occupations. Even when the returns to these personal efforts appear to be small on the aggregate, their contribution to the income and consumption of the individual in question may be crucial. The "separateness" of household members refers to this least inclusive level of personal production.

We often assume that in Africa the less inclusive level production units have recently emerged from the weakening or partial dissolution of the more inclusive ones, which in turn are only the relics of a more authentic state of affairs. We should not lose sight, however, that even in the most inclusive units of production, obligations and responsibilities are sometimes phrased in such a way as to reveal a highly individualistic facet. One hears traditionalist Mossi farmers announce that family members are fed from the common granary only on days in which they provide work on the joint field (cf. Jones 1986: 108). This establishes a continuity between joint household projects, work parties in which non-kin participate, and outright wage work.

The relatively straightforward model of nested units is complicated by overlapping ties that cut across them. In some societies spouses have much more important and lasting ties to their respective kinship groups than to each other, as in the Ashanti case modeled by Wilk (this volume). In others, kinship ties simply add a different set of relations to those individuals maintain within the farming unit. Nor is kinship the sole basis for conflicting loyalties and solidarities blurring the boundaries of conjugal sets. Age groups, religious affiliation, and gender consciousness can also provide grounds for them. The possibility for the formation of gender blocs dividing all production units right in the middle should not be underestimated; in protest movements or rituals of reversal (Van Allen 1972; Ardener 1973) such blocs manifest a strikingly physical reality. In any case, there are always more than one frame of organization on which people can rely or shift loyalties for support and relief. Because of this multiplicity of potential options the long term patterns between kinsmen and conjugal partners involve some level of negotiation (Jones 1986; Cloud 1986). To some extent members of production and residence units decide for themselves to work and live together.

Development and urban migration may affect relations between spouses and kinsmen in a variety of ways. At least in some instances the scope for women's autonomy is enlarged (Ottenberg 1957; Peil 1975; Dinan 1977; Sanjek 1982; Robertson 1974). The outcome depends in part on what kind opportunities women find in the new economic environment. It also depends on what goes on within the conjugal units—on what some time ago Netting aptly called the "politics of domesticity" (Netting 1969). Even in situations which one would think are least conducive to autonomy women have managed to carve for themselves a large area of economic independence, as shown by the fascinating accounts of the trade activities of secluded women in Kano (Remy 1975; Schildkrout 1982).

Once the "separateness" of spouses and other family members is recognized we can address the economic nexus established by the social relationship of marriage and coresidence. By the terms of their marriage contract women are usually obliged not only to provide work on the joint farm, but also to produce special crops and condiments on their own, or to find the cash needed to fulfill their assigned responsibilities (Jiggins 1986: 11). Thus, adult women are not only allowed but often encouraged to earn autonomous income. However, the extent to which these activities will enable them to fulfill and liberate themselves depends on a number of factors, social structural ones, but also the specific circumstances in which they find themselves, such as their age, the support of kinsmen and children, or the position of their husband.

As economic agents men and women adopt different production strategies. These largely reflect varying endowments by virtue of control of labor. Women usually do not have as easy access to labor as heads of household do. If they manage fields of their own the work has to be done after contributing a significant amount of labor to the joint fields managed by the head of the more inclusive production unit. From these joint fields women and other dependents derive in turn a large part of their food needs. Women also engage in strenuous tasks of social reproduction such as cooking and child care. They may be freed from most of these obligations during old age, but they must also shoulder full responsibility for their own livelihood (Obbo 1986). For some women old age is the apex of an independent career, for others it is a period in which they are reduced to the status of wage workers.

Adult women's obligations to more inclusive units largely circumscribe their autonomy and also shape their options. McCall noted that Akan women will choose trading rather than farming if they have a choice (1961: 291). This remains true whenever women find themselves at a comparative disadvantage in terms of labor. But the frequency with which and the scale at which women are able to trade, brew beer, or process other foods also depends on the income of the husband or the contributions of other kinsmen to her and her children's sustenance. Schildkrout observed that in Kano, despite very little pooling of resources, the amount of personal income that a woman is able to reinvest in business or gift exchange depends on how much of it she has to use to feed and clothe her family, which in turn depends on the husband's income (1979: 76–7). As I will discuss below, the husband's high income may also motivate women to reduce their autonomous activities.

There is, however, one further facet to the conjugal relationship. The economic autonomy of the partners may result in situations in which they belong to different income strata. Sanjek has shown that in Adabraka, relations of social reproduction, consumption, sexual union, and social-ization of children crisscross and bind together class groups defined in terms of their relation to the control of production (Sanjek 1982: 99). The marriage of the poor girl to the rich man is a staple theme of European romance literature, but after the union we expect the parties to come to the same level, at least in terms of consumption standards, and they certainly can inherit from each other what they do not share in life. This does not necessarily hold true in African cases. What is more interesting for a western audience, however, is that sometimes thanks to their autonomous activities women can achieve higher income and wealth than their men. Hill pointed out that the wife's economic autonomy is often sufficient to insulate her from her husband's poverty (1969: 398). Going beyond that, some West African women can achieve real prosperity (Şaul 1981), lend money to their husbands (Netting 1969: 1038), or become capitalists who hire their husbands as crew members (Le Cours Grandmaison 1979: 162).

There were some, albeit few, women who achieved such glory in the village described in this chapter. Most women, however, had at least a few personal concerns, even if those were at a more modest scale. My purpose here is to compare these autonomous activities of adult women to those of important males in their residential unit. I try to sort out the factors that influence women's choices and account for the varying scale of their income generating occupations. This study complements a previous one on consumption expenditure in the same village (Şaul 1989a). The site of research, Bare, is a farming community in southern Bobo country in Burkina Faso.[2] The Bobo have a dual descent organization which links matrilineal clans to the control of money and herds, but where farming and residence units are patrifilially constituted.

People in this part of Africa have had contact with "long distance" trade for several centuries. Until recently, however, the currency-generating gathering and manufacturing work was organized by matrilineal cor-porations, and personal control over possessions was very limited. Farm production and dwelling groups were internally differentiated because their members, being of separate matrilineages, were subject to the claims of different sets of elderly men and women for their work power and allegiance. Every person was, therefore, a member of a number of overlapping corporate institutions which complemented each other to provide a nexus for production and exchange. Some autonomy was possible in the interstices of these corporate structures, but the opportunity opened only with age seniority. Even though kinship and community structures are still of importance, in recent decades the domain of personal control has generally widened at the expense of corporate units. For middle aged women this change has been facilitated by growing involvement in farming and processing activities outside of matrilineal production and pooling units, and by the concurrent reduction in the genealogical span of matrilineal cooperation groups. Mothers now have greater access to their daughters' and sons' help, whereas in the past a greater proportion of these dependents' efforts were spent on collective matrilineal projects which fed corporate funds held by segment elders. Twenty or thirty years ago, many of women's income-generating activities discussed in this article either were not undertaken by the women of farming clans (brewing or gathering wood for sale) or were under the exclusive control of lineage elders (as in the processing of shea oil).

One of the unexpected findings of this study is that wives of the most prosperous male farmers undertake less autonomous production than other women. Perhaps the peasant household with the "single sum" controlled by the husband is emerging after all. It might be that what we have here is a trajectory of development to a well-known destination (the "household firm") via an unusual detour. The increasing personal autonomy rendered possible by the loosening of the hegemony of corporate units may in fact be only a transitory episode in the growth of a new configuration—one in which family members are far more organically integrated to the joint production activities managed by heads of intermediate range production units. My conclusion, however, is that we should not rush in relegating the individual autonomy of Bobo women and male dependents to the eccentricity of a swiftly disappearing order. The few prosperous farmers of the village sample do not give us the image of the future of the rest of the population. They represent only a small privileged stratum. They illustrate yet another possibility in the dynamics of conjugal relationships: that some women are willing to accept trade-offs by giving up some personal autonomy in exchange for being shielded from the common hardships of a strained rural population. This option is likely to be reversed rather than expanded under conditions of greater opportunity.

In the rest of this chapter I deal first with the farming and then with the non-farming activities that women of Bare undertake on their own account. My purpose is to isolate the factors that affect the scale of these operations. I am excluding from this discussion the few Zara women who specialize in trade (and who are the truly prosperous people in the village), and concentrate on the Bobo women living in farming compounds who constitute the overwhelming majority. The sample on which this information is based covers about one quarter of a village population of approximately 1900 people.[3]

Farming

Women's plots account for a very small proportion (less than 4 percent) of the total farmed area in the sample. Women cultivate some sauce plants and okra on the edge of the joint fields, but if they have personal parcels these are exclusively devoted to peanuts and groundpeas (*Voandzea subterranea,* also called Bambara nuts). Of the 59 parcels belonging to the women of the sample, only one was under cotton cultivation and a few very small ones were under cereals. The parcels of all dependent members, men or women, are generally small. The two largest fields owned by women are slightly under 1 ha, while the smallest ones are no larger than a hundred square meters. Nevertheless, these crops (especially groundpeas) are relatively high value crops and the income from the harvest may be important in relative terms for the woman who grows it, particularly when she does not sell the produce as is, but processes it for retailing in the market. Some young women, particularly those married to young men who are themselves dependent members in an elder's production unit, may intercrop some red sorghum in their husband's personal plots. In this way they benefit from the joint weeding effort on this plot. Because of the demands made on their labor for both the joint farms of the head of the more inclusive production unit and for the personal farm of their own husband, often this is the only personal farming young women can do at all.

The average size of women's plots is smaller than that of other (male) dependents. The circumstances were somewhat special, however, during the year in which the survey was conducted. In 1983 there was an initiation for boys which occurs every six or seven years, and the candidates for initiation were expected to produce large amounts of peanuts and ground peas (as well as meat and other produce) as a test of their valor and as a contribution to the stores that are distributed among members of senior age sets during the ceremonies. In other years young males would be less interested in personal farming. Furthermore, a good part of these boys' parcels were planted and tended by their mothers and sisters, so that the initiation-related farming effort may have reduced women's aggregate autonomous farming area.

Women receive some help from their sons, brothers and husbands in clearing land for groundpea cultivation, while peanut gardens are usually made on abandoned cereal fields with no large vegetation and no need to clear. The land that married women use is usually allocated by the head of the more inclusive production unit (who in turn either receives it as a member of an agnatic group or borrows it). Some women may prefer to use somebody else's land with permission (because of convenience of location, for example). They are also always welcome to use the land of their own agnatic or matrilateral relatives. In Bare, women's fields are so small that finding enough land does not present a serious difficulty. The more critical problem is to find the time or the help to accomplish the planting and weeding. Most women do the majority of the work themselves. Frequently co-wives work as a team taking turns at each other's gardens. Daughters and sisters come to contribute, but all the work on women's autonomous parcels is done after the day's work on the joint household fields is completed or on rest days.

For the women who have the largest fields, these sources of labor are not sufficient. The most common way to increase the labor input is to invite a work team. Bobo villagers establish a great variety of work teams on the basis of generation, sex and membership in ward or agnatic groups. The services of such teams can be hired for the day. A member of the team pays a discounted rate to host the group, but also pays an absenteeism fee for the days he or she fails to join when they are hired elsewhere or engage in collective projects. Many women who have autonomous farms are members of a work team whose services they hire on their own garden. In order to participate in such work teams, married women have to obtain the permission of their husband who then releases them from work on the days the team meets.

A few women cultivating more than half a hectare rent a plow or a tractor before sowing. If a woman's brother owns a plow, or if her husband owns a plow and she has an adult son with sufficient time, she can obtain this service for free. The women who operate the largest farms therefore have relatively significant cash expenses. Meeting these costs is possible only if they engage in farming with the purpose of selling a large part of their produce or processing it as market foods. Consequently, the scale of a woman's personal farming is not a direct result of the labor force available within the household or of the economic strength of her husband. A good example of this involves a farming unit including two of the women with the most important autonomous farming activity. The head of the household in this case is a 44 year old farmer who cultivates 2.6 ha. His two wives, 42 and 39 years of age, cultivate .48 and .93 ha each (together constituting 35 percent of the household total). The only other person present in the household is a 9 year old boy. The women have their fields prepared with a rented plow, and also invite the work group to which they belong to help with the weeding. They use funds from their considerable processing and trade activities, and also market the produce of their gardens. In this case the wives definitely possess a firmer economic position than their husband, but this is not typical.

Overall, wives of the men with the largest farms engage in little autonomous production. The 51 units in the sample were divided into two strata on the basis of the amount of land the head himself manages. Twenty units where the head cultivates more than 6 hectare are labeled large farm units, and the rest small farm units. The large farm units include a high number of women who do not engage in personal farming at all. The aggregated personal farm area of all dependents is also a smaller proportion of the total (Şaul 1988). These observations are supported by another finding in the study of expenditure patterns of the same sample. There I found that women of large farm units spend less money on what could be considered farming investment than their counterparts in small farm units (Şaul 1989a). A similar conclusion can be reached by grouping the data in a different way. Of the 14 women who possess the largest (more than .36 ha) personal parcels in the sample, the majority (10) live in small farm households which represent about half the sample population.

One would expect that wives of better-off farmers would be in a better position to pursue personal projects; the observation that they undertake less farming is somewhat puzzling. They do not have to use as much of their personal resources on feeding and clothing their own family than wives of poorer men. Usually they receive more frequent and generous gifts from their husbands. They also live in residences where there are more women who can share and organize chores, leaving more free time for each one of them. In light of the ideas presented in the early part of this chapter one could anticipate two arguments to explain this situation.

The first one is that women may be engaging in farming primarily to protect themselves from the husband's poverty. This would explain why women who live in households with greater food security would reduce their scale or give up altogether personal farming. This argument is not supported by my observations. In Bare, most men and women are driven to increase production not to prevent starvation, but rather to raise personal income. The most productive female and male farmers sell a large part of their harvests. Wives in average production units do not suffer from underconsumption, whereas wives of prosperous farmers would certainly welcome additional income. The greater initiative of women in the small farm stratum cannot be fully explained by the husbands' inability to produce sufficient food; one also has to consider the women's desire for greater autonomy in deciding how to spend their income.

The second argument would be that women in large farm households prefer trading and processing foodstuffs to farming. I will discuss this possibility in greater detail below in the section on monetary income. I would like to move here to a third explanation, one that has been inspired by fieldwork itself.

The differences in the scale of women's personal farming are linked to the production orientation of the husband. Heads of household who are efficient farmers absorb their dependent members more fully into their own operations than other men. They can do this thanks to the greater resources they possess, but their success in this respect is also a factor helping them enlarge their farm. The cycle of growth of large farm operators is based not only on knowledge, careful investment, hard work, and access to labor through positional advantage, but also on skilled manipulation of the politics of domesticity. They increase their work force by capturing a larger part of the labor power of dependent members who in turn have to settle for less autonomy. This involves some measure of renegotiation of roles and responsibilities between the conjugal partners.

Coercion is not absent in negotiation. Nevertheless, power is partly grounded in productive success. Force can be effectively manipulated only with a high standing in the community, usually associated with strength in one's economic position. Otherwise individuals are driven to seek support in alternative relations or institutions, and the limits of personal coercion can be quickly reached. A suffering or mal-treated wife will leave the house, either for a lover or for her father. Village men do possess collective means of coping with competition among themselves and of preventing this from happening too frequently (by means of various cults and by adjudication). But collective coercion also can go only so far. Many problems have to be solved by mutual (tacit) consent between the individual parties. Some husbands try to limit their wife's involvement in autonomous production, for example, by forbidding her to join a work team. This effectively cuts the amount of her own farming by increasing the monetary cost of outside labor. If a husband wants to restrict his wife's autonomous production in this manner, however, he has to bear the full cost of her and her children's consumption, and usually offer some kind of compensation for her loss of autonomy also. Not all husbands are willing or able to do that. Others encourage their wives to produce food which relieves them from part of their obligations. There is no doubt that the difference is to some extent a matter of personal disposition; but it is also related to how much labor and investment funds the husband currently controls, both of which have further links to many other factors.

Besides the willingness of husbands to allow their wives enough time for their concerns, the very way successful heads of household organize farming may present difficulties for the women living with them. Farms are sometimes far from the village where road access is better. Most household members have to spend a longer part of the year in the houses constructed on these farms rather than living in the permanent house in the nucleated village. Large farm operators frequently participate to a lesser extent in the social life of the village. This tends to isolate women from their network of friends and kin, and make it more difficult to organize personal farming as well as market and trade activities. Women will usually only accept these conditions, however, if they are somewhat satisfied with their life conditions.

In sum, some heads of production unit manage to negotiate with success a greater contribution by dependent members. They use both tangible and non-tangible rewards to achieve this, but possessing a large productive potential makes things easier for them. This success in turn enables them to grow even further, creating a snowball effect. Life in these households, far from being full of drudgery, may be attractive to spouses. Prosperous farmers can often attract the wives of less successful farmers, first as lovers and later as residents in their own compound.

Production units may also include women who are not wives of the head, such as divorced relatives or wives of kinsmen who migrated for work. The difference between large and small farm operators is even clearer in such cases. For example, one of the small farm units in the sample included the wife of the head's absent brother; she was provided with a substantial amount of support in labor to help her produce in her own field most of the food she needed. The head of a large farm unit would instead probably try to absorb her into his own work team, and also provide directly for her consumption. The ability to follow such a strategy is somewhat linked to the authority a man derives from high rank in the kinship and community system, but not completely, and a farmer will be motivated to attempt such incorporation only if he already has the economic strength to compensate for her lost opportunity in autonomous production.

Age and Autonomous Farming

Turning to factors related to the life cycle, age seems to be the variable most consistently related to the scale of autonomous production among women (cf. Peil 1975). The most successful autonomous women farmers in the sample are between the ages 24 and 45. Nine of the 14 women who have personal farms of more than .36 ha are within this age range. Few women below the age of 20 and above the age of 60 have autonomous gardens. Young women are expected to help mothers and other matrilineal relatives. The strong solidarity characteristic of matrilineal nuclei in Bobo society are not motivated only by filial piety. These networks store money for collective projects, help new mothers acquire what they need, and support men and women throughout their life. Young married women are further constrained by the need to care for babies, especially if they are not close to a cluster of kinswomen who can help them with that task.

The case of old women is more difficult to understand. Since they no longer have children to care for, they have fewer personal needs, and perhaps smaller ambitions. Elderly Bobo women also have the advantage of holding matrilineal offices which potentially give them some control over accumulated cash. Their lack of interest in farming is not, however, necessarily the result of an insufficiency of physical vigor. Needy old women do provide farm work in the fields of prosperous farmers on a contractual basis. (In fact, this is one of the principal types of non-household labor available to enterprising farmers in the village.)

Monetary Income

The income figures in the present analysis are estimates calculated on the basis of interviews with women. Thirty nine adult women gave me detailed information on the trade and processing activities they undertook, the gifts they received, and the products they sold within the year. This information was later converted into monetary values by using prices collected in the village and profitability estimates calculated for major processing activities from carefully monitored experiments. I chose to rely on these income estimates rather than including direct questions about monetary receipts in the weekly questionnaires during the survey because income data collected as part of sequential interview schedules are not always reliable. Of course, such estimates can be only indicative of trends. They should be used with care, especially concerning topics such as monetary gifts which is a delicate area to tackle regardless of the method used. These income estimates, however, also inspire confidence because they are consistent with the expenditure data collected for the same individuals in an altogether different manner. These data, which have been partially analyzed in Şaul (1989a), were recorded by enumerators in weekly questionnaire forms. For the 39 women discussed here there is a strong and statistically significant correlation between my yearly income estimates and total and trade expenses (Pearson's R between women's income and yearly total expenditures is .70, between income and trade expenditures is .72, $p < .0001$).

The relationship between the scale of farming and monetary income from non-farming sources is a complex one. When the husband works away from the village and sends regular sums of money back home, a young woman may have a small farm but relatively high cash income. Conversely, some middle age women who command the labor of sons and sons-in-law have relatively large farms while they engage in very little in the way of non-farming activity. Nevertheless, for women, high non-farming income and large autonomous farming are associated (Pearson's R = .48, p < .01).

Women derive non-farming income from processing activities, from the sale of gathered products such as firewood, shea nuts, locust beans and wild leaves and fruits, from small scale trading, and occasionally from the sale of chickens and eggs. From their kinsmen as well as from their husbands women may also receive post-harvest gifts of grain, part of which they can sell. In addition, some women receive money from sons or other relatives abroad. Among processing activities the brewing of sorghum beer, the production of mead from honey, and the sale of firewood were reported by many women to be the most important sources of money earnings. I should make it clear that the brewers in Bare operate on a smaller scale than the large brewers in Mossi villages or those in large cities. A woman Bare rarely mashes more than 70 kg of sorghum at a time. Nevertheless, even brewing at this scale constitutes for the village a very significant enterprise that necessitates the control of considerable resources.

In contrast, for a few women who had the largest gardens the sale of peanuts and groundpeas yielded larger earnings than processing or fire wood collecting, and for them this was the largest source of personal income. However, sale of crops never results in very remarkable incomes for women in Bare. Even those who have the largest personal gardens rarely earn more than 15,000 F CFA by marketing their own crops. This is a modest sum when compared to what other women in the village can earn by brewing beer.

Unlike processing activities which require some capital, gathering requires little more than effort and time and can be undertaken by anybody. The sale of shea nuts and locust beans brings important revenues, but these products are difficult to transport because they are heavy. Locust beans must also be collected from trees, which is dangerous. Shea nuts and locust beans also require processing (drying, pounding, and sifting) before sale.

Some of the gathering activities are onerous because of the small returns. For example, in June 1984 I observed a woman spend one hour collecting a large basin full of leaves of the *ta* plant (used to sour the water in which the porridge is cooked); she put in another 4 hours to pound and dry them, and then had to walk for 3 hours round-trip to take the product to the market. The return on this venture was 100 F CFA (about 25 cents).

As would be expected, some women are more successful in processing activities (brewing beer, preparing mead, producing shea butter, fermented locust beans [*soumbala*], cooking food for sale) while others concentrate on gathering wild products for lack of resources or helpers. Usually, however, most women do some of both types of activities and income from the two categories are correlated (Pearson's R = .37, p < .01).

The woman for whom I have the largest income estimate in the subsample makes more than 150,000 F CFA a year. Yet 54 percent of the women earn less than 44,000 F CFA, and 5 women (13 percent) earn less than 10,000 F CFA (all income sources combined). The relationship of monetary income to age is even more pronounced than is the case with farming. The most successful women entrepreneurs are generally between the ages 24–45. Of the 8 women who make more than 85,000 F CFA a year, 7 are in this age range. In contrast, only 6 (29 percent) of the women who earn from 10,000 to 44,000 F CFA and none of those who earn less than 10,000 F CFA are in this age range.

We need to consider a number of social organizational and historical factors in order to interpret this finding. I mentioned above that among the Bobo matrilineal institutions have an important bearing on women's money-making activities. The gathering of shea nuts and locust beans are still undertaken by restricted uterine segments consisting of an elderly woman, her daughter(s), and a few other young women matrilineally related to her, such as daughters-in-law or a classificatory sisters (see Şaul 1989b). The young women in this group bring all the shea nuts and beans they have collected to the old woman. She decides how much of the total is to be processed (which is also undertaken collectively) and how much is to be sold to traders. The part earmarked for consumption is distributed to the young women of the group for their cooking needs.

Part of the funds deriving from sales are kept by the old woman herself and used when necessary for the needs of the women of the group. Part of the money is passed on to other women who are heads of matrilineal segments of larger genealogical span for more important projects. Although the control of these funds does give financial clout to elderly women, it was not possible for me to judge with confidence the magnitude of such corporate funds. The primary purpose of my interviews was to establish the amount women sold as individuals. A whole range of corporate transactions escaped quantification. It may be that some elderly women are in a less precarious financial position than it appears on the basis of personal transactions. My feeling is, however, that the greatest value in matrilineal funds consists of hoarded treasures (cowries and valuable ritual objects) and goats, and that liquid funds held by elderly matrilineage matrons are not as important as those of successful middle age women entrepreneurs. The same corporate structures impose constraints on young women's activities. The wild produce they gather and the product of processing activities in which they participate are not all personal income. Elder women distribute a portion of the collective production to individual junior women for sale, but many young women explained that the amount that they have available for sale is at the discretion of their woman elder. Some negotiation goes on in these lineage relations as well, because the very distribution of the result of the joint effort for personal sales is a very recent development and a response to growing demands for individual autonomy.

The most remunerative processing activities, the collection of wood for sale to urban middlemen, the brewing of beer, the preparation of mead, and cooking food for sale, are all undertaken outside of matrilineal structures. Bobo women of farm households did not engage in these activities for profit until recent times because these services and simple trade were relegated exclusively to the women of groups that specialize in market transactions, such as the Zara and the Jula. For example, Bobo men occasionally express doubt that their women are as skilled in brewing as women of some other groups, and in cosmopolitan centers such as Bobo-Dioulasso, Bobo women cannot compete in this activity with women of other regions. In Bare, some women have access to the brewing utensils that are matrilineal property, but most women now either purchase them with their own means, or use pots acquired by their husbands that will be transmitted with the house to his agnatic descendants.

The recentness of and the slow pace at which women have been emancipated from matrilineal structures also helps in understanding the distribution of monetary income along age strata. The older women in the sub-sample may simply not have had the chance to build the necessary capital in their prime age which would then allow them to increase their scale of processing when they became free of child rearing activities and labor contributions to their husband's fields. Thus, the absence of elderly women from the high income group may be related to the lack of opportunity in the past and not to factors related to life cycle in general. The pattern is likely to be different in the future; the successful young and middle age women entrepreneurs of today probably will not cut down their production and trade when they become older. On the contrary, many of them are trying to insert themselves in the retailing of urban products such as bottled drinks and manufactured products, a highly remunerative activity that requires little physical effort, but one that is also highly capital intensive, and therefore largely relegated to the few professional traders of Zara origin in the village.

Personal Non-Farming Income
in Small and Large Farm Units

The comparison of women's non-farming incomes in the small and the large farm units reveals a pattern similar to that in the scale of autonomous farming. The women in small farm households have a larger mean income from non-farming occupations than those in large farm households. While the comparison is statistically significant (T = .3693 p < .05), in view of the large variation within both groups it is necessary to elaborate on this relationship.

Because access to monetary capital is critical in the pursuit of the most remunerative activities, women who are in a position to receive important sums of money as gifts frequently also have high incomes from processing activities. This opportunity is not directly related to a woman's conjugal connections, but may be the result of her having a child, a brother, or a father who is employed in the wage sector. An atypical case is that of a 53 year old widow leviratically re-married in the well-connected and crowded compound of her former husband. She is the only woman of advanced age in my top autonomous income group. Nominally she receives a pension because her deceased husband was a retired soldier. I did not take into consideration this income in estimating her non-farming income because even though the exact arrangement was never made clear to me, the agnates of her deceased husband (who are the adult males of her present household) also receive a share of these payments. She has a daughter who is a school teacher in Bobo-Dioulasso, and an educated son who is on and off salaried employment. She derives most of her monetary income from brewing and market cooking, the large scale of which is undoubtedly made possible by her cash resources from her unusual situation. She is also one of the largest autonomous farmers (.68 ha under cultivation) in the sub-sample, whereas the head of her household has only an average farming operation.

A contrasting case is that of a 28 year old woman who lives in the household of her father-in-law. Her husband is in the military, but sends large sums of money to his father, partly to contribute for her share of subsistence expenses. He also sends her regular monthly payments (which this time have been given with sufficient precision to be figured into her income). The major part of her autonomous earnings, however, are the result of her own activities. What makes her case more unusual is that a large proportion of this income is the result of retail trading in condiments and vegetables purchased in Bobo-Dioulasso and transported to the village. This makes her one of the few farming household women able to emulate the pattern of professional Zara trading women. A further similarity is that, unlike the woman in the first case, her autonomous farming activity is negligible.

One would expect wives of prosperous farmers to also possess an advantage and have high non-farming income, but this is not always the case. They benefit, for example, from more generous post-harvest gifts (the amount of which is at the discretion of the husband). Besides, enterprising male farmers take an interest in marketing and trade ventures which can be expedient for the women of the household. For example, if the grain is to be sold in the market place, it is the wives who conduct the transaction and normally they retain a portion of the proceeds for their services. Two types of contracts among conjugal partners were identified in urban Dakar with respect to the marketing of vegetables (Le Cours Grandmaison 1979: 161). Either the man gives the product to his wife and they share the proceeds, or the woman pays a wholesale purchase price to her husband and keeps the profit from retailing, taking also a greater burden of risk. The two seem to imply a different relationship between the parties qua economic partners, and are probably associated with dissimilar relative wealth standings and scales of operation among the spouses. In the rural areas of the Voltaic savanna one finds a third type contract that is intermediate between the two and resembles a commission. The husband gives his wife a product for sale (immediately or after processing) with the expectation of fetching a reasonable current rate, but the exact price is determined only after the transaction, with the understanding that she will realize a small profit for her effort.[4]

Successful farmers, however, sell most of their marketed crop in bulk directly to trading agents, which means that the women's share in these transactions is small. Some men do have their wives brew sorghum for the husband's account. They do this to raise money for production expenses that are paid early in the harvest season, such as input credits received from the extension agency. Such instances provide an income opportunity for women, but not at a level comparable to those of the women who brew their own or purchased grain. Wives of prosperous men may have advantages in other forms. A pensioned ex-soldier, for example, gave his wives 2–4 mango trees from which they generated a moderate income by selling the fruits.

On the other hand, being the wife of a successful farmer may also have its disadvantages. Because she must brew and cook for her husband, for work parties in the rainy season, and in the post harvest season to raise cash, the amount of time she has left to work on her own projects is reduced considerably. In addition, the necessity of having to spend a longer period of the year at a farm location far from the village further reduces her opportunity to acquire personal income. These disadvantages may be compensated for by privileges negotiated from the husband, such as a higher standard of living, or gifts in durables, grain, or cash. Yet this may mean a relegation of a greater share of her work power to the joint production enterprise managed by her husband.

One example is provided by the household of a 35 year old man who is one of the most successful farmers in my sample (11.6 ha under cultivation). This is a typically small production unit including the head himself, his two wives and his aging mother (and children who do little work). Most work on the vast fields is done by a permanent hired worker and by occasional daily workers and work groups. The man also makes bricks for sale, using hired labor which is unusual. He also raises pigs and produces honey. His two wives brew beer for him and produce mead out of his honey, but he also gives them 140 and 170 kg of grain per person and some honey to help them earn cash. Despite these opportunities, all three women in the residence have small scale operations generating little autonomous income. In this case, however, the two wives are very young (17 and 19 years of age) and the mother is elderly (67).

There were only three women who had high non-farm income in the group of large farm units. Two of them were co-wives of the same man, a fifty year old veteran with a modern outlook who revealed his unconventional nature in the matter of farming and investment innovations as well as in his being one of the few Muslims in this staunchly traditionalist community. The wives were in their prime age (42 and 44 years old) and had successfully combined large autonomous farms with a booming beer and mead business. The husband entertained hopes of opening a village bar one day (a wish indicating that his attachment to Islam was not necessarily out of piousness); his pleasure in observing his wives success was perhaps not unrelated to that project. The third woman entrepreneur was the young daughter-in-law (24 years old) of an old patriarch on the verge of senility. She did not have a plot of her own, but had planted some sorghum in her husband's personal parcel. Her success in her monetary activities was not the result of her being a member of large farm unit.

Conclusion

In Bare, the scale of women's autonomous economic activities is related to that of their husbands in complex ways. Women can benefit from the prosperity generated by joint activities under the management of the head of the farming group. But, paradoxically, wives of successful farmers generally have less autonomy, in the case of both farming and non-farming endeavors. Less autonomy, however, does not imply lower standards of living. On the contrary, by joining their husbands' activities more fully some of these women seem to have partially traded off their productive independence for security in high consumption levels and the prestige of being associated with a successful man.

Overall, resources contributed by close kin (sons, daughters, brothers, fathers, mothers), especially those who are in wage employment, appear to be much more critical in providing a woman with a basis for entrepreneurial activity than her husband's level of income. Such occasional or periodic contributions enhance her and her children's well-being directly, but especially effect a raise in her permanent income when the woman can transform them into capital for local ventures. A woman can use such opportunities to great advantage, and access to pecuniary assistance from people outside the production unit accounts for most of the differentiation observed among women who are otherwise similarly situated. Age is another predictor of the range of a woman's autonomous income. Nevertheless, to a large extent it is women's own management capabilities, effort, and choices in terms of negotiating a conjugal role that explain varying achievements in autonomous economic position.

Notes

1. Insensitivity to autonomy versus joint production can be misleading in other ways as well. In an article showing that women's education in rural Burkina Faso is hampered by longer working hours than men, McSweeney and Freedman (1982: 91) compare the time allocation by sex. Women's brewing, food processing, marketing, midwifery, farming and other activities are indiscriminately aggregated. Yet, some of these activities are undertaken by women on their own account, and some others for the head of the production group. Adult women have more choice to allocate time for attending educational activities than implied by McSweeney and Freedman. The conclusion that women have heavy obligations to members of their production and consumption unit is well supported by other research, but it is clear that this method of accounting is not sufficiently sensitive to illuminate the underlying structure of decisions.

2. Fieldwork in Bobo country was carried out in the village of Bare in 1983–84, with grants from the National Science Foundation (BNS 83-05394), the Wenner-Gren Foundation for Anthropological Research, and the University of Illinois Research Board. I want to thank these institutions, the villagers of Bare, many people who helped in Burkina Faso, and Steve Bridgeman who provided research assistance.

3. The sample includes 51 sampling units. These were "intermediate level" production units, defined as a group consisting of people who produce jointly and store together most of the grain they consume. In most cases this corresponds to a married man, his wife(ves), his children, and perhaps one or two other close relatives who depend on the man. One unit in the sample consists of a middle age man who farms by himself, while the most crowded units include married sons or divorced daughters and their children. Women, even if unmarried, are not considered heads of residential or farming units and are always represented

in formal affairs by a man; but if this man is a young adult son the mother can have a great influence on him. The demographic composition of these units changes frequently, even within the same farming season. They are not bounded, or self sufficient in terms of production or consumption. Nor are they always the most important arena for people's social lives.

4. See the way Wilk has modeled exchanges between conjugal partners among the Effetu fisherfolk in Ghana (this volume). However, it should be noted that the existence of formal contracts among spouses does not mean that there is no communality in other respects. In fact, members of Euro-American households too can enter into formal legal contracts with each other. In other instances (when there is no *formal* contract) contractuality may be one dimension of a multifaceted relationship. We can choose to stress its contractual facet or the communal aspect depending on the modality of our explanation. An example is the Mossi doctrine, mentioned earlier, concerning the relationship between eating from the central granary and working on the fields.

References Cited

Abu, Katharine. 1983. "The Separateness of Spouses: Conjugal Resources in an Ashanti Town," in C. Oppong (ed.), *Female and Male in West Africa*. London: George Allen & Unwin. Pp. 156–168.

Ardener, S. G. 1973. "Sexual Insult and Female Militancy." *Man* 8(3): 422–40.

Beauvoir, Simone de. 1968. [1949] *The Second Sex*. New York: Random House.

Burton, M. and D. R. White. 1984. "Sexual Division of Labor in Agriculture." *American Anthropologist* 86: 568–83.

Cloud, Kathleen. 1986. "Women's Productivity in Agricultural Systems: Consideration for Project Design," in C. Overholt et al. (eds.), *Gender Roles in Development Projects: A Case Book*. West Hartford, Connecticut: Kumarian Press. Pp. 17–55.

Dinan, Carmel. 1977. "Pragmatists or Feminists? The Professional 'Single' Women of Accra, Ghana." *Cahiers d'Études Africaines* 17:65: 155–76.

Dupire, Marguerite. 1956. "Organisation sociale du travail dans la palmeraie Adioukrou (Bass Côte d'Ivoire)." *Revue de l'Institut de Sociologie Solvan, Bruxelles* 2–3: 271–92.

Fortes, M., R. W. Steel and P. Ady. 1947. "Ashanti Survey 1945–46: An Experiment in Social Research." *The Geographical Journal* 110(4–6): 149–79.

Friedmann, Harriet. 1978. "World Market, State, and Family Farm: Social Bases of Household Production in the Era of Wage Labor." *Comparative Studies in Society and History* 20: 545–86.

Hill, Polly. 1969. "Hidden Trade in Hausaland." *Man* 4: 392–409.

Jiggins, Janice. 1986. "Women and Seasonality: Coping with Crisis and Calamity." *IDS Bulletin* 17(3): 9–18.

Jones, Christine W. 1986. "Intra-Household Bargaining in Response to the Introduction of New Crops: A Case Study from North Cameroon," in J. L.

Moock (ed.), *Understanding Africa's Rural Households and Farming Systems*. Boulder, Co.: Westview. Pp. 105–23.

Le Cour Grandmaison, Colette. 1979. "Contrats économiques entre époux dans l'Ouest Africain." *L'Homme* 19(3–4): 159–170.

MacCormack, Carol. 1982. "Control of Land, Labor and Capital in Rural Southern Sierra Leone," in Edna G. Bay (ed.), *Women and Work in Africa*. Boulder, Co.: Westview. Pp. 35–53.

McCall, D. F. 1961. "Trade and the Role of Wife in a Modern West African Town," in A. Southall (ed.), *Social Change in Modern Africa*. Oxford: Oxford University Press.

McSweeney, B. G. and M. Freedman. 1982. "Lack of Time as an Obstacle to Women's Education: The Case of Upper Volta," in G. P. Kelly and C. M. Elliot (eds.), *Women's Education in the Third World*. Albany: State University of New York Press. Pp. 88–103.

Meillassoux, Claude. 1981. *Maidens, Meal and Money: Capitalism and the Domestic Community*. Cambridge: University Press.

Netting, Robert McC. 1969. "Marital Relations in the Jos Plateau of Nigeria: The Politics of Domesticity among the Kofyar." *American Anthropologist* 71: 1037–47.

Obbo, Christine. 1986. "Some East African Widows," in B. Potash (ed.), *Widows in African Societies: Choices and Constraints*. Stanford: University Press. Pp. 84–106.

Ottenberg, Phoebe. 1959. "The Changing Economic Position of Women among the Afikpo Ibo," in W. R. Bascom and M. Herskovits (eds.), *Continuity and Change in African Cultures*. Chicago: University of Chicago Press.

Oppong, Christine, ed. 1983. *Female and Male in West Africa*. London: George Allen & Unwin.

Paulme, Denise. 1963. [1960] *Women in Tropical Africa*. Trans. by H. M. Wright. Berkeley: University of California Press.

Peil, Margaret. 1975. "Female Roles in West African Towns," in J. Goody (ed.), *Changing Social Structure in Ghana*. London: International African Institute. Pp. 73–90.

Pollet, E. and G. Winter. 1968. "L'Organisation sociale du travail agricole des Soninke (Dyahunu, Mali)." *Cahiers d'Études Africaines* 32: 509–34.

Remy, Dorothy. 1975. "Underdevelopment and the Experience of Women: A Nigerian Case Study," in R. R. Reiter (ed.), *Toward an Anthropology of Women*. New York: Monthly Review Press. Pp. 358–71.

Robertson, Claire. 1974. "Economic Woman in Africa: Profit Making Techniques of Accra Market Women." *Journal of Modern African Studies* 12: 657–664.

Sanday, Peggy R. 1973. "Toward a Theory of the Status of Women." *American Anthropologist* 75: 1682–973.

Sanjek, Roger. 1982. "The Organization of Households in Adabraka: Toward a Wider Comparative Perspective." *Comparative Studies in Society and History* 24(1): 57–103.

Şaul, Mahir. 1981. "Beer, Sorghum and Women: Production for the Market in Rural Upper Volta." *Africa* 51(3): 746–64.

———. 1988. "Money and Land Tenure as Factors in Farm Size Differentiation in Burkina Faso," in R. E. Downs and S. P. Reyna (eds.), *Land and Society in Contemporary Africa*. Hanover and London: University Press of New England. Pp. 243–77.

———. 1989a. "Expenditure and Intrahousehold Patterns among the Southern Bobo of Burkina Faso," in B. S. Orlove and H. Rutz (eds.), *The Social Economy of Consumption*. Lanham: Society for Economic Anthropology and University Press of America.

———. 1989b. "Corporate Authority, Exchange, and Personal Opposition in Bobo Marriages," *American Ethnologist* 16(1): 58–76.

Schildkrout, Enid. 1979. "Women's Work and Children's Work: Variations among Moslems in Kano," in S. Wallman (ed.), *Social Anthropology of Work*. London: Academic Press. Pp. 69–85.

———. 1982. "Dependence and Autonomy: The Economic Activities of Secluded Hausa Women in Kano, Nigeria," in E. G. Bay (ed.), *Women and Work in Africa*. Boulder, Co.: Westview, Pp. 55–81.

Sudarkasa, Niara. 1973. *Where Women Work: A Study of Yoruba Women in the Marketplace and in the Home*. Ann Arbor: University of Michigan, Museum of Anthropology papers, no. 53.

Van Allen, J. 1972. "'Sitting on A Man': Colonialism and the Lost Political Institutions of Igbo Women." *Canadian Journal of African Studies* 6(2): 165–81.

PART THREE

Implications of Household Processes for Agricultural Development

10

Tubuai Women Potato Planters and the Political Economy of Intra-Household Gender Relations

Victoria S. Lockwood

In assessing community responses to development and the potential impact of development on rural peasant societies, households are often taken as the basic socioeconomic unit of analysis, and are treated as internally undifferentiated and homogeneous structures. However, recent studies of women's roles in development have demonstrated that this approach is limited in its explanatory power because it fails to recognize that peasant households are internally stratified by gender. Consequently, the economic and political conditions under which men and women operate in the household are different. In many cases, the determinants, as well as the implications, of male and female behavior are substantially different.

More specifically, in the commodity producing peasant household, a form generated by the penetration of capitalist relations of production (see Cook 1982; Gibbon and Neocosmos 1985), men control major market-oriented economic activities and wealth producing resources, and women are usually economically dependent and politically subordinate (see Fernandez-Kelly 1981; Nash 1977). Patterns of gender stratification characteristic of this household type encompass not only gender-structured roles and activities, but also differential access to household resources and capital, and unequal participation in household decision-making and authority. In order, then, to isolate the particular forces which shape women's economic choices and strategies and to understand why these may be different from those of men, the economic and political dimensions of women's structural position in the peasant household must be documented.

Table 1

Tubuai Potato Cultivation 1980–1987*

| | Numbers of Planters | | | | | Average Cultivation Scale (kg./planted) | |
Year	Males	Females	Total	% Increase Males	% Increase Females	Males	Females
1980	37	4	41			1,780 kg.	625 kg.
1981	39	8	47	+ 5%	+100%	2,750 kg.	1,200 kg.
1983	82	20	102	**	**	1,300 kg.	770 kg.
1984	102	33	135	+48%	+65%	1,210 kg.	869 kg.
1985	125	47	172	+22%	+42%	1,030 kg.	766 kg.
1986	152	65	217	+21%	+38%	1,070 kg.	810 kg.
1987	186	93	279	+22%	+43%	1,260 kg.	870 kg.

* Information provided by the Service de l'Économie Rurale, Tubuai; information for 1982 is not available.

** Because information for 1982 is not available, the rate of increase in numbers of planters for 1983 was not calculated.

My aim in this chapter is to analyze a case of rural women's participation in development, that of Tubuai (French Polynesia) women potato cultivators.[1] I will show that island women's rapid and unexpected movement into potato cash-cropping is a phenomenon which can only be understood in terms of the political economy of intra-household gender relations.

In the late 1970s, a government-sponsored project for developing potato cultivation was implemented on Tubuai, a rural outer island in French Polynesia (population 1700 persons, approximately 300 households).[2] While the number of farmers participating in the project has steadily grown since 1979, the rate of increase in new female planters each year has been almost double that of male planters. By 1987, women farmers had become a third of all program participants (see Table 1).

Tubuai women's potato cultivation is notable for several reasons. First, reported cases of successful, independent female participation in planned agricultural development programs are relatively rare. Second, on Tubuai (as throughout the Tahitian culture area), men are culturally defined as the primary cultivators, while women's work centers on maintaining the household and child care. Most significantly, on Tubuai males dominate market-oriented economic activities and control cash income. By adopting potato cultivation, women have taken on an independent role in commodity production, a role they have not previously occupied, and have acquired a lucrative source of cash income which they personally control.

Tubuai women's participation in development thus raises important questions related to development and gender studies. These include the impact of development on women's traditional roles, the nature of the structural conditions under which female development participation is promoted and facilitated, and the factors which specifically motivate women, as one segment of society, to take part. The Tubuai case also reflects on the broader political implications of development participation and autonomous control of income for women's status in male-dominated peasant societies.

I will first outline the major structural features of women's position in commodity producing peasant households. I then describe the political economy of intra-household gender relations on Tubuai, including the organization of the sexual division of labor, household relations of production, patterns of resource and income control, and differential authority and decision-making. I next look specifically at Tubuai women potato planters, analyzing their socioeconomic characteristics and describing the particular features of the potato program which have facilitated women's involvement. Using household socioeconomic data and information from structured interviews of male and female cultivators, I then set out the factors which have motivated women's participation in development and argue that it represents a reaction against their economic subordination in the Tahitian household. Finally, I assess the potential long-term implications of women's cultivation and control of income for the present structure of Tubuai gender relations, and for the development process itself.

Gender Stratification in Commodity Producing Peasant Households

As more traditional communities are incorporated into market systems, households are transformed into petty commodity producers for regional and world markets (see Smith 1984). In many rural areas of the Third World these commodities are agricultural products (e.g. coffee, copra, cocoa, etc.). The typical peasant household economy is mixed and generalized, combining subsistence-oriented production of indigenous crops with the cultivation of cash crops. In some communities, wage labor or craft earnings may contribute to household income. The small-holder rural household frequently owns its own land (and other means of production) and uses mostly family labor.

The commodity producing peasant household, a capitalist form, combines in one unit the functions of capital (ownership of the means of production) and of wage labor (production). As a result, it embodies internal contradictions (see Cook 1982; Gibbon and Neocosmos 1985). According to Marx,

> The independent peasant or handicraftsman is cut up into two persons. As owner of the means of production he is a capitalist, as laborer he is his own wage-laborer. As capitalist he therefore pays himself his wages and draws his profit on his capital; that is he exploits himself as wage-laborer, and pays himself in the surplus-value, the tribute that labor owes to capital. (Marx 1969:408, cited in Gibbon and Neocosmos 1985:177)

Inherent in the petty commodity producing household is the potential for internal stratification based on role/status differences and the *de facto* concentration of the functions of capital among particular members of the household. Research from diverse third world areas now documents what appears to be a general pattern associated with the penetration of capitalist relations of production: in traditional communities incorporated into market systems, males come to dominate market-oriented production and achieve effective "ownership" of wealth-producing resources. As a result, they can also control the products of family labor and the income earned from their sale (see Fernandez-Kelly 1981; Nash 1977; Caulfield 1981; Reiter 1975; Afonja 1981; Sacks 1974; Linares 1984; Bossen 1975, 1984). This is true even where women make substantial labor investments in the production of commodities. At the same time, women's labor in reproduction and domestic activities is devalued and unremunerated because, in capitalist systems, the "concept of labor [is] reserved for activity that produces surplus value" (i.e. cash-earning activities) (Mies 1982:2).[3]

A critical facet of this pattern of intra-household gender stratification is that differential power (i.e. decision-making and authority) in the household is derived from, and inextricably linked to, control of the means and rewards of production (as in all capitalist systems). Thus, the material foundation of male domination in commodity producing peasant households is male control of capital. This foundation may be reinforced by social institutions, religious beliefs, or ideologies which socially justify male pre-eminence.

The strength of the relationship between male dominance and male control of capital in the household is, however, weakened in peasant societies traditionally structured by bilateral principles (e.g. Tahitian society). Here, women are defined as the jural owners of some resources, and although these may be controlled by men (e.g. agricultural lands), women nevertheless have some economic clout. Michaelson and Gold-schmidt (1971) have proposed, for example, that in Latin American peasant communities male economic control is threatened by female inheritance of land and that the machismo complex is an ideological device that reinforces male dominance. Women's economic power is also bolstered where women make major labor contributions in the production of commodities and male household heads are dependent on these contributions; wives may be able to make claims to some portion of the product of their labor, although it is "owned" by men. Because male economic control is not absolute, women may also be able, at least on a situational basis, to challenge male authority when their own interests dictate it.

Peasant women's responses to their relative subordination varies with the degree to which they actively perceive themselves as subordinate and dependent, and on available mechanisms for response. They will also be influenced by women's perception of their economic interests and priorities as different from those of male household heads. Recent studies have suggested such interests frequently diverge, particularly in the area of consumption expenditures. Once household subsistence needs are met, males and females typically spend money differently: men purchase consumer luxuries (e.g. radios, liquor, bicycles) and women purchase items for the household and children (e.g. clothing, food, etc.) (see Schuster 1983; Browner 1986; Nash 1977).

Women in some peasant societies are able to pursue their own small-scale, secondary economic activities, such as craft production or local marketing, acquiring some income of their own. An important feature of these pursuits, however, is that they do not directly compete with male activities (i.e. use the same set of resources, etc.). Most often, the major input is a woman's own labor.

The *Wok Meri* movement of the Eastern Highlands of Papua New Guinea is an interesting example of women's economic response to their subordination in a strongly male-dominated society (Sexton 1984). Sexton documents how, following the introduction of coffee cultivation, wage labor, and commercial enterprises, men took over these activities and achieved control of coffee lands and earnings. She proposes that through *Wok Meri*, a highly ritualized women's savings and investment system, "women attempt to redress the imbalance they perceive between their labor contributions and their lack of control over products." (1984:146) Women save and invest small amounts of money they earn by selling vegetables and coffee, gradually building a personal store of wealth and acquiring some economic autonomy.

Women's Structural Position
in the Tubuai Household

Throughout the 1800s and early 1900s, smallholder households on Tubuai made their living from subsistence farming (taro and tree crops) and fishing, earning limited amounts of cash income by selling copra, coffee, manioc starch and fresh foods to merchants on passing schooners. Starting in the early 1960s the French/Territorial government implemented a major program for regional development and modernization, generating new economic opportunities (and social services) in rural areas. Tubuai, located 700 kilometers due south of Tahiti, was designated as a target for agricultural development and as a government administrative center for the Austral Islands group. The cultivation of European vegetables was introduced and they became important cash crops which were exported and marketed in Tahiti under the auspices of the Territorial Agricultural Service. A number of wage jobs was also created with new branches of various government agencies (Public Works, Agricultural Service, etc.) and in the new local administration. Islanders were also incorporated into the French family welfare system and families began receiving monthly welfare payments based on the number of children in the household.

The adoption of new cash crops and wage employment brought about a substantial rise in the island's standard of living and in household incomes. Relative to other outer-islands in the Territory, Tubuai is known today as a "wealthy" island. Average annual family incomes in 1987 were about $12,000–$15,000.

This prosperity has caused little change in the organization of the household economy, including the sexual division of labor and relations of production and income/resource control. The majority of contemporary Tubuai households, including high income families, continues to adhere to a generalized pattern which combines subsistence agriculture (taro and tree crops) and fishing with commodity production (for local sales or export) and wage labor (Joralemon 1986; Lockwood 1988a). Island families typically pursue a range of economic options to maximize their access to cash income, and thus increase their ability to purchase the large number of expensive, imported consumer items now deemed necessities (e.g. trucks, televisions, etc.).

Access to land continues to be regulated through a traditionally-derived, collective (familial), tenure system (Ravault 1979; Joralemon 1983). In this bilateral system, landholdings are inherited equally by all offspring as a group in each generation. Thus, each parcel is owned collectively by a group of kin which usually consists of three generations. Co-owners possess undifferentiated use and "ownership" rights. Individuals also have rights to use the familial lands of a spouse. Because at marriage couples choose to reside with approximately equal frequency on the bride's and groom's familial lands, it is not uncommon for men to plant gardens on their wive's land and vice versa.

In addition, long-standing Tahitian principles of rights to gardens and plantations remain in place. These assign rights to control garden products to the individual who created (planted) the garden or plantation, and in capitalist peasant society this control has become translated into garden "ownership." The ownership of gardens, however, is a separate jural issue from the ownership of the land itself.

Most Tubuai households (76 percent) are composed of nuclear families; the rest are composed of extended (13 percent) or composite families (11 percent).[4] Extended family households usually include an elderly grandparent or other permanently attached relative. Composite households are temporarily extended families which most often include young, married offspring (and possibly their children) who will establish their own households when they are economically able to do so. For the most part, the economic affairs of conjugal units within a composite household are kept separate, although the degree of financial dependence of units on each other varies a great deal. Average household size is six members, with a range of from one to fourteen members.

The distribution of Tubuai households in 1987 in terms of their primary economic activity and annual income is presented in Table 2. Low income households (16 percent of all households; coded L) are predominantly subsistence-oriented (i.e. they do not include an employed member and market less than $200/month in household products: taro, fish, vegetables, etc.). Households designated as low/middle income households (20 percent of all households; L/M) rely on government retirement benefits and pensions for their livelihood. These are usually families whose male household head is over the age of 60. Middle income households (35 percent of all households) are of two types: those that rely mainly on wage employment (M2) and those that market substantial quantities (> $200/month) of household products (M1). High income households (28 percent of all households) are of several types: 1) those that include a member with skilled employment (H0), 2) those in which both spouses are employed (H1), 3) those which combine wage employment with substantial market production (H2), and 4) those in which members market/export large quantities of household products (i.e. vegetables), or act as entrepreneurial middlemen and arrange vegetable

Table 2

Distribution of Households by Income and Primary Occupation (1987)*

Economic Code	Income Level/ Primary Occupation	# of Households	% of All Households
L	Low Income	46	16%
	(<$4,500/year)		
LM	Low/Middle Income	58	21%
	($2,000-16,000/year)		
	Middle Income		
	($4,500-16,000/year)		
M1	a. Major Marketer	27	10%
M2	b. Employed	72	25%
	High Income		
	($16,000-35,000/year)		
H0	a. Skilled employment	35	12%
H1	b. dual spouse employment	25	9%
H2	c. employed and markets	12	4%
H3	d. exporter/marketer	9	3%
	Totals	284	100%

*Composite households are classified by the highest income level of their constituent units.

exports to Tahiti (H3). This last specialization has appeared in only the last two years.

Intra-Household Relations of Production and Product/Income Control

In Tahitian commodity producing households, males dominate the major productive tasks, agriculture and fishing, and they also hold the majority of wage jobs on the island. In the division of labor, men plant and perform most of the work required in taro, vegetable, and tree crop (coconuts and bananas) production. Fishing has been considered, since pre-contact times, to be a specialized male task, although women do occasionally fish on the reef. Men also cook food, particularly on feast occasions, and maintain the household yard and buildings.

Women's work is concentrated in the household and includes food preparation, maintaining the house, and child care. Each morning after children are sent off to school, a woman completes her ménage (housework). Later hours in the day are taken up with food preparation for the day's large meal, sewing, weaving (pandanus), washing clothes, and work in gardens. Although men invest more labor than women in agricultural production, women's overall labor inputs are significant; men depend on their wives to contribute to numerous tasks that they, working alone, would be unable to complete. Women weed and fertilize gardens, mound potatoes, and perform general plant care (e.g. thinning carrot seedlings, tying up tomato vines, etc.).

Most jobs on the island are unskilled or semi-skilled, in maintenance, public works, or agriculture with government agencies (e.g. Travaux Publiques, Service de l'Économie Rurale, etc.). There are approximately 194 jobs on the island of which 142 (73 percent) are held by men and 52 (27 percent) are held by women. Employed men work in their gardens and fish either after hours or on weekends. The few jobs held by women are for school teachers, local administration secretaries, maids and school cooks.

Through their domination of most cash-earning activities, men are able to control the earnings from those activities. Because men plant most gardens (cash crops and subsistence crops), they "own" the products of those gardens and consider the income from their sale to be theirs. Even though women may own the land on which gardens are planted and contribute necessary labor in production, they control no part of the product, nor participate in production decisions. This pattern is not a new one. Men controlled income earned from vanilla and copra production in the Tahitian peasant household during the 1950s; this has been documented in an ethnographic reconstruction of the household economy of this era (Lockwood 1988b).

In addition to income acquired from selling garden produce, male household heads usually control income from sales of other household products, such as fish, manioc starch, and prepared foods. A limited local market in household products exists, and some families produce surpluses of these items specifically for sale to other households or to the island's schools. The schools, which prepare meals for students, are the largest bulk purchaser of household products. The 1981 purchase records of the high school show that the 25–30 individuals who regularly sold household products were all male.

Women consider themselves to be financially dependent on their husbands, and most attempt to reduce that dependence by earning their own money. Prior to the potato program, however, few economic opportunities existed for women. Many wove and sold pandanus mats, hats and satchels, sewed dresses for other women, or sold snacks. The scale of production of these items is small because of competing domestic demands on a woman's time, because the household's major productive activities (directed by male household heads) have first call on women's labor, and because local demand for these items is limited. As a result, a woman's typical monthly earnings from her own economic activities rarely exceeded $50–100.

As a result of a recent government policy shift, women are now the direct recipients of family allocations. Previously, these welfare funds (approximately $55/month/child in 1987) were deposited into an account in the name of the male household head. Islanders, who were not informed about the government's reasons for the change, attribute it to the fact that men (in their assessment) did not use the money as it was intended, to buy needed items (food, clothing, school supplies, etc.) for children, but instead spent it on liquor, gambling, and consumer luxuries. Both men and women now assert that mothers use the money appropriately and that they should receive it.

The majority of island women, then, control income from only two sources, their own small-scale economic activities and family allocations. These earnings comprise approximately 10–20 percent of all familial cash income. This percentage is slightly higher for low income households where government family allocations may be as much as 30–50 percent of total income.

Typically, Tubuai husbands and wives keep separate incomes; each considers the funds which he/she controls (i.e. from employment, sales of household products, family allocations, etc.) to belong to him or herself, as an individual. Once the family's subsistence needs are met, any remaining income is used to purchase imported luxuries, such as trucks, motorbikes, televisions, washing machines, etc. The high cost of these coveted items makes cash extremely scarce and forces families to set priorities among their diverse and competing demands. Islanders say that money is a frequent source of conflict between spouses because there is never enough of it to meet all consumer demands, priorities frequently differ, and men unilaterally control the disposition of most of the family's cash. Husbands may or may not consult wives regarding expenditures, and many Tubuai wives openly express their discontent with the extent to which they are excluded from financial decision making.

Within the Tahitian household, patterns of differential authority are closely linked to control of cash income. Finney (1973) has described this relationship in 'A'ou'a, a community on the island of Tahiti. In 'A'ou'a, located on a major road into Papeete, wage work had become the most important source of income by the early 1960s, and jobs were available for men and some women. When both spouses held jobs Finney says, "Such a division of income earning is often accompanied by a weakening of the husband's authority, and, in a few extreme cases where the wife has become the main provider in the family [i.e. the husband earned less money or did not have a job], by women of the household assuming major authority." (1973:83) He goes on to say, "This gain in authority is resisted by some men, and disagreements over family authority between a working man and his wife appear to be the cause of many recent family quarrels." (1973:84) In short, and as one of Finney's Tahitian women informants noted, "Money gives authority." (1973:84)

The strength of the relationship between income control and authority in the Tahitian household appears to be related both to the general importance of money and consumer goods, and to the weakness of other non-economic bases of authority. Male pre-eminence in the family, once justified by religious principles in pre-contact society, is, in the peasant community, backed mainly by Christian norms which designate men as family heads.

These norms can be described as weakly-entrenched because Tahitian women are socially assertive and are frequently willing to challenge male authority when in a position to do so. This is true to the extent that Oliver's description of ancient Tahitian women as ". . . anything but a passive, deferential, submissive lot; certainly not in domestic matters and often not in 'public' affairs either," (1974:604) could be applied equally to contemporary peasant women. Tubuai women's assertiveness is readily observable, for example, at the frequently volatile meetings of the island's agricultural cooperative where women are just as likely as men to be outspoken verbal advocates of their opinions on coop affairs.

Tubuai Women and the Potato Cultivation Project

It was into this context of intra-household relations of production and consumption that the potato program, the most recent phase of vegetable cash-cropping on Tubuai, was introduced in the late 1970s. In 1979 a small group of about 30 male farmers signed up to cultivate the new crop during the three month winter (June–August) season. By 1987, 279 farmers (93 women and 186 men representing 192 households) were participating in the program, and 68 percent of all island households included one or more potato planters.

Between 1980 and 1987 the structure of program participation changed dramatically. Whereas in the early years (1980–1981) most potato planters were male household heads of middle and high income, members of "market-oriented" households (Joralemon 1986), by 1987 potato cul-

Table 3

Distribution of Households of Male and Female Potato Cultivators
by Income/Occupation

Economic Code	Income/ Occupation	Female Cultivators' Households*	Male Cultivators' Households	No Potatoes	Totals
L	Low Income/ Subsistence	18	23	5	46
LM	Low/Middle: retired	13	10	35	58
M1	Middle/ Marketer	3	18	6	27
M2	Middle/ Employed	25	33	14	72
HO	High/skilled Employment	9	13	13	35
H1	High/dual employment	4	5	16	25
H2	High/employed and markets	5	5	2	12
H3	Exporter/ marketer	3	5	1	9
	Totals	80	112	92	284
	% of all Households	28%	39%	32%	100%

*These households may also include a male cultivator.

tivation had become a widespread activity of both men and women, who represented households of all income levels and occupational specializations.[5] Only retired, elderly families and those in which both spouses were employed had a low rate of involvement. The distribution of male and female potato cultivators among households of different socioeconomic types is presented in Table 3.

Most households (67 percent) include only one potato planter, either the male household head (in 46 percent of all cultivating households), wife, a female household head who is widowed or separated, or other household member (see Table 4). The other third of all households include two or more planters; 9 percent of potato planting households had husbands and wives who grew their own independent gardens. In other cases, other household members (e.g. a father and an adult son, or a widow and her son-in-law) planted independently.

Table 4

Potato Cultivators in Tubuai Households (1987)

Planter(s)	Number of Households	Frequency
One Planter		
Male household head only	88	46%
Wife only	31	16%
Female household head only (widowed/separated/divorced)	10	5%
Other household member (i.e., neither the male household head, nor his wife)	13	7%
Multiple Planters		
Husband and Wife	18	9%
Male household head and other member (i.e., not his wife)	20	11%
Wife and other member (i.e., not the male household head)	4	2%
Female Household head and other member	4	2%
Other household members	4	2%
Totals	192	100%

The widespread involvement of islanders in potato farming can be attributed to the manner in which the program has been implemented, as well as to the availability of agricultural land and flexible tenure principles. The program was set up in such a way that potential obstacles to participation, particularly access to capital and labor, would be removed or minimized. While this has made cultivation feasible for many segments of the population, it has particularly benefited women who, for structural reasons, have substantially less access to these factors of production (capital and labor) than men.

To plant, a farmer simply signs up with the Agricultural Service and all necessary inputs, including seed potatoes, fertilizers, and insecticides are provided (at subsidized prices) and are charged against an account in that person's name. Capital investments are not required to start cultivation. When a farmer harvests his/her crop it is sold to a local development agency (Société de Dévéloppement d'Agriculture et de la

Peche/SDAP) which then subtracts the accrued charges from the total value of the crop.

The Agricultural Service and SDAP also make cultivation machinery (operated by employees of the agency), including a tractor, bulldozer and planting/harvesting equipment, available to islanders at subsidized prices. Access to this equipment greatly reduces the labor expenditures required for land clearing and preparation and for planting and harvesting, the most labor-intensive phases of production.

Women's participation in the program is also facilitated by their access to land through the bilateral, collective land tenure system. Women have rights to use any parcel in which they, as individuals, have inherited co-ownership rights, as well as rights to use any parcel in which a husband has co-ownership rights. These rights may be activated at any time, even if a women has not previously planted her own gardens. Although pressure on land is increasing, the average scale of potato cultivation is small (about 0.4 hectares) and land is still sufficiently abundant that, in general, access to land is not a factor which constrains either male or female farmers (see Joralemon 1983; Lockwood 1988a).

Once a woman has decided to plant potatoes, her production strategy differs little from that of male planters, except that women cultivate on a smaller scale, approximately 70 percent that of men (see Table 1). The average scale of cultivation for men is about 0.5 hectares for men and 0.3 hectares for women. Women planters say that their daily responsibilities for maintenance of the household and child care interfere with potato cultivation and that they must plant on a small scale. Domestic tasks are considered to be women's work and are rarely assumed by men. Even if employed, men are able to devote sizable periods of otherwise un-distracted time to their fields during afternoons and on weekends.

At this scale of cultivation (0.3 hectares/800 kilograms of seed potatoes planted) a woman will be able to earn approximately $1,000 profit in a moderately successful season. All planters, however, encounter cultivation risks and there have been several years when many farmers did poorly. If a farmer cannot repay the cultivation costs incurred, he/she goes into debt to the agency which finances the program. Although such debts can usually be paid back in the next season, women, whose access to capital is significantly limited, have greater difficulty getting out of debt than men.

Women Potato Planters and Their Households

Female potato planters are a diverse group of all ages, marital statuses, and family situations (see Tables 5 and 6). The typical female cultivator

Table 5

Family Structure and Size of Households of Female Cultivators and
Male Cultivators (N = 191)

	Family Structure			Household Size			
	Nuclear	Extended	Composite	1-3	4-6	7-9	10-14
Households of Female Cultivators	55	11	14	9	38	25	8
Households of Male Cultivators	84	14	13	20	55	23	13
Totals	139	25	27	29	93	48	21

Family Structure: Chi-Square = 1.45, p = .4833.
Household Size: Chi-Square = 3.162, p = .3058.

Table 6

Households of Male and Female Cultivators: Stage in the Developmental
Cycle of the Family (N=191)

Stage in the Family Cycle	Households of Female Cultivators*	Households of Male Cultivators	Totals
A	22	42	64
B	33	40	73
C	10	16	26
Composite Households	15	13	28
Totals	80	111	191

*Households may also include a male cultivator.

(Chi-Square = 3.50; p = .3195)

A = Household heads are less than 40 years of age; still
reproductively active; household includes small children.

B = Household heads are middle-aged (40-60 years); children are
teenagers; may include small adopted grandchildren and/or
adult children's young spouses.

C = Household heads are over 60 years of age; may include small
adopted children and/or adult children with their families.

is, however, a married woman between the ages of 20 and 40 who has small or teenaged children.

There are no major socioeconomic characteristics, such as income level, occupation, family structure, etc., which distinguish the households of male and female cultivators. Because the potato program has removed the structural obstacles, particularly access to capital and labor, which constrain farmers, one would expect that male and female cultivators would come from households of virtually all socioeconomic types and they do. There are, however, minor differences in male and female households that shed some light on the structural constraints which affect men and women cultivators differently.

There is no statistically significant difference between female and male cultivators' households in family structure or household size (Table 5), or in stage in the developmental cycle of the family (Table 6). However, as the data in Table 6 show, "young" families (developmental stage A) produce slightly fewer female planters than expected, but the numbers of female planters (relative to males) increases as families mature. Reproductively active women with small children are hampered in their ability to plant potatoes; this, however, is not a significant constraint and 34 percent of all female cultivators are of this type.

Households that are slightly larger than the average, those with seven to nine members, are more likely to have a female planter than smaller households (see Table 5). This does not hold, however, for the largest families (10–14 members), who produce fewer female cultivators. Composite households produce more female than male planters, the only case for which this is true (Table 6).

There is also no statistically significant difference between the households of male and female planters in total income and primary economic occupation (see Table 3). Although low/middle income households (LM) have the lowest rate of program participation, these households have more female than male cultivators. In most of these cases, males are over the age of 60 and retired.

One can also see in Table 3 that households in which both spouses are employed also have a low rate of potato cultivation. This raises the question of how employment affects potential male and female cultivators. In 1987, 42 percent of all employed males (52/142) cultivated potatoes, whereas only 15 percent of employed females cultivated (8/52). I believe that women cannot successfully combine their domestic responsibilities, employment, and potato cultivation, but that men can mix employment and potato cultivation.

While employed men (M2 and H2 households—see Table 3) are often potato cultivators, their wives also have a greater than expected rate of participation. In fact, some of the households with the highest rates of female cultivation (about 36 percent) include those in which males are employed, but females are not. At the same time, households which have the lowest frequency of female cultivation (about 11 percent) are those in which the male household head is a major commodity producer/ marketer (M1 households). Put together, these two facts suggest that when men are major producers, women will not be, and that when men are not major producers (because they are employed), women may be. In the former case, women's cultivation would compete directly with men's productive activities for the same set of household resources (land, labor, etc.).

While the factors that have just been discussed tell us something about the various structural constraints upon women, they tell us little about why some women are motivated to plant, but not others. Because so many obstacles to potato cultivation have been removed, the majority of island women are theoretically able to plant if they choose to do so.

A representative sample (N=45) of women planters was interviewed regarding their household situations, their motives for planting, and their economic goals. It became apparent that women planters are of two types: 1) non-married, female household heads (widowed, separated or divorced) who are supporting their families (N=16), and 2) married women (N=60) (see Table 7). The first group cultivates out of economic necessity; 81 percent of the households of these women are in the low/ low-middle income ranges, and potatoes are the household's major source of income.

The forces driving married women planters are substantially different. As Table 7 shows, many of these planters come from middle and high income households. Most married women described their decision to plant as one they had made independently and as an act of personal volition. Some mentioned specific consumption goals, such as the purchase of a sewing or washing machine, as the motivating factor, while others stated that they wanted to earn money for general household expenses. Consistent themes in female cultivator's comments, however, were: 1) their desire to have their own money which they could spend as they wished and 2) their desire to be less financially dependent on their husbands. Some women expressed their disapproval of how their husbands spent money, and others explained that their husbands refused to purchase (or put off the purchase of) items for them, the house, or the children.

Clearly, many married women who cultivate potatoes perceive their economic priorities to be different from their husband's and believe that they are excluded from household financial decision-making. By earning their own money they can achieve some personal financial autonomy. These attitudes, as well as sufficient drive to redress the situation by independently cultivating potatoes, appear to be the most significant

Table 7

Female Cultivators' Marital Status and Household Incomes/Occupations (1987)

Household Economic Code	Married*	Single Female Household Heads	Totals
L	13	8	21
LM	12	5	17
M1	5	0	5
M2	21	3	24
H0	6	0	6
H1	3	0	3
H2	6	0	6
H3	3	0	3
Totals	69	16	85

*This category includes nine cultivators who are single daughters or grandaughters of the household; there are actually 60 married women in this group.

factors which distinguish female cultivators from non-cultivators. The forces which move women to plant, then, emanate from within the household and reflect conditions unique to women's structurally subordinate position there. If island women were not able to retain independent control of their potato earnings, there would be fewer participating in this program.

Although these may be women's motives, husbands do not impede a wife's decision to cultivate, recognizing that this is a decision which she can make and carry through on her own. Most husbands cooperate with a potato planting wife and will work with her in her fields during the most labor intensive phases of planting and harvesting; women, however, perform the bulk of the required labor. Husbands consider a wife's potato field to be "her affair" and will refer questions about it to her.

In some cases husbands do not cooperate with their wives. This is most common when both a husband and wife each plant their own separate fields during the same season. In 1987 this happened in 18 households, or for 20 percent of all women planters. Separate cultivation by spouses is a clear statement of overt divergence of economic interests, and in some cases, active economic conflict.

Implications

The rapid movement of Tubuai women into potato cultivation at a rate almost double that of men, as well as their strong motivation to earn their own money, suggests that women will continue to be major participants in this development program. The question of greatest importance is what impact this phenomenon will have on intra-household gender stratification, the organization of the household economy, and on the development process itself.

Women cultivators' autonomous control of income gives them some financial independence which undermines male authority in the Tahitian household. But Tubuai women have always earned and controlled small amounts of money and this has not previously constituted a challenge to male dominance on the island. A challenge would be posed, however, if a wife's income were greater than her husband's. As mentioned above, Finney noted that in 'A'ou'a, ". . . cases where the wife has become the main provider in the family" were associated with ". . . women of the household assuming major authority." (1973:83) What is of relevance, then, about women's control of income (from whatever source) is not whether or not women control any money, but how much they control relative to male household heads.

Women's cultivation and independent earnings will therefore have different economic, and thus political, ramifications in households of different socioeconomic types. In the vast majority of island households, male household heads are either employed or they produce and market household products. In these households, average annual income is about $15,000 and woman's potato profits (about $1,000) constitute only 6 percent of the total. Even in low-middle income households where the major source of income is a male's retirement benefits (average $8,000/ year), a woman's potato earnings constitute only 11 percent of all income.

It is only in low income households (16 percent of all households; average annual income is less than $4,500) that a woman's potato profits, plus the funds she controls through family allocations, might be the bulk of the family's total cash income. If this happens, a wife can become the main provider in the household and exercise considerable authority. Because men hold most wage jobs and "own" gardens and thus household products, they will continue to control the vast majority of all household income. Because women's earnings are such a small proportion of total income for most families, one can predict that women's potato cultivation will have little affect on present patterns of male authority and intra-household gender relations.

It is unlikely that women will expand production and earn what might be significant sums of money relative to husbands' earnings. While many women have access to sufficient agricultural land to expand, they do not have access to sufficient labor, mainly because of the extensive pre-existing calls on a woman's own labor. Supervision of extensive potato fields would greatly diminish a woman's ability to perform her domestic duties. Women recognize this constraint and are for the most part content with the small sums of money they earn from potato cultivation. Most believe that the acquisition of a sewing machine or extra money for household expenses is a satisfactory and sufficient accomplishment for one potato season.

Although it appears that women's participation in potato cultivation will not alter the present structure of male domination and female subordination in the Tubuaian commodity producing peasant household, it has put more land under cultivation and raised overall levels of production. This has generated additional income for island families and augmented familial consumption levels.

The long term potential for women's participation in the program is, however, not clear. As more and more farmers adopt potato cultivation pressure on agricultural lands will increase. As land availability declines, farmers will begin to compete for land. It is difficult to predict what might happen if men and women were placed in the position of competing with each other for land. While women's rights in land are theoretically equivalent to those of men, it is probable that because men dominate production and possess overarching authority in the household, their demands for land would receive priority. While at the present time the number of female planters is increasing, a critical point of land scarcity may be reached in coming years and their number may start to decline rapidly.

The increase in the number of new, small-scale planters (mainly women and low income cultivators) over the last few years has also placed strain on the resources of the agricultural agencies which organize the project. Tractors and bulldozers are insufficient to deal with the number of fields which must be prepared for planting each season. Agricultural officials in Papeete and on Tubuai attribute this strain to the proliferation of what they call "non-serious" planters, i.e. small farmers whose livelihoods do not depend on potato cultivation but who earn small amounts of money each season. According to these criteria, women form a large contingent of these "non-serious" cultivators. Officials hint that if cutbacks must be made, these planters may be discouraged from cultivating. In short, as the program expands and resources (including land) become scarce, female participants' situation may deteriorate much more rapidly than that of men.

Conclusions

Two conclusions can be drawn from this analysis. The first is that in many cases it is not household units, but individual members of the household, who respond to new economic opportunities. Because peasant households are differentiated internally, particularly along lines of gender, household members are not equivalent actors, nor are they equally endowed in their ability to make economic decisions and utilize household resources. Moreover, one member's economic decisions need not necessarily reflect the interests or economic priorities of other household members.

Thus, in order to understand responses to development by various household members, we must analyze the structure of intra-household political and economic relations and document the conditions under which different categories of members (e.g. husbands, wives, etc.) operate. Only then is it possible to isolate the factors which differentially shape the economic behavior of those categories of members and to assess the implications of that behavior for relative status in the household and community.

The second conclusion concerns the broader issue of the relationship between women's participation in development and their social status. There is substantial evidence that women's status in a society is related in part to the degree to which they participate in production and control the distribution of valued products (see Friedl 1975). For this reason, it often believed that if women can achieve a greater role in development this will improve their overall socioeconomic position and status relative to men.

On Tubuai, women have achieved an important role in development, but this will have little affect on the present structure of gender stratification or on patterns of male domination in the household. Women may achieve a limited degree of personal financial autonomy and this is certainly worthwhile, but it will not alter (in any significant way) women's position of economic and political subordination. Only structural changes related to a more egalitarian distribution of control over the means of production and income among household members can reduce that subordination.

Notes

1. Fieldwork was conducted on Tubuai in 1980–1981, 1985 and 1987. I would like to gratefully acknowledge a research grant from the National Science Foundation (#BNS 8507861) which supported field research in 1985 and 1987. The data which form the basis of this paper were gathered as part of a larger project concerned with the relationship between agricultural development and

the growth of social stratification on Tubuai. I would also like to thank the
Haut-Commissaire de la République en Polynésie Française for permission to
pursue the research, as well as the staff of the Office de la Recherche Scientifique
et Technique Outre-Mer (ORSTOM, Papeete, Tahiti) and of Le Service de
l'Économie Rurale (Papeete and Tubuai) for their help and guidance.

2. According to a government census, there are approximately 330 households
on Tubuai. About 30 of these belong to French residents (government officials,
teachers, the island's doctor, etc.) or to families from Tahiti who work for the
administration and are residing on the island temporarily. I was able to gather
socioeconomic census data on 292 "Tubuai" households in 1987. These household
data form the basis for the discussion presented here.

3. Surplus value is defined (following Roseberry 1976:50) as the difference
between the value of the product of labor (usually measured as market value)
and the value of the labor power that produced the product. Capitalists retain
the surplus value while labor receives only wages, the market value of its labor.
Women's domestic/reproductive labor creates no marketable product and thus
no surplus value in a capitalist system.

4. Information on Tubuai households was gathered during 1987 during an
island-wide socioeconomic census. A household is defined as that group of
individuals which occupies the same eating and sleeping quarters, sharing a
common set of economic resources and pooling (for joint benefit) a least a
portion of products produced by members.

5. "Market-oriented" households are defined as those who regularly market
household products (> $200/month) and rely on this as the primary source
of income.

References Cited

Afonja, Simi. 1981. "Changing Modes of Production and the Sexual Division
    of Labor Among the Yoruba." *Signs* 7(2): 299–313.
Bossen, Laurel. 1975. "Women in Modernizing Societies." *American Ethnologist*
    2(4): 587–601.
———. 1984. *The Redivision of Labor: Women and Economic Choice in Four
    Guatemalan Communities.* Albany: State University of New York Press.
Browner, Carol. 1986. "Gender Roles and Social Change: A Mexican Case Study."
    Ethnology 25(2): 89–106.
Caulfield, Mina. 1981. "Equality, Sex, and the Mode of Production," in G.
    Berremen (ed.), *Social Inequality: Comparative and Developmental Approaches.*
    New York: Academic Press. Pp. 201–219.
Charlton, Sue Ellen. 1984. *Women in Third World Development.* Boulder: Westview
    Press.
Cook, Scott. 1982. *Zapotec Stoneworkers: The Dynamics of Rural Simple Commodity
    Production in Modern Mexican Capitalism.* Washington, D.C.: University Press
    of America.
Fernandez-Kelly, Maria. 1981. "The Sexual Division of Labor, Development, and
    Women's Status." *Current Anthropology* 22(4): 414–419.

Finney, Ben. 1973. *Polynesian Peasants and Proletarians.* Cambridge, Ma.: Schenkman.

Gibbon, P. and M. Neocosmos. 1985. "Some Problems in the Political Economy of 'African Socialism'," in H. Bernstein and B. Campbell (eds.), *Contradictions in Accumulation in Africa.* Beverly Hills: Sage. Pp. 153–206.

Joralemon, Victoria Lockwood. 1983. "Collective Land Tenure and Agricultural Development: A Polynesian Case." *Human Organization* 42(2): 95–105.

––––––. 1986a. "Development and Inequity: The Case of Tubuai, A Welfare Economy in Rural French Polynesia." *Human Organization* 45(4): 283–295.

Lockwood, Victoria Joralemon. 1988a. "Development, French Neocolonialism, and the Structure of the Tubuai Economy." *Oceania* 58(3): 176–192.

––––––. 1988b. "Capitalist Development and the Socioeconomic Position of Tahitian Peasant Women." *Journal of Anthropological Research* 44(3): 263–285.

Linares, O. 1984. "Households Among the Diola of Senegal: Should Norms Enter by the Front or the Back Door?" in R. Netting, R. Wilk, and E. Arnould (eds.), *Households: Comparative and Historical Studies of the Domestic Group.* Berkeley: University of California Press. Pp. 407–445.

Marx, Karl. 1969. *Theories of Surplus Value, Part I.* Moscow: Progress.

Michaelson, E.J. and W. Goldschmidt. 1971. "Female Roles and Male Dominance Among Peasants." *Southwestern Journal of Anthropology* 27: 330–352.

Mies, Maria. 1982. "The Dynamics of the Sexual Division of Labor and the Integration of Rural Women into the World Market," in L. Beneria (ed.), *Women and Development: The Sexual Division of Labor in Rural Societies.* New York: Praeger. Pp. 1–28.

Nash, June. 1977. "Women and Development: Dependency and Exploitation." *Development and Change* 8: 161–182.

Oliver, Douglas. 1974. *Ancient Tahitian Society* (3 volumes). Honolulu: University Press of Hawaii.

––––––. 1981. *Two Tahitian Villages: A Study in Comparison.* Honolulu: The Institute for Polynesian Studies.

Ravault, Francois. 1979. *Le Régime Foncier de la Polynésie Française.* Centre ORSTOM de Papeete. Paris: Office de la Recherche Scientifique et Technique Outre-Mer.

Reiter, Rayna. 1975. "Men and Women in the South of France: Public and Private Domains," in R. Rapp (ed.), *Toward an Anthropology of Women.* New York: Monthly Review Press. Pp. 252–282.

Roseberry, William. 1976. "Rent, Differentiation, and the Development of Capitalism Among Peasants." *American Anthropologist* 78(1): 45–58.

Sacks, Karen. 1974. "Engels Revisited: Women, the Organization of Production, and Private Property," in M. Rosaldo and L. Lamphere (eds.), *Woman, Culture and Society.* Stanford: Stanford University Press. Pp. 207–222.

––––––. 1979. *Sisters and Wives.* Westport: Greenwood Press.

Schuster, Ilsa. 1982. "Recent Research on Women in Development." *Journal of Development Studies* 18(4): 511–535.

Sexton, Lorraine. 1984. "Pigs, Pearlshells, and 'Women's Work': Collective Response to Change in Highland Papua New Guinea," in D. O'Brien and S. Tiffany (eds.), *Rethinking Women's Roles: Perspectives From the Pacific.* Berkeley: University of California Press. Pp. 120–152.

Smith, Carol. 1984. "Forms of Production in Practice." *Journal of Peasant Studies* 11:200–221.

11

Smallholders, Householders, Freeholders: Why the Family Farm Works Well Worldwide

Robert McC. Netting

An overwhelming percentage of the world's farmers, perhaps 80 percent by one FAO estimate (Wilken 1987), are smallholders with one or two hectares (perhaps 5 acres) of land under cultivation at any one time (Ruthenberg 1985). They produce much of their own subsistence as well as some food or fiber to sell, supplying labor largely from their own households, and possessing continuing, heritable rights to their own resources. These are *not* characteristics of all agriculturalists. They do not apply to shifting cultivators, practicing long-fallow or slash-and-burn farming where land is still plentiful and population density low in some parts of the humid tropics. It doesn't fit herders, whether the nomadic pastoralists of East Africa or the ranchers of Texas. And, for reasons we will examine, it doesn't match the geographical and social relations of dry wheat monocropping, sugar cane haciendas, cotton plantations with slaves, or California agribusinesses. Rather the farming system we are concerned with is *intensive agriculture,* producing relatively high annual or multicrop yields from permanent fields that are seldom or never rested, with fertility restored and maintained by practices such as deep tillage, crop diversification and rotation, animal husbandry, fertilization, land surface modification such as ridging or terracing, irrigation, and drainage. We are not talking about amber waves of grain but about gardens and orchards, rice paddies and *chinampas.*

The small intensive farm as an economic enterprise is closely related to the form and functioning of the resident household social unit. Definable elements of productive activities, labor mobilization, consumption, and tenure cohere in a pattern that recurs in time and space. Unlike the preceding closely observed ethnographic cases in this volume, this chapter will adopt an ethnological stance, suggesting the possibility of generalization through comparison. Rather than testing the bounds of standard definitions of the household and rejecting stereotypes of harmoniously pooled resources or egalitarian gender roles (Clark, this volume), I will treat the morphology of domestic units as relatively unproblematic and emphasize the common characteristics of a widespread and familiar type of production that regularly occurs in a household context. I will argue that the distinctive qualities of work, sharing, management, and transmission that smallholder farming implies make the family household a more effective, utilitarian institution than the agricultural business, the commune, or the estate. None of these groups are immune from internal conflict, inequity, or inefficiency, but the benefits of family farming as an enduring solution to problems of production and reproduction in an environment of scarce resources are often overlooked. By and large the household does work, even when, as is often the case, it is not one big, happy, non-authoritarian family.

The Smallholder and the Practice of Intensive Agriculture

I am going to contend that smallholders practicing intensive agriculture present a set of cross-cultural regularities in population, land use, and social organization despite tremendous variability in local environment, technology, culture, and politics. These common features form a definable cultural ecosystem with its own evolutionary patterns and probabilities of change. Our smallholders are alike in that for all of them land is a scarce good, agrarian production per unit area is relatively high and fields are permanent, work is hard and long, and the farmer has continuing rights to the land and its fruits.

Not all food producers by any means are intensive cultivators. We can predict that we will find them in situations where arable land is limited and the demand is greater than the supply. The demand may arise from the pressure of population on resources, as in Ester Boserup's (1965) now classic model of agricultural intensification. This farming system may appear anywhere that rural population densities reach 150 to 250 per square mile (Netting n.d.). A land shortage may also result from a demand for market production and cash crops (Turner and Brush 1987). On the other hand, there are still places in Africa where shifting cultivation with long fallow regeneration of the forest holds sway. Slash-and-burn farmers like the Tiv of Nigeria, could expand when virgin land became unproductive after a few years of use. They told Paul and Laura Bohannan (1968) that they had no boundaries, only arguments, and they obviously preferred fighting to the switch to a more stable farming adaptation. In fact, our own Midwest was won by some rather shiftless shifting cultivators. Abe Lincoln's father went from one wilderness clearing to another, blaming bad luck but getting crops with a minimum of effort and moving when the hunting declined. Lincoln's famous rail splitting fenced fields from pastures, establishing permanent farms with some of the extra labor his father avoided. Only when a frontier fills up is the farmer constrained from making the obvious (and economically rational) choice of seeking new fertile land. When there is no place to go and one's own children must compete with each other and the neighbors for a homestead, there will inevitably be a settling in and putting down of roots. Smallholders may not want to be small and stable, but the prevalence of people has closed off the options of unfettered growth and easy migration.

Once fixed in place and competing for a dwindling supply of land the cultivator must intensify, that is, raise the production per unit area over the long run. Even if one year's yield is less than from the same plot under slash-and-burn, minimizing or eliminating fallow means that there is a crop every year. Further intensification keeps the land in continuous production, as in the triple cropping of transplanted rice in some Asian irrigated paddy systems. I once watched Portuguese farmers cut and bind the sheaves of winter rye from a vine-bordered terrace, plow the area with oxen, break the clods by hand, and plant the summer crop of corn. The land was out of use, technically fallow, for about half an hour.

The knowledge and techniques of intensification may be complex and highly integrated, but they are not necessarily reliant on modern science, machines, or sources of energy. In fact, plots that are small and irregular may cause a farmer to down-size from a tractor and metal plow to a scratch plow and donkey and finally to a hand-held hoe or spade. Does simple technology mean that yields go down? On the contrary, innumerable studies show an *inverse* relation between farm size and productivity per unit land (Bachman and Christensen 1967; Ellis 1988: 191–209). Smallholders regularly get higher and more dependable yields from their plots than do the large farmers in the same environment. They do this with an amazing bag of techniques and an expert, practical grasp of their own farms' micro-ecology.

How Intensive Cultivators Do It: Techniques, Labor, and Tenure

To raise total production, reduce competition from weeds and pests, and limit risks of seasonally-specific crop failure, intensive agriculturalists may intercrop plants with different planting and harvest times and with different spatial niches from below-ground tubers, through vegetable bushes, stalky cereals, and climbing vines, to trees that stratify the air space (Stoler 1981). The Kofyar on the Jos Plateau in Nigeria plant early millet with later maturing sorghum, and ground-hugging cowpeas under oil palm trees in their homestead farms, and they provide a dependable subsistence for a family from about an acre and a half (Netting 1968). To do this on a permanent basis, the soil must be thoroughly tilled—turned over, ridged, mounded, or levelled—and organic material system-atically restored to the soil. Livestock manure is the intensive cultivator's gold, but concentrating it requires penning and stall-feeding the animals, providing them with absorbent bedding, and hauling the composted material to the field. The Kofyar do it with goats, but they also collect and use the ash from their cooking fires. The alpine Swiss (Netting 1981) used pine needles from the forest floor to supplement straw in their cow barns and then raked, dried, and recycled the compost that remained on the soil surface. The collection and distribution of night soil from Chinese cities to the country is an age-old and still thriving enterprise.

Water, another requisite for plant growth, must also be tapped or impounded, controlled, divided, applied in precise, scheduled amounts, and drained for maximum crop yields. The Swiss watered their hay meadows from systems of ditches, the most recent of which was built in 1280. Irrigation as exemplified by the serried slopes of Ifugao rice terraces in highland Luzon (Conklin 1980) exhibits intensification at its most dramatic, ponding water that brings dissolved nutrients, providing an even bed for precisely spaced transplanted seedlings, and preventing erosion.

The success of smallholder cultivation is not only its large and dependable production but its ecological continuity and conservation, its *sustainability,* in the currently popular phrase. No intensive cultivator can afford to degrade his resources for short-term gains. The Swiss who packed soil from the foot of their gardens to the top of the slope every spring could bring the wrath of the entire community on any citizen careless enough to cause a landslide from an untended irrigation ditch, and overgrazing of the communal alp was prevented by local regulations inscribed on parchment in 1483 and still observed. Peasant smallholders who ruined their fragile resources were not merely convicted by morality and law; they and their posterity were as good as dead.

The skills and devices of agricultural intensification appear worldwide, reflecting similar solutions to the problems of populations utilizing and conserving scarce resources, but it is less evident what else these techniques have in common—they all require more *time, labor,* and *management* than extensive means of food production. *The cost of economizing on resources is expending more energy in production.* We, who see evolutionary progress as essentially labor-saving, may forget that what smallholders do is a lot of work. More people, including women and children, have tasks on the farm, they work more hours per day and more days per year, and they do it with care, attention, and discipline. The marginal returns on this labor may actually decline. In comparison, shifting cultivators have it easy. One group in Cameroon produce the staple cassava for a family's needs by just 16 days of hoeing each by the husband and wife (Burnham 1980). In contrast, people with livestock and poultry must feed, water, milk, gather eggs, and possibly clean stalls *every day* or twice a day. The "chores" as they are called on American farms don't go away, and the farmers can't take holidays. Our own proverbial wisdom deals with seasonal labor bottlenecks, "Make hay while the sun shines," and diligence, "Early to bed and early to rise . . ." A Bangladeshi man who puts in an average of 3,487 hours a year (3,797 to 3,844 hours for females) would undoubtedly voice similar sentiments (Wallace et al. 1987). One estimate has intensive farming systems demanding some 3.5 hours more work per day for men and 4 hours for women as compared to extensive cultivation under conditions of low population pressure (Minge-Klevana 1980).

When people want to further raise production because there is a new mouth to feed in the household or because more cash-crops are desired, they schedule their time and allocate more duties so as to increase their labor. Kofyar farmers introduced yams and rice into a traditional system of grains and legumes, filling in troughs between peak demands for cereal planting and harvesting and using formerly slack dry season periods for yam mounding and digging the ripe tubers (Stone et al. 1988). Most field tasks are done by men and women working side by side, and total farm labor input is about 50/50. A Kofyar adult puts in an average of 1,549 hours over the 50 weeks we kept records. This is almost three times as much as a Hausa male farmer in a somewhat drier but similar environment, and Hausa women in Islamic seclusion do almost no agricultural fieldwork. Substituting animal traction and the plow for the hoe may reduce person-hours in the field but it increases herding and fodder-crop labor and enjoins the production of a surplus to buy replacement draft animals, their barns, and the plow or other implements they draw. The diversity of crop and livestock activities means that smallholders are almost always busy, and, if they lack sufficient land to occupy them, they must intensify *out of agriculture,* devoting labor to crafts, service occupations, trade, or wage work for others. Part-time farming with some household members engaged in petty commodity production or off-farm paid labor is probably the rule rather than the exception among peasant smallholders (Poats et al., this volume; Lockwood, this volume).

Intensive cultivation also implies something about tenure and property, what the smallholder *holds.* This may not be private property like deeded land with a money price and rights of permanent sale or alienation. But it does mean that the smallholder has some continuing, secure rights to the means of production. If there are returns to extra labor and superior skill in intensive agriculture, the worker who makes the effort and has the ability must receive tangible rewards in increased products and higher value resources. Intensive agriculturalists invest their time and energy in soil improvement and conservation, in orchards that may not bear for years, and in the infrastructure of irrigation works, roads, fences, and barns that support future yields and reduce the risks of environmental fluctuations. Is it any wonder that developed farmland is the smallholder's most cherished possession, the goal of youth, the shelter of age, and the hope of progeny? Valuable property rights are transmitted across generations, and the primal, potentially tragic, drama of peasant life is inheritance or retirement with its tensions and conflicts.

It is not a testimony to individual selfishness or greed that people invest their energy and plan for the future most prudently when they are assured of a commensurate return from the land or livestock that they tend. Therefore we find that scarce land that can be intensively utilized to give adequate, reliable crops and that can be kept in production for long periods is held by individuals or households (Netting 1982a; Feder and Noronha 1987). Rights of tenure are asserted and defended by intensive agriculturalists in both states and stateless polities, whether under courts or customary laws, in ancient and in modern societies. In the same Swiss village where vineyards, gardens, grainfields, and meadows are carefully marked properties, jealously guarded, reverently inherited, and occasionally sold for many francs per square meter, other extensively used lands with low production like the alp and the forest are administered by the community (Netting 1976). Private and communal property exist side by side over centuries of history, but it is land use and the logic of smallholder intensification that dictate the form of land tenure.

Claiming to find significant similarities among smallholder intensive cultivators across cultures and through time may seem an act of radical (or reactionary) typologizing because it blurs the established categories of political-economy, Marxism, and cultural evolutionism. There is in this formulation no industrial revolution as a great divide between traditional and modern. There are recognizable smallholders in kin-ordered, tributary, and capitalist modes of production (Wolf 1982). They frequently combine individual and communal ownership of resources and subsistence with market activities. While using their own means of production in tools and land as partly self-sufficient households, they both sell and buy labor power. Their surpluses may stay largely at home as replacement and ceremonial funds or they may be removed in part as funds of rent and taxation (Wolf 1966). They seldom voluntarily under-produce, use household labor unintensively, or rely on the largesse of Big Men or patrons as the "domestic mode of production" would imply (Sahlins 1972, but cf. Minge-Klevana 1977; Roseberry 1985).[1] And, despite constant attrition as some former farmers become city-dwellers or factory workers or a rural proletariat, smallholders do not go away. It is the elements of this distinctive and persistent agro-economic system with its particular blend of household labor organization and control of resources that we wish to elucidate.

Why Small Is Beautiful, and Less Is More

But what does sustainable, labor-intensive agriculture on scarce land with definable rights of tenure have to do with little farms? Can't the same agrarian technological and economic system be carried on at any scale from the widow's cabbage patch to the feudal manor, the plantation, or the collective farm? No! It doesn't work that well. This is true despite the fact that we prefer bigness, we idolize growth, and the economies of scale are a glib article of faith. Big agriculture is appropriate, no doubt, where land is abundant, energy cheap, and labor expensive, in every respect the opposite of those areas where intensive cultivation is dominant. Some types of agriculture, even with modern methods, remain land extensive. Cattle ranching in semi-arid zones is one, and a "ranchette" is an oxymoron. Growing dry winter wheat in Sicily or Andalusia or North Dakota may require alternate years of fallow and have highly variable yields, so that only a latifundia can produce enough in good years to tide the owner over bad ones. Sugar cane gives phenomenal caloric yields, but efficient milling demands large areas that grow nothing else in a highly regimented fashion. Modern estates and large farms may make do with little labor, but they must pour in gas, fertilizer, pesticides, and machines to the point where according to David Pimentel (1973) U.S. corn cultivation returns less than three units for every unit of energy input, and the American farm as a whole has the negative energy ratio of ten calories expended for every calorie produced (Evenari 1968). And the quality of the land gets worse.

Where big, industrial agriculture dependent on a world market and purchased inputs has become dominant, the "goals of food system stability and sustainability that prevail in most other subsistence adaptations are superseded by a growth ethic based on constant innovation," as Peggy Barlett (1987a) points out. Resource mining with top soil erosion, ground water exhaustion, and chemical pollution mean that industrial methods use resources faster than they can be replaced, and at some point the system will have to move toward a less energy-intensive adaptation. Large-scale agriculture, far from being an invariant model of progressive development, may, in a crowded world, be a prescription for extensive, declining production, higher energy costs, more risk and volatility, and environmental degradation.

What does the old-fashioned, indigenous solution, the smallholder alternative, have going for it? More specifically, why does the farm family, the smallholder household, appear so regularly as the social group that carries on intensive cultivation? Comparative data now suggest that there is indeed such a correlation which we may provisionally explain by (1) the effectiveness of the household in mobilizing long-term labor of high quantity *and* quality, (2) the flexibility of the household in accommodating itself to available resources, and (3) the autonomy of the household as a unit of decision making, economic accumulation, and security, despite community and state control.

Household Farm Labor:
Home Economics Where It Counts

Why should households be so persistently associated with small farms even in market economies with wage labor and urban dominance? Isn't the necessary trajectory of capitalist penetration into the countryside a polarization of landholdings into the very large and the tiny and the development of a landless rural proletariat, as Lenin prophesied (Hart 1986: 5)? Intensive cultivation, especially the diversified, low energy, sustainable variant we are discussing, is by nature small rather than big business. The household is simply a better way to mobilize skilled, responsible, high-quality labor in substantial but carefully calibrated amounts.

We have discussed the fact that intensive cultivation calls for more total labor more regularly applied through the year, and that marginal returns on those additional units of work are not high. When an agricultural economist breaks down the costs and benefits of peasant farming, the household enterprise looks like a going concern (little capital, modest "tradable inputs," high returns on land). If, however, total labor is credited at the opportunity cost of market wages, small farms go into the deficit column and appear to be inherently unprofitable (Fox and Finan 1987). The stubborn desire of Portuguese rural people to buy one or two hectares of land, often paying what seem to be highly inflated prices, and then to raise a little corn, potatoes, wine grapes, and kale along with a few milk cows, chickens, and rabbits becomes by definition economically irrational behavior. But if labor costs were to reflect the much lower returns acceptable to men working part-time or as elderly retired farmers, women combining gardening at odd hours with child care and domestic duties, and children doing chores after school, the family farm makes sense. Intensive cultivators the world over do other things besides farming, and their choice of maintaining agriculture as a household endeavor reflects a decision that the extra work and the quite modest returns to labor it brings are worth it—you eat better, live more securely through the risks of unemployment, sickness, and old age, and, according to the Georgia part-time farmers Peggy Barlett (1987b) interviewed, you derive pleasure and satisfaction from making things grow. Doing what serves the survival and long-range interests of the domestic kin group is a better strategy than the maximizing of short-term rationality. The factory job and the city slum or the vulnerability of landless rural poor are worse than smallholder work, periodic drudgery perhaps, but an occupation or avocation willingly opted for by millions.

The reasons for household members performing the tasks of smallholder cultivation more effectively than wage laborers is not just the comparative cheapness of their labor, what Marxists refer to as self-exploitation.[2] It also has to do with organization, motivation, and just plain quality of work. It is true that household members have to be fed, clothed, and housed for years, even when they are too young, too sick, or too old to contribute much. But these costs may be more than compensated by the absence of recruitment problems—residents are readily available, they don't haggle for pay, and they don't leave before the job is finished. They think nothing of doing ten different things in the course of a day and working late or taking off from a formal sector job to meet bottleneck demands on the farm.

The household work force also has the benefit of years of on-the-job training and experience, both in social cooperation and in the needs of their own specific fields, animals, and tasks. The male/female division of labor, the socialization of children, the authority to direct and the willingness to follow instructions are taught and exemplified in the fundamental activities of the household—for smallholders, social reproduction and economic production are part of a seamless cultural fabric.

Family members know each other's capabilities and idiosyncrasies, whereas such information on outsiders is expensive to acquire. The personal supervision so necessary for hired laborers may be minimal in the household. Diverse and discontinuous tasks can go on simultaneously in different parts of the farm with individual responsibility freeing the household head from direct overseeing, and the returns on this work enter a family pool to be shared. The risks of crop failure or individual incapacity are also shared by the household, and internal consumption can be regulated to stretch food supplies to the maximum. Curtailing expenditures is a coping strategy sensitive to economic pressures, and a household can only persist as an independent management unit if it adjusts its level of consumption to the available resources. Self-sufficient Swiss families survived the Great Depression on cheese and potatoes with next to no cash and coffee only on Christmas eve. A successful householder was one who "hat einfach und sparsam gelebt," had lived simply and frugally. It is only in the household unit that the socialist dictum of "from each according to his abilities, to each according to his needs" may be in fact realized.[3]

Supervision and other transaction costs are minimized in the household because the incentive problem is reduced. The development economists, Hans Binswanger and Mark Rosensweig (1986), point out that the family members who share farm work are sole residual claimants to farm profits. If labor is hired to cultivate on piece work rates, haste may lead to missing weeds and damaging crops unless the process is closely monitored. The interest of a smallholder family member is different. There the link between work and livelihood is clear, and those disciplined additional efforts so vital to intensive cultivation will directly benefit the individual who makes them. When I tried to determine Kofyar attitudes toward work, I showed a picture of a boy watching some people farm. People insisted the youngster was on an errand and had just stopped to greet the workers, but when I said that he was indeed refusing to work, they reacted with shocked disbelief. In such a hypothetical case of blatant laziness, their solution was simple: "If the child does not work, we will not feed him." With such stern but not unusual sanctions and the fact that members depend for both immediate subsistence and long-term insurance on the household, it is no wonder that they and other small-holders display a full-blown Protestant ethic regardless of the theology they profess. Households may and do hire labor during peak periods and send their own members out to work elsewhere during slack times, but a heavy reliance on wage workers may be not only costly but risky. Intensive cultivators must cope with the synchronic timing of operations across farms and the importance of timeliness of operations (Binswanger and Rosensweig 1986). An optimal and skilled permanent labor force is there quickly when you need them and when neighboring smallholders are too busy at home to help you.

Our contention is merely that the household is peculiarly adapted to the critical requirements of smallholder agriculture. Household management succeeds in reducing labor, recruitment, and supervision costs, increasing incentives for responsible work, sharing risks, and mobilizing the co-residential kin-group's potential for education, administration, and cooperative production.

Household Flexibility and Fit

Where people depend on agrarian resources for a significant part of their livelihoods, household size and composition will conform in general to economic levels of production, whether measured by land areas, livestock ownership, wealth, or tax valuations. By household, Wilk and I (Wilk and Netting 1984) mean a socially recognized domestic group whose members usually share a residence and both organize and carry on a range of production, consumption, inheritance, and reproductive activities whose specific contents varies by society, stage in the life cycle, and economic status. Household inhabitants may be kin, but they may include friends, lodgers, and servants, and there are certainly family members, who are not co-resident and cooperating.

When demographers or anthropologists tabulate household size, they find it varies directly with farm size (Netting 1982b). A Japanese village with records from five census years between 1716 and 1823 showed small landholders averaging 3.7 member households, medium having 4.2, and large 5.3 (Smith 1977: 124). Numbers varied from year to year, but the ranking was unchanged. A large sample of Russian peasant households exhibited a pronounced stratification from those with less than 0.1 desitinas of land, no horses, and 3 members to those with 16.1 to 25.0 desitinas, 1.8 horses, and 9.9 members (Shanin 1972: 64). Where land is plentiful, households can expand the areas they farm to feed more dependent children as the great Russian agricultural economist, Chayanov, pointed out. This is most feasible when fallow land exists in abundance, when grain farming is extensive, and when land can be reallocated yearly to match household consumption and labor, exactly the case in the historic Russian repartitional commune. As land supplies become more constricted, average household sizes may shrink and even fertility may decline from initially high rates to one approaching replacement as it did with the closing frontier in the northern United States (Easterlin 1976).

The Kofyar have transformed their households before my eyes since I first lived among them in 1960. Originally the households of these terraced homestead farmers were small, about 5.1 people, and there were few examples of multiple family households having two or more co-resident married couples. When the Kofyar migrated to the largely vacant Benue Valley to grow crops for the market, their need for labor induced rapid household growth, peaking at an average of over 11 members for those households with 25 to 30 years in the new lands (Stone et al. 1984). The Kofyar recruited temporary work groups by hosting big beer parties and by hiring outsiders, but their basic strategy was to add permanent household members through increasingly frequent polygynous marriage and keeping married sons in their natal households. The French farm family proved equally resilient after the frightful population crash of the Black Death. LeRoy Ladurie (1984) chronicles the assembling of the survivors into extended family groups such as the frérèche of married brothers, their expanded land use, and the improvement of the diet before Malthusian pressures returned. Both the Kofyar frontier and the French rural population vacuum were temporary states. Once competition for land, declining average farm size, and more intensive agriculture re-emerged, households contracted in size, and the era of smallholders returned.

Lineages, Communes, and Businesses: Alternatives to the Household

Does this direct, seemingly determinist relationship between resources and household size strike you as too simple, somehow reductionist? Can't other units that aren't households do the job of intensive agriculture just as well? The household itself may be created relatively recently out of the requirements for capital accumulation on a world scale, or so Emmanuel Wallerstein (Smith et al. 1984, but cf. Rutz, this volume) contends. The lineage mode of production, as defined by Terray (1972), Meillassoux (1981), and the French neo-Marxists, comprises descent group work teams whose produce goes into communal granaries and whose food is allocated by elders. Livestock is communal rather than private property. Lineage elders control iron tools, marriage, and trade as representatives of the group. A supposedly weak and stagnant technology meant that lineage elders exercised little direct authority in agricultural production but appropriated the surplus generated by women and younger males by controlling the process of reproduction through bridewealth (Geschiere 1985). The size of the group and its internal articulation, whether as a large multiple family household or a set of kin-linked cooperating residence units, remain unclear, but the members of actual African lineages referred to seem always to be engaged in extensive agriculture with little scarcity of land.[4]

I know of no cases anywhere where a descent group above the level of the household is a primary unit of agricultural production and consumption. Even the necessarily communal task of clearing high forest for the milpas of Kekchi Maya shifting cultivators, in which the males of entire villages cooperate, produces corn from household fields for residential family use (Wilk 1984). Descent groups or local communities may control large areas of potentially arable and fallow land, redistributing it among their members as required for temporary usufruct and prohibiting trespass by outsiders (Netting 1982a). But when land for shifting cultivation gets scarce, the lineage as a mechanism for allocation and territorial defense breaks down (Harner 1970; Collier 1975). Households farm and eat separately, providing for their own reproduction, and protecting rights in valuable, heritable property. A variety of reciprocal exchange and festive labor groups may be maintained, even after wage labor is initiated (Saul 1983; Erasmus 1956; Netting et al. n.d.).[5] Frequently the multiple family household residential group fissions, with nuclear families adopting dispersed settlement on their own plots (Udo 1965). With intensive cultivation, rights to hold and transfer land and livestock become rigidly defined at the household and individual level, even in the absence of major market influences or state legal systems. Hobbled by the lack of sound comparative data in evolutionary formulations and the "wistful romanticism" of the nineteenth century, Marx "clearly failed to realize the complexity of rights over property, including property in land, characteristic of a primitive agricultural community." (Firth 1973: 36) Not even the ghost of primitive communism lingers among the individualistic Kofyar or Philippine Ifugao terrace farmers, though both were until recently innocent of chiefdoms and states, as well as being staunch pre-capitalists.

Any mode-of-production analysis must engage the fact that smallholder intensive agriculture as we portray it here can include a variety of forces of production (crops, technologies, farming systems) and a range of political-economic relations of production, though the household core unit continues to play a key role. Our heresy is in espousing a socioeconomic type that maintains a functional identity transcending the kinship/tributary/capitalist modes of production, the use/exchange dichotomy, and the peasant/farmer opposition. Indeed the cases we cite combine some degree of household self-provisioning of goods and services for self-consumption with production for market exchange (Lockwood, this volume) as well as non-agricultural, extra-household labor. The larger social formations in which most smallholders exist are capitalistic in the sense that monetary wealth is enabled to buy labor power, but the fact that a smallholder retains rights to his own means of production sufficient to provide a minimal sustenance (cf. Wolf 1982: 77) does not mean that he will remain outside the market or forgo its attractive commodities. As Rutz (this volume) points out, the household is not shaped solely by the capitalistic need to reproduce cheap labor nor can its internal norms of sharing and consumption be reduced to variable combinations of wage and non-wage labor. The objective scarcities of land, resources, tools, labor, and capital that constrain the smallholder household produce similarities in the social organization of production that can be recognized across cultures, temporal periods, and social formations.

If a postulated lineage control of resources appears antithetical to smallholder intensive production, why doesn't farming, especially the high-tech modern variety, go in the direction of corporate or collective institutions where capital and centralized, scientific management replace labor? Such a solution appears as obvious as it is historically inevitable, and even the great East/West ideological oppositions of our time seem to dissolve in *de facto* agreement about the virtues of large-scale mechanized agriculture. The day-to-day workings of the collective wheat farm on the Russian steppe or the Cornbelt grain and soybeans agribusiness may not be all that different, once issues of ownership of the means of production are put aside. In contrast to the smallholder strategy, big contemporary farms are not just energy intensive but energy inefficient. Cheap fossil fuels for making fertilizers, pesticides, and herbicides, manufacturing and running tractors, pumps, trucks, lights, and all those other labor-saving devices, mean that we can happily transform oil or coal energy into many fewer but edible calories.

A Russian collective farm of 3,144 hectares in the Moscow district has almost 1,700 arable hectares of which 93 percent are under collective use with 7 percent as private plots. Bayliss-Smith (1982) in his energy comparison of various traditional and modern agricultural systems estimates that over half of all household labor time is devoted to the small family plots, achieving per hectare yields of 6 times the level of collective fields at a probable efficiency of 11.2:1. The collective gets energy returns of 1.09 for each calorie of input, a ratio much lower than the 17 to 1 of Thai rice cultivation but higher than the 1 to 4 of U.S. egg production and the 1 to 600 of greenhouse vegetables (Evenari 1988). Wisconsin Amish have energy ratios four times higher than the 0.3 to 0.4 of their mechanized neighbors (Johnson et al. 1977). The Russian private plot is a good analog for the smallholder mini-farm because it is near the house, receives constant care and attention, is heavily manured, and has diversified plant and animal production. Decisions concerning these small operations are made by the household, with women playing a more important role. On the collective, however, "Any response by farmers to signals from their environment must, in all important respects, be made with reference to instructions from a remote bureaucracy, instructions which cannot foresee all the local vagaries of weather, disease, and soil conditions." (Bayliss-Smith 1982: 97)

The contradiction between smallholder efficiency and communist ideology has finally been recognized in Gorbachev's recent call for freeing Soviet farmers from the state-run system of collective agriculture. "Comrades, the most important thing today is to stop the process of de-peasantization and to return the man back to the land as its real master." (New York Times 10/14/88)

An even better example of the ecological and economic problems of collectivization is that of the Chinese farm communes. High population density and wet rice cultivation, integrated with pig, mulberry-silkworm, and fishpond production, have made China perhaps the most intensively and continuously farmed area in the world. Using historical data, Wen Dazhong and David Pimentel (1986) model a seventeenth century local system with labor power inputs of 3,700 hour per hectare and nutrient recycling so efficient in terms of energy that the agroecosystem was indefinitely sustainable. Mechanized rice production in contrast requires 2 to 10 times as much energy expenditure. Wet rice multicropping with controlled irrigation and the recycling of everything from silkworm and duck droppings to human excrement, house sweepings, and carbon-blackened heating stoves (Yang 1945) has enormous potential for increasing land productivity, but it involves higher levels of individual skills and experience as well as manual labor rather than capital inputs.

As the economic historian, Francesca Bray, so cogently points out, the economies of scale characteristic of European agriculture did not apply, and most production in China since the medieval period has been on the small family farm (Bray 1986: xv, 115, 196). Even under large-scale ownership by aristocrats or gentry, household small holdings remained the basic unit of both farm management and rural commodity production (Bray 1986: 179). Farmers would only devote the extra work and skill to their fields if they received the fruits of their efforts. Thus rents remained stable even while production climbed, and the tenants in sixteenth century Fujian described by Evelyn Rawski (1972) could inherit and sub-lease land from which the landlords could not evict them. Where skill and careful work counted more than capital (Bray 1986: 115), no one had to remain a landless laborer over his entire life. Neither communal tenure nor feudal manors seem to occur in this agrarian system (Chao 1986; Hsu 1980: 10), and serfdom is probably incompatible with intensive rice cultivation (Bray 1986: 177). Only under frontier conditions of sparse population, abundant land, and poor markets were peasants highly vulnerable to exploitation by rich landlords or the commanders of military garrisons (Hsu 1980).

History's lessons were lost on a Communist regime that insisted on combining households into integrated work teams and erasing field boundaries. William Hinton (1983), both a long-term participant observer and a partisan of the commune movement, describes unending meetings to assign work points for particular tasks and provide consistent accounting. The difficulty of tying rewards to work input was colossal, especially in intensive agriculture where a multitude of exacting tasks vary with time of day, season, and soil conditions and with the worker's age, sex, physical strength, and special skills (Putterman 1985). Is it any wonder that a national agricultural policy of *baogan daohu,* household responsibility, was begun in 1979, encompassed the majority of Chinese villages by 1982, and was all but universal by 1984 (Smil 1985).[6] Officially, land remained collectively owned, but households contracted to fill quotas for delivery of certain products at fixed prices to the state in return for the right to dispose of their entire surpluses on the free market (Perkins and Yusuf 1984). Linking rewards with output and encouraging household initiative, innovation, investment, efficiency, and risk taking has explosively raised production and effected what has been called "the most far reaching and orderly socioeconomic transformation of the 20th century." (Smil 1985: 118) The market incentives to increased household production have been protected by the government's refusal to raise taxes or labor obligations (Putterman 1985). Peasants are getting rich, and by all accounts, they like it.

Household ascendancy in agricultural organization is less obvious where resources are less constricted and capital is abundant. But even in the homeland of the hog and the dollar, family farms (Bennett 1982) may resist being turned into maximizing businesses. Sonya Salamon (1985) distinguishes two kinds of farm enterprises in central Illinois, the Yankee entrepreneurial variety with large monocropped grain fields, often rented, worked for short-term profits by efficient individualists, and the yeoman types, of German-Catholic ancestry cultivating smaller diversified dairy-hog-beef-grain farms that stay in the family for generations. The yeomen manage their operations with a labor-intensive strategy and careful stewardship, avoiding debt and conserving the resources that will support them and their children. Both midwestern farming patterns have persisted in the same environment for a century, but Salamon (1985: 338) suggests that the small-scale yeoman orientation "which entails close family cooperation and relatively modest financial goals may be particularly adaptive under uncertain economic conditions."

Household Autonomy vs. the State

Given scarce resources and population pressure with its inherent competition, smallholders are forever fine-tuning and tinkering with a host of variables that make every household farm different in some respects from its neighbors. A cultivator confronts micro-environmental differences of soil, slope, moisture, and exposure to sun and wind, often within a single field. Decisions on crop mix, seeding rates, interplanting, rotation, and timing of various operations are further influenced by the vicissitudes of climate in any particular year. Absolute quantities of land, irrigation water, manure, and draft animals must enter his calculations, along with the possibility of supplementing these factors by purchase, rent, barter, or borrowing. Household and non-household sources of labor must be critically assessed for their availability, skill, and cost. As Murray Leaf (1972) emphasizes for Sikh farmers in the Punjab, the amount of information a farmer must gather and assess along with the accumulated experience from a farm and a family in the past make for an extremely complex and individually specific ecological perspective. The more intensive the cultivation, the more this knowledge and the resulting management decisions affect the viability and the comparative success of the enterprise. Marx was not a farm boy, and he was wrong when he said that peasants are as like one another as potatoes in a sack.

When an attempt is made to standardize practices over large areas and maximize production by hierarchical decisions on crops, mechanization, and labor allocation in terms of rigid scientific or economic logic, the small-scale flexibility and with it the responsiveness and resilience of the smallholders, those expert, garden-variety ecologists, is lost. National governments with their massive development schemes, land consolidation plans, and collectives do not believe this, and they systematically sabotage their own smallholders. The rural autonomy of smallholders who need and want to be their own bosses collides with administrations that Michael Mortimore (1987) terms "remote in location, bureaucratic in organization, centrist in style, interventionist in mode." I am convinced that the voluntary migration and successful entrance of perhaps 4,000 Kofyar households into the Nigerian cash-crop economy was based in large measure on their freedom from government assistance and control (Netting et al. n.d.). The state never knew they were there.

Smallholder interests also suffer, sometimes tragically, when the state forcibly rearranges their settlement pattern. As part of their strategy of intensive land use, smallholders often live dispersed in the fields and orchards they tend. This reduces travel time, makes possible guarding of crops and livestock, and asserts tenure rights by permanent occupation. Governments seem always to discourage such economically reasonable settlement. The official claim is that civic services—schools, clinics, utilities—can only be provided to concentrated population enclaves. Both the British colonial government and the Tanzanian state promoted villagization, and in the latter case, centralized communal agriculture with the community functioning as an ideal cooperative *ujamaa* household was the goal (Hyden 1980). Farmers who resisted, sometimes violently, this nucleation realized they were giving up the benefits of living on their own plots in exchange for inevitably onerous (and economically maladaptive) government control. When the rationale for concentrating formerly dispersed populations is military security and counterinsurgency, as it was in the strategic hamlets of Viet Nam and in the Development Pole villages of Guatemala today, direct coercion counters and often destroys the economic rationale of independent, largely self-sufficient householders. For former freeholders, forced consolidation of settlement may be at best an impediment, at worst a trap with military domination and famine in wait. Both the settlement system and farm level manipulation of resources are areas of action in which external control inevitably restricts smallholder latitude for choice and individual enterprise. Production suffers as freedom wanes.

Can we speak of freeholders when even the most cursory examination of intensive cultivators reveals inequality in rights to the means of production? Limitations on resource availability and individualized property holding means that at any point in time there will be rich and poor farmers, and there may be landless laborers and craftsmen who are not smallholders at all. We might go so far as to say that there will always be clear economic differentiation within any society of intensive cultivators. The Ifugao of highland Luzon restrict major inheritance of irrigated rice terraces to the first son and first daughter of a marriage, and these heirs are more likely to have further wealth in livestock, brass gongs, and heirloom Chinese porcelains (Conklin 1980). Even where, as in the Swiss community of Törbel, partible inheritance gives every male and female child an equal share in the estate, we found significant difference in the eventual wealth of full siblings, and parents' land valuation predicted only 4 percent of the variation in children's property (McGuire and Netting 1982). Evidently there was considerable mobility up and down the ladder of wealth, due to personal abilities as well as to marriage, non-agricultural earnings, and chance.

Even on farms of equal size and potential, some intensive agriculturalists will consistently out-produce others. Ruthenberg (1968: 329) found only a weak correlation between Sukumaland cotton inputs (including labor) and outputs, crediting this "principally to the essential factor, namely the differing entrepreneurial qualities of the farmers." The role played by management in the planning and careful calculation of intensive cultivation seems especially significant for smallholders (Matlon 1981; Eder 1982). The so-called levelling mechanisms that redistribute peasant wealth seem never to erase these distinctions, and the prosperity of larger farmers appears frequently to be attained in the course of the family cycle rather than merely passed on within a rural upper class (Greenhalgh 1985).

Why then is not a polarization into dominant large holders and landless dependents the order of the day? There seem to be several factors that lead toward internal stratification and mobility over the life course rather than rigid and impenetrable class boundaries. Smallholder land has been improved by long term investment and produces dependable, relatively high yields. The demand within the community for the small supply of available property is heavy, and prices per square meter are unbelievably expensive. Shortly after the turn of the century, a Swiss agricultural economist marveled that a steep meadow in Törbel cost more than a similar area of level wheatland in other cantons. The hay gave such a low monetary return that alpine farmland was a poor capital investment. Medieval petty nobles recognized this fact, often selling off their mountain lands to engage in trans-Alpine trade or the lucrative mercenary service. The heavy work inputs, the low marginal returns on labor, and the difficulty of hiring workers to replace or extend the household labor force all work against the large holder as well. It is true that military or legal/political power can dispossess smallholders, often *dis*intensifying land use in the direction of cattle ranches or monocropped plantations, but this economic devolution is achieved only by abrogating the freedom of the smallholder and destroying his livelihood. If left alone, smallholders may create elaborate systems of local stratification while allowing economic mobility in both directions and moderating the extremes of wealth and poverty.

Smallholders can indeed be threatened by outside forces that deprive them of land, tax away their surplus, relocate their settlements, or conscript their manpower. Yet we find the smallholder adaptation under every conceivable regime from independent villages and chiefdoms to monarchies and socialist states. As a household-based system of land use, labor organization, and resource control, it exhibits a persistent formal-functional pattern, though it may be articulated with a variety of contrasting dominant modes of production. There may also be a number of consistent similarities at the level of local integration beyond the household. Neighborhood, voluntary association, and village labor exchange and coordination are economically significant. The internal business of the local community is often conducted by groups of citizens, regulating access to common property resources such as the forest or the mountain pastures, managing the irrigation system, deciding the block rotation of field crops, and resolving land and water disputes. Just as the householder must make decisions on his own basket of resources, the community must handle the cooperation and conflict at the next level of interaction. Semi-autonomous possessors of property and ecological knowledge recognize common interests (or interests in the commons) and they gather to talk, to dispute, to judge, and perhaps to vote. They can tolerate inequality but not the domination that deprives them of their holdings or denies them their right to make economic choices for the welfare of their households. If there is a locus for agrarian democracy, this is it. Smallholders flourish best with a modicum of freedom. Intensive agriculture is wonderfully fruitful, but it is no bowl of cherries. With enough work, skill, and management it can produce plenty of food from few resources, conserving both non-renewable energy and avoiding the degradation of those plots of highly limited earth. The familiar households that all of us know and love seem to do this job best, adjusting their numbers, mobilizing domestic labor, administering their own property, and managing their own enterprise. So long as they are free to do that, the family farm will sustain the land, the smallholder, and, if we are fortunate, the rest of us too.

Acknowledgments

An earlier version of this chapter was presented as the Scott-Hawkins Lecture at Dedman College, Southern Methodist University in Sept., 1988. I appreciated the comments of David Weber and other members of the Departments of History and Anthropology on that occasion. Research was conducted in part during my year as a Fellow at the Center for Advanced Study in the Behavioral Sciences with financial support from National Science Foundation grant #BNS 84–11738.

Notes

1. Sahlins sees an absolutely fundamental division between primitive society whose dominant institutional locus is kinship as analyzed by social anthropology and modern society whose capitalist economy is explicated by some form of Marxism (Stromberg n.d.). By definition, land and labor is not scarce in "archaic economies," and pressure on land is not a function of technology and resources but of social access to the means of livelihood, a "specification of the cultural system" (Sahlins 1972: 49). The domestic mode of production is intrinsically an "anti-surplus system" resisting the socio-political pressures to secure the intensification of labor (Sahlins 1972: 82). When production for exchange and profit replaces production for use, and state coercion dictates labor, both society and the household can never be the same again.

2. Is it useful to insist with Marx that the commodity producing peasant embodies the contradiction of being both the capitalist owner of the means of production and the laborer who produces surplus value (see Lockwood, this volume)? Where options of minor artisanal or mercantile occupations or agricultural wage labor exist, it is clear that smallholder work on own land or even as a sharecropper has higher marginal returns (Nag, White, and Peet 1978). Exploitation is present across the board, but the smallholder realistically appraises the opportunities and makes what appears to be a rational economic choice.

3. This is not an attempt to reinstate the Western myth of patriarchal harmony in the household to which Barlett (this volume) refers. Nor is it an effort to ignore age and gender inequality, lack of economic pooling (Clark, this volume), and internal stratification (Wilk, Lockwood, this volume). Rather it reflects a sense that the small farm household enterprise manages despite conflict and occasional inequities to mobilize the energies of its members toward shared goals and to provide satisfactions, both physical and emotional, that maintain their

long-term allegiance. True generalized reciprocity remains a powerful, if never completely achieved, ideal.

4. This appears to characterize the Bobo (Saul, this volume) with long fallow, rain-fed agriculture and, as yet, little scarcity of land. Even in this case, the demands of higher market production with presumably increasing individual labor inputs are reducing cooperation within corporate matrilineal descent units and the control of jointly produced goods by lineage matrons and elders. For the case of Gbaya shifting cultivators with no gerontocratic exploitation, no lineage collective labor, and no corporate property, see Burnham (1980: 167–173).

5. There is no evidence that reciprocal work groups appear only where the lineage has been weakened due to secession, migration, trade, or war (Terray 1972). Deductive reasoning from the postulates of an antiquated evolutionism unfortunately vitiates some of the insights of world-economy theorists.

6. The plan itself was not a new one. In 1962 Deng Xiaoping first unsuccessfully proposed to the Central Committee that households be the principal productive units (Putterman 1985: 72).

References Cited

Bachman, K. L. and R. P. Christensen. 1967. "The Economics of Farm Size," in H. M. Southworth and B. F. Johnston (eds.), *Agricultural Development and Economic Growth*. Ithaca: Cornell University Press. Pp. 234–257.

Barlett, Peggy F. 1987a. "Industrial Agriculture in Evolutionary Perspective." *Cultural Anthropology* 2: 137–154.

———. 1987b. "The Crisis in Family Farming: Who Will Serve?" in Michael Chibnik (ed.), *Farmwork and Fieldwork: American Agriculture in Anthropological Perspective*. Ithaca: Cornell University Press. Pp. 29–57.

Bayliss-Smith, T. P. 1982. *The Ecology of Agricultural Systems*. Cambridge: Cambridge University Press.

Bennett, John. 1982. *Of Time and the Enterprise: North American Family Farm Management in a Context of Resource Marginality*. Minneapolis: University of Minnesota Press.

Binswanger, Hans P. and Mark R. Rosenzweig. 1986. "Behavioural and Material Determinants of Production Relations in Agriculture." *Journal of Development Studies* 22: 503–539.

Bohannan, Paul and Laura. 1968. *Tiv Economy*. Evanston: Northwestern University Press.

Boserup, Ester. 1965. *The Conditions of Agricultural Growth*. Chicago: Aldine.

Burnham, Philip. 1980. *Opportunity and Constraint in a Savanna Society*. New York: Academic Press.

Chao, Kang. 1986. *Man and Land in Chinese History: An Economic Analysis*. Stanford: Stanford University Press.

Clark, Colin and M. R. Haswell. 1967. *The Economics of Subsistence Agriculture*. London: Macmillan.

Collier, George A. 1975. *Fields of The Tzotzil*. Austin: University of Texas Press.

Conklin, H. C. 1980. *Ethnographic Atlas of Ifugao: A Study of Environment, Culture, and Society in Northern Luzon.* New Haven: Yale University Press.

Easterlin, R. A. 1976. "Population Change and Farm Settlement in the Northern United States." *Journal of Economic History* 36: 45–75.

Eder, James F. 1982. *Who Shall Succeed? Agricultural Development and Social Inequality on a Philippine Frontier.* Cambridge: Cambridge University Press.

Ellis, Frank. 1988. *Peasant Economics: Farm Households and Agrarian Development.* Cambridge: Cambridge University Press.

Erasmus, Charles. 1956. "Culture, Structure, and Process. The Occurrence and Disappearance of Reciprocal Farm Labor." *Southwestern Journal of Anthropology* 12: 444–469.

Evenari, Michael. 1988. "The Problem Posed: Elements of the Agricultural Crisis." *Kidma: Israel Journal of Development* 10, No. 2: 4–8.

Feder, Gershon and Raymond Noronha. 1987. "Land Rights Systems and Agricultural Development in Sub-Saharan Africa." *Research Observer* 2: 143–170.

Firth, Raymond. 1975. "The Skeptical Anthropologist," in M. Bloch (ed.), *Marxist Analyses and Social Anthropology.* Cambridge: Cambridge University Press.

Fox, Roger and Timothy J. Finan. 1987. "Patterns of Technical Change in the Northwest," in Scott R. Pearson, et al. (eds.), *Portuguese Agriculture in Transition.* Ithaca: Cornell University Press. Pp. 187–201.

Greenhalgh, Susan. 1985. "Is Inequality Demographically Induced? The Family Cycle and the Distribution of Income in Taiwan." *American Anthropologist* 87: 571–594.

Harber, Michael J. 1970. "Population Pressure and the Social Evolution of Agriculturalists." *Southwestern Journal of Anthropology* 26: 67–86.

Hart, Gillian. 1986. *Power, Labor, and Livelihood: Processes of Change in Rural Java.* Berkeley: University of California Press.

Hinton, William. 1983. *Shenfan.* New York: Vintage.

Hsu, Cho-yun. 1980. *Han Agriculture: the Formation of Early Chinese Agrarian Economy (206 B.C.–A.D. 220).* Seattle: University of Washington Press.

Hyden, Goran. 1980. *Beyond Ujamaa in Tanzania: Underdevelopment and an Uncaptured Peasantry.* London: Heinemann.

Johnson, Warren A., Victor Stoltzfus, Peter Craumer. 1977. "Energy Conservation in Amish Agriculture." *Science* 198: 373–378.

Leaf, Murray J. 1972. *Information and Behavior in a Sikh Village.* Berkeley: University of California Press.

LeRoy Ladurie E. 1974. *The Peasants of Languedoc.* Urbana: University of Illinois Press.

Matlon, D. J. 1981. "The Structure of Production and Rural Incomes in Northern Nigeria: Results of Three Village Case Studies," in H. Bienen and V. P. Diejomaoh (eds.), *The Political Economy of Income Distribution in Nigeria.* New York: Holmes and Meier.

Meillassoux, Claude. 1981. *Maidens, Meal and Money: Capitalism and the Domestic Community.* Cambridge: Cambridge University Press.

Minge-Klevana, Wanda. 1977. "On the Theory and Measurement of Domestic Labor Intensity." *American Ethnologist* 4: 273–284.

———. 1980. "Does Labor Time Decrease with Industrialization? A Survey of Time-Allocation Studies." *Current Anthropology* 21: 279–298.

Mortimore, Michael. 1987. "Shifting Sands and Human Sorrow: Social Response to Drought and Desertification." *Desertification Control Bulletin* 14: 1–14.

Nag, Moni, B. N. F. White, and R. C. Peet. 1978. "An Anthropological Approach to the Study of the Economic Value of Children in Java and Nepal." *Current Anthropology* 19: 293–306.

Netting, Robert McC. 1968. *Hill Farmers of Nigeria: Cultural Ecology of the Kofyar of the Jos Plateau.* Seattle: University of Washington Press.

———. 1976. "What Peasants Have in Common: Observations on Communal Tenure in a Swiss Village." *Human Ecology* 4: 135–146.

———. 1981. *Balancing on an Alp: Ecological Change and Continuity in a Swiss Mountain Community.* Cambridge: Cambridge University Press.

———. 1982a. "Territory, Property, and Tenure," in R. McC. Adams, M. J. Smelser, and D. J. Treinman (eds.), *Behavioral and Social Science Research: A National Resource.* Washington, D. C.: National Academy Press. Pp. 446–502.

———. 1982b. "Some Home Truths on Household Size and Wealth." *American Behavioral Scientist* 25: 641–662.

———. 1988. "Agricultural Expansion, Intensification, and Market Participation among the Kofyar, Jos Plateau, Nigeria." Manuscript for the Workshop on Population Growth and Agricultural Change in Sub-Saharan Africa. University of Florida, Gainesville.

Netting, R. McC., M. P. Stone, and G. D. Stone. n.d. "Kofyar Cash-Cropping: Choice and Change in Indigenous Agricultural Development." Ms. Department of Anthropology, University of Arizona.

Perkins, Dwight and Shahid Yusuf. 1984. *Rural Development in China.* Baltimore: Johns Hopkins University Press.

Pimentel, David, et al. 1973. "Food Production and the Energy Crisis." *Science* 182: 443–449.

Putterman, Louis. 1985. "The Restoration of the Peasant Household as Farm Production Unit in China: Some Incentive Theoretic Analysis," in Elizabeth J. Perry and Christine Wang (eds.), *The Political Economy of Reform in Post-Mao China.* Cambridge: Council on East Asian Studies, Harvard University. Pp. 63–82.

Rawski, Eleanor S. 1972. *Agricultural Change and the Peasant Economy of South China.* Cambridge: Harvard University Press.

Roseberry, William. 1985. "Review Essay of E. R. Wolf, Europe and the people Without History." *Dialectical Anthropology* 10: 141– 153.

Ruthenberg, Hans. 1968. "Some Characteristics of Smallholder Farming in Tanzania," in Hans Ruthenberg (ed.), *Smallholder Farming and Smallholder Development in Tanzania.* Munchen: Weltforum Verlag.

———. 1985. *Innovation Policy for Small Farmers in the Tropics: The Economics of Technical Innovations for Agricultural Development.* Oxford: Clarendon Press.

Sahlins, Marshall. 1972. *Stone Age Economics*. Chicago: Aldine.

Salamon, Sonya. 1985. "Ethnic Communities and the Structure of Agriculture." *Rural Sociology* 50: 323–340.

Saul, Mahir. 1983. "Work Parties, Wages and Accumulation in a Voltaic Village." *American Ethnologist* 10: 77–96.

Shanin, T. 1972. *The Awkward Class*. London: Oxford University Press.

Smil, Vaclav. 1985. "China's Food." *Scientific American* 253, no. 6: 116– 124.

Smith, Joan, Immanuel Wallerstein, Hans-Dieter Evers, eds. 1984. *Households and the World Economy*. Beverly Hills: Sage.

Smith, T. C. 1977. *Nakahara: Family Farming and Population in a Japanese Village, 1717–1830*. Stanford: Stanford University Press.

Stoler, Anne L. 1981. "Garden Use and Household Economy in Java," in Gary E. Hansen (ed.), *Agricultural and Rural Development in Indonesia*. Boulder: Westview. Pp. 242–254.

Stone, G. D., M. P. Johnson-Stone, and R. McC. Netting. 1984. "Household Variability and Inequality in Kofyar Subsistence and Cash-Cropping Economies." *Journal of Anthropological Research* 40: 90–108.

Stone, Glenn D., R. McC. Netting, and M. Priscilla Stone. 1988. "Seasonality, Labor Scheduling, and Intensification in the Nigerian Savanna." Manuscript, University of Arizona, Department of Anthropology.

Terray, E. 1972. *Marxism and 'Primitive' Societies*. New York: Monthly Review Press.

Turner, B. L. and S. B. Brush. 1987. *Comparative Farming Systems*. New York: Guilford.

Udo, R. K. 1965. "Disintegration of Nucleated Settlement in Eastern Nigeria." *Geographical Review* 55: 53–67.

Wallace, Ben J., R. M. Ahsan, S. H. Hussain, and E. Ahsan. 1987. *The Invisible Resource: Women and Work in Rural Bangladesh*. Boulder: Westview.

Wen Dazhong and D. Pimentel. 1986. "Seventeenth Century Organic Agriculture in China." *Human Ecology* 14: 1–28.

Wilk, Richard R. and R. McC. Netting. 1984. "Households: Changing Forms and Functions," in R. McC. Netting, R. R. Wilk, and E. J. Arnould (eds.), *Households: Comparative and Historical Studies of the Domestic Group*. Berkeley: University of California Press. Pp. 1–28.

Wilken, Gene C. 1987. *Good Farmers: Traditional Agricultural Resource Management in Mexico and Central America*. Berkeley: University of California Press.

Wolf, Eric R. 1982. *Europe and the People Without History*. Berkeley: University of California Press.

Yang, M. C. 1945. *A Chinese Village: Taitou, Shantung Province*. New York: Columbia University Press.

12

Gender and Intra/Inter-Household Analysis in On-Farm Research and Experimentation

Susan V. Poats, Hilary S. Feldstein,
and Dianne E. Rocheleau[1]

Introduction

The chapters in this volume amply demonstrate that the household is "unreliable" as a unit of analysis. The degree of commonality varies considerably from the very brittle, fractured, Asanti household, where relations of production are dominated by matrilineal corporate groups, to the Tubai household in which male dominance is still the norm, but women have attained some degree of autonomous control of production and its benefits. As Şaul points out, among the Bobo the former dominance of production by matrilineal groups is giving way to increased individual autonomy. This is accompanied by flexibility and conditionality in establishing relations of production and in some cases to the stronger bonding of men and their wives as a production unit. All three cases demonstrate that traditional norms and behavior governing relations of production are undergoing change. Such a state of flux and the degree of flexibility and conditionality in a given system may make patterns of production more difficult to discern, but is itself data which needs to be taken into account when anticipating the likely acceptability and affect of an introduced change in agricultural production.

There have been significant steps taken to put before planners the evidence of the differential impact on women of development and the poor results which come of not understanding the gender allocation of roles and resources (Overholt et al. 1985; Carloni 1987; Population Council 1985). These attempts have two purposes. The first is equity—forcing attention to the unequal share for women of development resources and the uneven distribution of benefits from projects themselves. Greater equity requires that project planners explicitly take into account the distribution of project resources and benefits in project implementation. The second purpose is efficiency. Poor projects, failure to achieve projected outputs, frequently results from insufficient attention to the availability of local resources to carry out activities. Often the failure comes from not seeing that men's and women's activities and resources are not equivalent. Understanding the actual patterns would lead to better planning.

The application of Intra-Household or gender analysis (referred to hereafter as IHH analysis) to farming systems work and the design of on-farm trials grows out of the work of the Case Studies Project, a collaborative effort of the Population Council and the Farming Systems Support Project (University of Florida).[2] The project objective is to provide materials to farming systems practitioners which will assist them in taking account of intra-household relations and gender in designing and disseminating agricultural innovations. The written products of that collaboration are a conceptual framework and a set of training type case studies used to train agricultural researchers, both social and technical scientists (Feldstein and Poats 1989) and a methodologies handbook containing first person accounts on collecting and presenting IHH data within agricultural research projects (Feldstein and Jiggins 1989). The unwritten product is a growing network of technically oriented scientists who are incorporating IHH into their work and from whom we have learned.

Planning On-Farm Research and Experimentation

The approach and methodology of Farming Systems Research and Extension (FSR/E) has most often been used to generate appropriate, adoptable technology for low-resource farmers. The technologies being developed and tested are drawn principally from the biological sciences. They include such changes as breeding new varieties of crops to fit specific environments, assessing appropriate levels of local or purchased fertilizers or pesticides, introduction of new cropping patterns involving new varieties and sequencing of production, and changes in cultural practices such as timing and mechanisms for land preparation, weeding, harvesting, etc.

To understand agricultural production, constraints and opportunities for improvement in a given area, FSR/E looks at the whole farm system in order to understand production patterns in terms of enterprise responsibility, time (absolutely and over the year or seasonally), resource flows, and farmers' perceptions of benefits or risks. The resources of particular interest to agricultural research are land (especially topography and soil type), water, germ plasm, equipment or implements, local or purchased fertilizers and pesticides, cash or credit, and knowledge or information.

FSR/E is undertaken in stages: diagnosis, planning, design, experimentation, and recommendations (Norman and Collinson 1986; FSSP 1987; Fresco and Poats 1986; Hildebrand and Poey 1985; Tripp 1986). *Diagnosis* is the formal and informal collection of information about farmers and the farming system in a given zone or project area. Diagnosis is finding out what people are doing, what problems they are confronting and how they might already be dealing with these problems. In recent years, there has been a greater emphasis on asking whether or not farmers are already experimenting with alternative solutions to problems in their farming systems. Many involved in FSR/E believe that these experiments or solutions are the best basis for broader interventions and on-farm research. Throughout information gathering the important question is *who* does what and has the critical resources and knowledge. Diagnosis results in an approximation of the farming system and a picture of the resources and stakes of different household members.

During the *design* stage priority problems identified during diagnosis are "channeled" to destinations where appropriate solutions can be sought or implemented. These destinations can include: on-farm experimentation, on-station and laboratory research, referrals to policy or decision-makers or, in the case of solutions that have already proven acceptable to farmers, direct to extension (Tripp 1986). First the problems are subjected to further scrutiny to clearly trace probable causes and linkages. Next, possible solutions are screened for compatibility with the farming system. One result of this sorting procedure is a list of problems for which on-farm research can be conducted. On-farm research can include experiments to test solutions or derive technical alternatives for problems related not only to crop production but also to livestock, marketing, environmental conservation, and post-harvest management. Further screening is usually needed to match desirable trials with project resources.

The next step is the *design* of trials, usually conducted on-farm. On-farm trials bring testing closer to farmer circumstances unlike trials on research stations which are usually better favored in terms of soil, water, and labor supply. In on-farm trials, one or more treatments, "a dosage of material or method that is to be tested" (Little and Hills 1978 in Shaner et al. 1981), is put into farmers' fields and data is collected with which to measure and evaluate production. A "treatment" may be a crop variety, fertilizer dosage, weeding regime, etc. At the design stage, researchers, sometimes in collaboration with farmers, specify what treatments, the number of replications, criteria for selecting farmer collaborators, and the data to be collected. The criteria for such decisions are heavily weighted to the demands of statistical analysis.

Experimentation is the implementation of trials. It has evolved as the difficulties and limitations of classical experiments focusing on yield and marginal rate of return have become apparent. Experimentation is beginning to incorporate other desirable outcomes such as reduced risk, improved nutrition, better labor allocation or alternate uses of scarce resources. Evaluation of results provides the basis for *recommendations* to researchers concerning further experimentation, to extension for dissemination to farmers, and, often, to policy makers on desirable changes in infrastructure (credit, markets, input supply) which condition agricultural enterprises.

On-farm testing stands at the heart of FSR/E. We have written elsewhere on the application of IHH analysis to the whole stream of FSR/E decision-making (Feldstein and Poats 1989). This paper focuses specifically on that most challenging of tasks, translating the insights from IHH analysis into the design of on-farm trials, generally regarded as a strictly technical exercise.

On-farm research promotes understanding of the considerable variability in environments, farm management, and the decision-making characteristics of limited resource farms. Commonly, while paying more attention to the human as well as field side of agricultural production, researchers have considered the household as an undifferentiated unit of production and consumption. This has led to miscalculation about the availability of resources, especially labor and cash, for changes in production associated with new technologies. Often overlooked is availability of women's labor for a particular task or at a particular time of the year. As both Saul and Lockwood's papers demonstrate, a woman's work in child rearing and home production severely constrain her availability for either autonomous or household agricultural production. Their papers along with Jones' work in Cameroon (Jones 1986) show that women's balance of time between autonomous and male directed household production also varies for a variety of reasons, including incentives, economic class, and stages in the life cycle.

A more productive approach to FSR/E is one which looks carefully at the *actual* pattern of intra- and inter-household relations, particularly as defined by gender, as part of on-going diagnostic and experimental research. This is a recent methodological development within the FSR/E approach (McKee 1984; Flora 1984). For many of our technical science colleagues, this is a difficult notion—they are unsure of its legitimacy in improving their research and bogged down by their own data gathering requirements, reluctant to add to that burden. While appreciative of some anthropological insights, they are wary of long term research which is not timely and which addresses questions outside their need for improving agricultural production with technical solutions. It is not within their province to get at the intricacies of intra-household bargaining. It is within their scope of work to understand and refine the general pattern of roles and resources so that they can design and test technologies which "fit." The objective of the conceptual framework and mode of analysis proposed in this paper is to assist agricultural researchers to ask the right questions and organize their information. They can then use the resulting analysis to inform their decisions about research priorities, appropriateness of specific technologies, farmer selection, design of trials and associated data collection, and recommendations concerning extension and policy.

Framework for IHH Analysis

IHH analysis provides the means for relating household structure and dynamics to technology development. It examines differences in household structures (such as male-headed and female-headed), different activities and resources of members of the household, and linkages between households. Cloud (1988) has described succinctly the patterns of variation in gender responsibility in agriculture. Household members frequently engage in different activities. For example, they may grow *separate crops* with men growing maize and women growing beans; they may have *separate tasks* with men preparing land, women selecting seed and planting, and children and women weeding; or men and women may grow the same crop on *separate fields* with different management practices. In some West African farming systems, women labor on their fields only after they have worked on communal fields and those of their husband. Their management and output will differ because of the labor constraint (Jackson 1985). Men and women may *share tasks* and this may be an index to the flexibility within the system for meeting labor demands. Finally, *women-managed farms* may represent special circumstances in terms of farm level constraints. *De facto* women-managed farms are those whose husbands are usually absent; resources may be available, but women lack the legal authority to sign credit agreements and commit resources. *De jure* women-managed farms are those that are legally headed by women, and are rapidly increasing in number. They are frequently among the poorest of farm households with few resources and severe labor constraints (Due and White 1984).

In low-resource households, individual and household welfare usually depend on activities other than farm production. Thus, to understand a whole farm system, attention must be paid to household maintenance, household production and off-farm activities. Household maintenance refers to child care, food preparation, collecting of fuelwood and water, household repair, etc.. Household production refers to preparation within the household of items which may be for sale. Frequently the raw materials for such items come from farm production, such as sorghum for beer brewing or rattan for baskets. Off-farm activities refers to wage labor, marketing, or other enterprises which produce income for household members.

Household production and off-farm labor or enterprises may contribute capital to farm production, but may also compete for resources and time. Şaul's paper illustrates this nicely in showing how with greater autonomy some women are engaging in more autonomous production (brewing beer), while others are allocating more time to husband-managed farm production. Understanding household production is important also because it sheds light on the post-harvest processing and uses of farm products. The end use of a product affects the desirability of specific changes, particularly in varieties. Within the household the activities of different members may be parallel but separate (as among the Asanti), complementary (an agreed upon division of labor), or conflicting. Farmers's decisions about adopting promising innovations will be influenced by the multiple objectives of members within the household and the internal bargaining to resolve them.

In order to learn about these relations, researchers must learn to ask *who*? Who does what? Who has what? Who benefits?

To organize the information collected from such questions, the Case Studies Project has developed a conceptual framework which focuses on three aspects underlying farmer decision making: the pattern of activities, access to and control of resources, and access to and control of benefits (Feldstein, Poats, Cloud, and Norem 1989). *Activity analysis* asks who does what and when do these activities occur. The whole range of household members' activities is included. Completing an agricultural calendar for the research area and identifying tasks by gender provide excellent tools for identifying labor problems and screening the possible impacts of technical solutions or cost of labor reallocation (see the sample calendar in Figure 1). An examination of the patterns of activities draws attention to the rigidity or flexibility of task assignment, labor constraints, and possible competing activities. The researcher can predict whose labor will be required or saved with any specific change.

Resource analysis identifies the necessary inputs to farm production and asks who has access to and control of each, and the conditions governing that access. Specifying who has knowledge about specific crops directs the researcher to farmers' own best practices and experiments. *Benefit analysis* identifies who gains from or has a stake in primary and residual farm products. It asks how products are consumed or exchanged

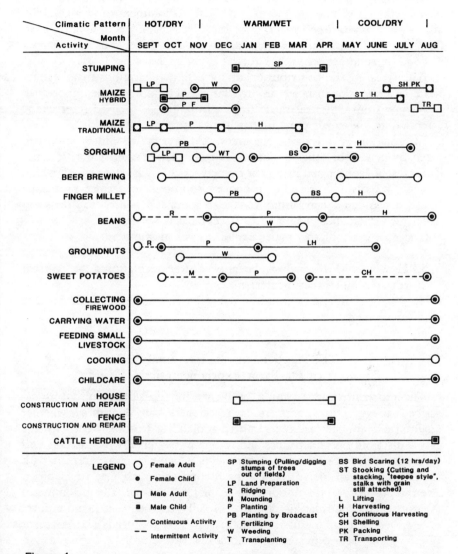

Figure 1
Example of an African Farming Systems Calendar Disaggregated by Gender

and what characteristics are preferred by the product users. Benefits and incentives analysis help the researcher anticipate whether or not those asked to invest additional labor or resources in a particular activity will benefit enough to have an incentive to make recommended changes. The analysis allows researchers to foresee the affect changes will have on crop characteristics important to users or processors. When benefits analysis is done in conjunction with a total picture of household or individual income streams, the contribution of some farm operations may become more apparent. For instance, in Sta. Barbara, Philippines, the importance of income from delicacies made from glutinous rice focused researchers' attention to the small plots of 'traditional rice'.

Information on activities, resources, and benefits should be disaggregated by gender or other important criteria such as age, seniority, class. This creates "conceptual maps" or frameworks of "who does what" which provide a basis for assessing proposed solutions to farmer problems. These assessments contribute to the researcher's ability to focus on experimentation most likely to be acceptable to farmers.

The remainder of this paper explores two questions:

1. How can IHH analysis be applied to the planning of on-farm research and experimentation?
2. What information should be collected in association with on-farm experiments?

The Application of IHH Analysis to On-Farm Experimentation

The procedure for screening problems and possible solutions is described above. During screening, researchers can determine whether assumptions about labor and resource availability are consistent with the actual distribution of activities and resources by gender? Researchers will then have a list of promising experiments which can be performed with the resources available to them. One further screening may be in order. Are the problems and solutions applicable to only one (albeit dominant) portion of the population or more broadly to the whole community? One way to approach this is to make sure that the needs and concerns of each group are addressed by at least one of the proposed innovations. For example, if resources allow for three lines of research, then a project serving men cultivators and women processors would pursue at least one research topic relevant to each.

On-farm trials can be classified in several ways. Three different criteria are used here: 1. the nature of the problem to be researched, 2. the respective roles of farmers and researchers in trial design and management, and 3. trial functions in a sequence aimed towards refining promising options. In each of these classification systems, IHH analysis can assist in selecting and designing on-farm research.

Nature of the Problem

Trials vary by the nature of the problem addressed. These include crop variety, cultural practices, plant nutrition and plant protection. Similarly, in livestock and agroforestry, the problems addressed are species screening, technology development and management, nutrition and protection, and land and water management. For each kind of problem there are points at which IHH analysis can be helpful. Below are a series of questions and examples that illustrate these possibilities.

Variety. Do specified breeding characteristics take current or desirable uses as defined by farmers and users into account?

- Activities analysis can show whether women and men have different management practices for the same crop. Both management practices should be included when testing the performance of new varieties.
- Activities analysis can also show how changes in the timing of labor associated with a new variety will affect labor allocation of different household members.
- Resource analysis finds out whether men and women use different cultivars. Both should be used in control plots to be compared with experimental varieties.
- Resource analysis also shows who maintains knowledge about native species and varieties. For instance among the Kpelle, in Liberia, women can name and describe over 100 varieties of rice seed while men's knowledge in this field is limited (Gay 1982). Similar division of knowledge about use of woodlands and trees-as-crops has been reported in Ghana (Owusu-Bempah 1988) and in other areas of West Africa (Hoskins 1983).
- Benefits analysis finds out which crops have several purposes and identifies the users of various products. Are all user preferences taken into account in specifying desirable characteristics for the breeder? For example, where young green leaves of cassava are used as snack foods, relish, or in brewing beer to pay laborers and late season leaves are used for fodder, are these uses included in the breeding program? (Jiggins 1988). Are the requirements of post-harvest storage and processing taken into account?

A good example of the application of IHH analysis to the identification of varieties for use in on-farm research comes from The Gambia (Caldwell et al. 1986). An open survey among men and women indicated vegetable marketing was a high priority, but there is sharp disaggregation of crop by gender. Men grow cereal crops while women grow vegetables on semi-communal plots with residual moisture during the dry season. Analysis of the market found it was desirable to look at changes in varieties of vegetable crops and subsequent experimentation was done with women farmers.

Cultural Practices. These include spacing, timing, sequencing, crop care (pruning, weeding, etc.), and land and water management.

- Activities analysis shows specifically who does what. If women's time for gender specific tasks is a constraint, perhaps attention should be paid to labor saving devices which would release women's labor. If women plant, and experimental treatments include row planting with different spacings, they must be consulted about trial feasibility and must learn the experimental technique. Their changes in labor inputs must be monitored. This may require plot sizes large enough to monitor labor inputs in a realistic manner.
- Resource analysis shows who already has equipment or the cash or credit needed to acquire new implements or use implements in new ways. In Botswana, the control of draft animal power determined the applicability of experiments with timely plowing in relation to rains. Poor households, predominantly female-headed, could not use these techniques, and over time the project developed experimental post-establishment practices that better fit the resource constraints of these farmers (Baker 1987).
- Resource analysis can determine access and control of fields and trees. Does the introduction of land extending technology threaten the sources of wild foods important to seasonal provisioning? Does intercropping of men's and women's crops on a given field change the ownership of a crop? Here we quote Janice Jiggins' report to the Consultative Group on International Agricultural Research Secretariat (CGIAR) on gender roles:
- "One of the biggest issues is the possible displacement of land or labor from crops/livestock/trees for self-provisioning in favor of market oriented cash crops with its incumbent risks of fluctuation in the market place and increasing dependence on the market for food (Jiggins 1986)."

Nutrition and Protection. This includes local and purchased fertilizers and pesticides, crops planted for purposes of improving soil nutrition or providing fodder, and the building or growing of fences.

- For both plant nutrition and plant protection, the analysis of resources comes into play in identifying who has control of local products or cash or credit needed to acquire purchased products. In Calamba, Philippines, though men apply pesticides, women managed household finances and were therefore included in the discussions about the merits of and techniques for integrated pest management (Adalla 1988). Is there competition for the use of local sources such as the use of manure for either fertilizer or fuel? Does access to proposed inputs limit the spread of new technologies or suggest a need for alternative labor-intensive approaches?
- Where new inputs are applied, activities analysis shows who is affected and who must be taught techniques of application. What new tasks are associated with applying the inputs? Are they labor saving or labor using? If fertilizer is applied in conjunction with weeding, and women weed, they need to be taught how to apply the experimental doses. Activity analysis can also indicate who is at risk from pesticides or who should be trained in pest management practices.
- Benefits analysis identifies the other products that might be at risk when herbicides or pesticides are introduced. In the Bukoba region of Tanzania, spraying of banana trees for nematodes destroyed interplanted beans used for subsistence (Tibaijuka 1985). In maize-cowpea intercrops in Kenya, application of recommended pesticides against maize pests can poison the cowpea leaves collected by women for use in relish. Finding out how women use plants and where these plants are located helps researchers anticipate negative consequences and to plan accordingly.

These examples show that screening proposed solutions against maps created by IHH analysis will help identify the costs and benefits of proposed changes. The analysis makes clear whose activities or resources should be monitored for evaluation of trials results. The method also can predict whether innovations are compatible with existing systems and can determine their likely efficiency and equity.

Roles of Farmers and Researchers in Trial Design and Management

Trials can also be classified by the degree of farmer (user) participation and the respective roles of farmers and researchers in the design and management of agronomic trials. The possibilities range from researcher-designed on-station trials to a farmer's own experiments that are simply "discovered" and documented by research institutions. Most agricultural research and development programs using the FSR/E approach are based on a more direct collaboration between the two groups, including a variety of roles for farmers and researchers in trial design and management. These include:

- Researcher-designed and managed, on-station. Farmers are consulted and farmers's problems are addressed, but farmer resources and management are not included in the research design and cannot be evaluated.
- Researcher-designed and managed on farmer's fields. Farmers are consulted, farmer problems are addressed, and farmers evaluate results, but there is little or no involvement of farmer resources nor management since all costs and labor are covered by the research entity.
- Researcher-designed and farmer-managed. These are the same as above, but farmers' resources and management are included in the trial, evaluation and feedback are continuous, and farmers' performance and judgment are part of experimental design.
- Researcher and farmer joint design and management. Farmer and researcher collaborate in the design of the trial and confer on management decisions. Farmers' management and decision-making are experimental variables and their feedback and evaluation are high priorities.
- Farmer-designed and managed, researcher consulting. The researcher enters into an on-going farmer's trial as consultant or collaborator.
- Farmer-designed and managed. The researcher observes and documents a farmer's existing experiment.

IHH analysis can play a crucial part in choosing the appropriate level of researcher involvement in a given trial for a particular group of participants. The researcher's role will be different if the research is conducted on men's versus women's fields, on the farms of literate versus non-literate farmers, or with sedentary farmers versus migratory or semi-pastoralists farmers.

The greater the involvement of farmers as collaborators and as researchers, the more important it is for researchers to concentrate on the form as well as the content of their interaction with farmers. Different research personnel may be required for work with specific groups, or it may require a different style and level of interaction. For example, in a situation where women researchers are not available and it is not feasible for women farmers to work with male researchers, women extension agents might be able to do liaison and data collection tasks in trial types requiring more intensive interaction with women farmers. In other cases with less strict prohibitions, male researchers working on women's farms might be better able to carry out researcher-designed and managed trials or farmer-designed and managed trials, which both require less continuous interaction than the other types of on-farm trials. In yet other situations, male researchers may take a consult-and-document approach to women's group experiments, while playing a more interactive role with male farmers collaborating in researcher-designed and managed trials.

IHH analysis can also help researchers to work more effectively with the various user groups involved in managing and assessing trials. By combining men and women or different groups in the community as collaborators in the design process, researchers may uncover different criteria for evaluating the same technology. The goal here is to insure that both men's and women's views are incorporated appropriately. What issues to address with either group and whether to work with them separately or together will depend on the locally specific conditions revealed by the initial IHH analysis.

Different approaches to farm trial design may further clarify the division of labor, knowledge, and interests at household or community level. For example, careful monitoring of a trial may lead to development of different versions of the same technology or to different ways of testing the same technology for different groups. For example, if men and women or other distinct groupings of farmers are part of one trial, the results may also be different than if they are part of separate, parallel trials. When combining two or more groups with different interests in a single trial, differences in their objectives or criteria for design would likely lead to a compromise which masks those differences. Whether this increases or decreases acceptability would be an important question in evaluating the results. In separate trials, the result might well lead to two distinct technologies for men and women or other groupings, or for two separate approaches to evaluating their results. The inclusion of both groups in joint farmer-researcher or researcher-consultant trials allows for the adaption of technology and the development of alternatives that fit the special needs of each group. If the trials were done only on men's fields, with subsequent extension to women's fields, women might reject the technology "package." If they are involved as researchers and designers, women may still reject a particular technology accepted by men, but they may also be able to develop an acceptable adaptation or alternative in collaboration with researchers. This would be most likely in trials with greater interaction between farmer and researcher or in independent experimentation.

The Function of Farm Trials

Though we have dealt principally with the classification of trials by their nature and by their management, trials can also be grouped according to three functions: exploratory, refinement, and verification. These *functional* types follow a sequence as knowledge about a technological intervention improves through the on-farm research process. (Further explanation and examples of these types of trial function can be found in the FSSP Training Manuals, Vol. II, Walecka 1987.)

Exploratory Trials. These trials are conducted when little is known about the area in which research is being conducted. Exploratory trials complement the characterization of a domain, will preceed refinement trials, and normally provide more qualitative than quantitative information about factors. One kind of exploratory trial exposes a large number of technologies to a season's testing to cut the list to the most promising alternatives. For instance, researchers interested in whether fertilization will make any difference in yields may place bands of quite different amounts across a field. The objective is to narrow the range of for later experiments to the range of levels most likely to have a positive effect. These trials are often superimposed on farmer's fields without the need for special preparation.

In another kind of exploratory trial a proposed technology is released immediately to a large number of farmers and researchers observe how farmers use it and with what results. The International Livestock Center for Africa's (ILCA) program in the 'Humid Zone' in Nigeria is an example of this type of experimentation. Original on-station research focused on high input livestock production for sale. Further research indicated that most small ruminants were kept in small numbers by poor farmers, predominantly by women, and were part of integrated crop-livestock systems. Vaccination was successful and stock began to grow in numbers, putting pressure on fodder sources. At this point, recognizing that production of fodder was critical, but that the region to be covered was large and varied, researchers conducted exploratory research throughout the region. Giving farmers seedlings of leguminous trees and showing them patterns of combining trees with crop production (alley cropping), they carefully monitored farmers' practices. Special efforts were taken to include women farmers.

As this illustrates, exploratory trials can incorporate different kinds of farmers into the experiment. Data collection for the trials should explicitly measure the similarities and differences between men and women or other groups, especially if they do the same tasks or produce the same crops but on separate lands. Exploratory trials can often be conducted with larger social groups, for example a community or a women's collective.

These trials offer the opportunity to explore first hand, who does what and why and refine the activity mapping done during diagnosis and planning.

Refinement Trials. The objective of refinement trials is to submit the most promising alternative solutions to rigorous agronomic testing, usually employing more complex experimental designs and fewer total numbers of trials. Initially these are specific to a few sites. Regional trials are a further refinement, designed to expose the best treatments from site-specific trials to a much wider range of environments and submit them to both agronomic and socio-economic analysis.

Refinement trials pose research questions of great detail and specificity. In addition to selecting an appropriate mix of farmers, the researcher must specify what data to collect for purposes of evaluation. Attention to the IHH distribution of activities and resources should assist in insuring that monitoring of time or expenditures is properly targeted. Economic analysis which on aggregated household level data may mask important differences in 'costs' to the producers. For instance, in Botswana, the addition of an early plowing before plow-planting of sorghum increased yields and returns. But when changes in labor demand are disaggregated by gender, the new practice is revealed as one which demands more labor from men (extra plowing) and less from women (less weeding). Such analysis foreshadowed the limited adoption of the technique except by richer farmers who hire plowing (Baker 1989).

In farming systems where women do not participate directly in the actual cultivation of a crop, they may make major decisions about processing, storage and marketing. Because innovations in production impinge directly on their activities, trial design should include a means of learning about and evaluating with their criteria.

Validation Testing. Validation trials take a promising technology and verify it on a scale closer to farmer reality in terms of time, space and management. Large plots with no replications within farms are used. The purpose is for farmers to compare the interventions with their own practices.

It is important to monitor the direct and indirect impact of the management of the technology. Are results measured as returns to land or are other measures employed such as returns to seed planted, labor, capital, inputs, animal power or time? Does the intervention result in less need to purchase food? Does it save cash by reducing the cost of production? Multiple evaluation criteria are often necessary and may vary by user group.

Care must be taken in assessing validation trials to observe possible "ripple effects" from new technology. Ripple effects are changes in one part of a farming or household system as a result of interventions in another part of the system. Clues to likely ripples may be found by reference to activity analysis. For example, does increased labor required for intensive maize production result in reduced or late effort (and lower production) in beans or groundnuts. How might this affect individual or household welfare? These effects may take time to surface, but researchers and those interested in the distribution of project benefits should monitor this as more farmers try out a new technology.

The design and implementation of on-farm experimentation is governed by the objective or nature of the trial, the roles of researcher and farmer, and the stage of experimentation. Within any set of parameters, reference to IHH analysis of roles in production and the use of outputs improves the reliability of the information collected.

Gathering Additional Information

Gathering and analysis of additional information continues along with the implementation and agronomic measurements of on-farm experiments. Three areas are important: (1) information complementary to the trials, (2) the on-going and final assessment of experiments by farmers and users, and (3) additional studies of the farming system.

Complementary Information

IHH analysis shows that factors other than yield and returns frequently affect the acceptability of proposed changes. Before carrying out a trial, an analysis of proposed changes will highlight other factors and unanswered questions which will affect farmer decision-making. How do farmers mobilize labor when the labor available from household members is not sufficient? Is the fertilizer applied inappropriately because of labor constraints or lack of instruction? Will new varieties be acceptable to users or processors? These questions mean the collection of additional information. It is therefore important at the onset in trial design to layout *all* the evaluation criteria and make plans for collecting whatever additional information will be necessary. For example, it may be useful to monitor areas not directly related to the trial such as who does new or additional tasks and what is left undone, the effects on cooking and other household tasks, or who among non-owners borrows or doesn't borrow draft animals.

Farmer's and User's Views

In addition to measurements and informal conversations in the field, formal discussions may be held with those affected as decision makers, including those who provide the labor and those who use the outputs.

Where those affected are women and there are cultural barriers between men and women, special techniques may be required. Sometimes, women researchers must conduct the work. In Zambia, separate field days for men and women has resulted in large turnouts for each. Researchers report that women's willingness to express their views was greater than in mixed groups. They learned that men and women had markedly different views on the current experiments and came away with better defined lines of inquiry for the next year's experimental programs. CARE/ Kenya trains men and women extension workers to pay particular attention to women in group discussions by directing specific questions to them on which they have expertise. They have also found that a week's wait between asking a question and getting an answer allows time for family and community level discussion and decision-making. This broader participation and time for reflection results in more indigenous knowledge being shared and in a more active role for women in technology development (Buck 1986; Sutherland 1984).

Additional Studies

Experience shows that initial diagnosis is not sufficient to characterize a farming system and IHH dynamics. During the planning phase, problems for which causes are not well understood are good topics for follow up research. This may mean focused studies on particular topics such as food processing techniques or more generalized studies which deepen or verify the researchers' initial understanding of the system within which farmers live. Such studies demand further collaboration between technical and social scientists so that the topics being addressed and the manner in which they are addressed will lead to insights useful to the technical scientists. Among the most promising methodologies for doing such research are mini-case studies on representative farms, participant observation, community studies, time allocation studies, and focus-group interviews. Another technique is multiple visit surveys along the chain from production to consumption to determine gender responsibility for activities and consumer preferences. Three examples of special studies conducted in different types of agricultural projects are summarized below.

In Sitiung, a transmigration site in Indonesia, a time allocation study found that a large amount of time was spent by women and children on fodder collection, thereby validating the importance of experiments with nitrogen producing fodders. The study also showed that a high proportion of both men's and women's labor was allocated to the home garden. Observation showed that fertilizer meant for paddy rice was also diverted to home gardening. This suggested that the garden itself, frequently ignored in FSR/E, deserved further study (Sigman et al. 1989).

In Colombia, the recognition that certain bean varieties being tested by the breeders were favored by women led to a short, six-week period of intensive participant observation with women in their kitchens to better understand the role of beans in household production and consumption. The researcher discovered that beans were important as food for laborers, thus reducing labor cost. The cooking characteristics of beans, particularly their swelling and taste, were considered important. This discovery resulted in considerable interest in a bean originally ranked low by the breeder because it lacked the color and size desired by urban consumers. The participant observation also helped differentiate between farmers by age and life cycle stage. Younger farmers, men and women with cash resources from off-farm labor and subsistence support from their parents, tended to be more innovative and cash oriented. Older male heads of household with extended families who hired labor gave priority to wives's preferences for varieties as well as varieties for urban markets (Ashby 1989).

In highland Peru, women are responsible for grazing animals, collecting fodder and curing animals. Early attempts to understand sheep production by meeting with men or organizing women's groups through the male dominated community assembly led nowhere. Finally, a meeting was called to deal directly with sheep production problems and the women active in this enterprise attended. Focused on this task, the group set priorities and designed on-farm research on the need for dry-season fodder. As a result of discussions about women's use of local plants for preventing certain diseases, researchers and the women's group have also begun investigating indigenous medicines for sheep (Fernandez 1988).

This chapter has illustrated several important ways that IHH analysis can be incorporated into on-farm research: (1) in planning what potential solutions should be tried on which farmer's fields and what issues require additional research; (2) in *ex-ante* analysis of proposed solutions, (3) in identifying whose interests are at stake in undertaking innovation and assuring that both males and females are involved in on-farm experimentation; and (4) in defining the desirable characteristics of new technologies and the criteria by which they may be evaluated.

The research in this volume and elsewhere has shown unequivocally that the household as the main locus of production or consumption cannot be assumed. Relations of production are complex and varied, but it is possible to discern patterns which will guide development efforts. As the body of successful experimentation grows, IHH analysis will eventually become simply a normal part of the process of conducting good agricultural research and development.

Notes

1. Former Associate Director of the Farming Systems Support Project at the University of Florida and currently a consultant for the Population Council, Consultant for the Population Council, and Project Officer at the Ford Foundation Office, Nairobi, Kenya. An earlier version of this paper was presented at the CIMMYT Networkshop on Intra-Household Dynamics and Farming, Lusaka, Zambia, April 25–30.

2. A collaborative project, running 1984–1987, between the Population Council and the Farming Systems Support Project, USAID/University of Florida.

References Cited

Adalla, Candida B. 1988. "Women in Rice IPM: the Philippine Experience." Paper presented at the 1988 Farming Systems Research/Extension Symposium, University of Arkansas, Fayetteville, Arkansas, October 9–12.

Ashby, J.A. and G. De Jong. 1982. "Farmer Field Preparation and Tillage Practices: Implications for Fertilizer Technology Research." *Soil & Tillage Research* 2: 331–346.

Ashby, J.A. 1989. "Production and Consumption Aspects of Technology Testing, Pescador, Colombia," in H.S. Feldstein and S.V. Poats (eds.), *Gender and Agriculture: Case Studies in Intra-Household Analysis.* West Hartford, Connecticut: Kumarian Press.

Baker, D. 1989. "On-Farm Experimentation in Botswana," in H.S. Feldstein and S.V. Poats (eds.), *Gender and Agriculture: Case Studies in Intra-Household Analysis.* West Hartford, Connecticut: Kumarian Press.

Barker, R., C. Lightfoot and D. Gibbon. 1986. "On-Farm Trials." Paper presented at the 1986 Farming Systems Research and Extension Symposium. Kansas State University.

Barker, T.C., C.A. Francis and G.F. Kraus. 1986. "Resource Efficient Experimental Designs for On-Farm Research." Paper presented at the 1986 Farming Systems Research and Extension Symposium. Kansas State University.

Buck, L. 1986. *Training Manual for Extension Workers.* Nairobi, Kenya: CARE.

Caldwell, J.S., G.O. Gaye and I. Jack. 1986. "Linking Farming Systems Research/Extension and Commodity Research: FSR/E Team Identification of Horticultural Research Priorities in the Gambia, West Africa." Paper presented at the 1986 Farming Systems Research and Extension Symposium. Kansas State University.

Carloni, Alice Stewart. 1987. *Women in Development: A.I.D.'s Experience, 1973–1985, Vol.1.* A.I.D. Program Evaluation Report No. 18. Washington, D.C.: United States Agency for International Development.

Cloud, Kathleen. 1988. "A Teaching Module on Women and Agriculture: Household Level Analysis." Prepared for the International Workshop on Women, Households and Development: Building a Data Base. University of Illinois, Champaign-Urbana.

Due, Jean and Marcia White. 1984. "Contrasts Between Joint and Female-Headed Farm Households in Zambia." *East Africa Economic Review* 2(1984): 94–96.

Feldstein, H.S. and Janice Jiggins, editors. 1989. *Field Methodologies for Gender Analysis in Agricultural Research.* In press.

Feldstein, H.S. and S.V. Poats, editors. 1989. *Gender and Agriculture: Case Studies in Intra-Household Analysis.* 2 volumes. West Hartford, Connecticut: Kumarian Press.

Feldstein, H.S., S.V. Poats, K. Cloud and R. Norem. 1989. "Intra-Household Dynamics and Farming Systems Research and Extension Conceptual Framework and Worksheets," in H.S. Feldstein and S.V. Poats (eds.), *Gender and Agriculture: Case Studies in Intra-Household Analysis.* West Hartford, Connecticut: Kumarian Press.

Fernandez, M.E. 1988. "Technological Domains of Women in Mixed Farming Systems of Andean Peasant Communities," in S. Poats, M. Schmink, and A. Spring (eds.), *Gender Issues in Farming Systems Research and Extension.* Boulder: Westview Press.

Fresco, L. and S.V. Poats. 1986. "Farming Systems Research and Extension: An Approach to Solving Food Problems in Africa," in A. Hansen and D.E. McMillan (eds.), *Food in Sub-Saharan Africa.* Boulder: Lynne Reinner Publishers, Inc..

Gay, J. 1982. *Liberia, Lesotho and Tanzania: Students of Survival.* Reading: AERDC Bulletin.

Hildebrand P.E. and F. Poey. 1985. *On-Farm Agronomic Trials in Farming Systems Research and Extension.* Boulder: Lynne Reinner Publishers, Inc..

Hoskins, M. 1983. *Rural Women, Forest Products and Forestry Outputs.* Rome: Community Forestry Office, FAO.

Huss-Ashmore, R. and J.J. Curry. 1986. "Nutritional Consequences to On-Farm Research in Swaziland." Paper presented at the 1986 Farming Systems Research and Extension Symposium. Kansas State University.

Jackson, Cecile. 1985. "The Kano River Irrigation Project," in *Volume 4, Cases for Planners: Women's Roles and Gender Differences in Development.* West Hartford, Connecticut: Kumarian Press.

Jiggins, J. 1988. "Problems of Understanding and Communication at the Interface of Knowledge Systems," in S. Poats, M. Schmink, and A. Spring (eds.), *Gender Issues in Farming Systems Research and Extension.* Boulder: Westview Press.

———. 1986. "Gender-Related Impacts and the Work of the International Agricultural Research Centers." CGIAR Study Paper Number 17. Washington D.C.: The World Bank.

Jiggins, J. and L. Fresco. 1984. "Sociological and Anthropological Aspects." in *Upland Rice Conference.* Djakarta: IRRI.

Jones, Christine W. 1986. "Intra-Household Bargaining in Response to the Introduction of New Crops: A Case Study from North Cameroon," in J. Moock (ed.), *Understanding Africa's Rural Households and Farming Systems.* Boulder: Westview Press.

Lightfoot, C., T. Cornick, R. Ayaso, Z. de la Rosa, E. Lapsanda, G. Aves, and R. Hipe. 1986. "A Short Methodological Account of a Dynamic Systems Field Experiment: The Case of Legume Enriched Fallows for the Restoration of Soil Fertility, Eradication of Imperata, Improvement of Pasture and Reduction in Labor for Cultivation, in the Philippines." Paper presented at the 1986 Farming Systems Research and Extension Symposium. Kansas State University.

Little, T. M. and F. J. Hills. 1978. *Agricultural Experimentation.* John Wiley and Sons: New York.

Low, A. 1986. "On Farm Research and Household Economics," in J. Moock (ed.), *Understanding Africa's Rural Households and Farming Systems.* Boulder: Westview Press.

Maxwell, S. 1984. "The Role of Case Studies in Farming Systems Research." Sussex: IDS Discussion Paper 198.

Nagy, J.G., H.W. Ohm and S. Sawadogo. 1989. "Burkina Faso: A Case Study of the Purdue University Farming Systems Project," in H.S. Feldstein and S.V. Poats (eds.), *Gender and Agriculture: Case Studies in Intra-Household Analysis.* West Hartford, Connecticut: Kumarian Press.

Norman, D. and M. Collinson. 1985. "Farming Systems Research in Theory and Practice," in J.V. Remenyi (ed.), *Agricultural Systems Research for Developing Countries.* ACIAR Proceedings No. 11, Canberra, Australia: Australian Centre for International Agricultural Research.

Okali, C. and H.C. Knipscheer. 1986. "Small Ruminant Production in Mixed Farming Systems: Case Studies in Research Design." Paper for the 1986 Farming Systems Research and Extension Symposium. Kansas State University.

Okali, C. and J.E. Sumberg. n.d. "Examining Divergent Strategies in Farming Systems Research." Mimeo.

Owusu-Bempah, K. 1988. "The Role of Women Farmers in Choosing Tree Species for Agroforestry Systems in Ghana," in S. Poats, M. Schmink, and A. Spring (eds.), *Gender Issues in Farming Systems Research and Extension.* Boulder: Westview Press.

Overholt, Catherine, Mary B. Anderson, Kathleen Cloud and James Austin. 1985. *Gender Roles in Development Projects: A Case Book.* West Hartford, Connecticut: Kumarian Press.

Paris, T.R. 1987. "Developing Appropriate Technologies for Women in a Rice Based Farming Systems Project: A Case in Pangasinan, Philippines." Paper presented at the Association for Women in Development, Moving Forward: Innovations in Development Policy, Action, and Research. Washington, DC., April 15–17.

Population Council. 1985. *Women's Roles and Gender Differences in Development: Cases for Planners.* Seven volumes. West Hartford, Connecticut: Kumarian Press.

Rocheleau, D. 1987. "The User Perspective and Agroforestry Research and Action Agenda," in H.L. Gholz (ed.), *Agroforestry: Realities, Possibilities and Potentials.* Dordrecht: Martinus Nijhoff Publishers.

Shaner, W. W., P.F. Philipp, and W. R. Schmehl. 1981. *Farming Systems Research and Development: Guidelines for Developing Countries.* Boulder: Westview Press.

Sigman, V., C. Colfer, K. Wilson, R. Yost, M.D. Rauch and M. Wade. 1989. "Farm Bases Research in the TROPSOILS Project, Sitiung, Indonesia," in H.S. Feldstein and S.V. Poats (eds.), *Gender and Agriculture: Case Studies in Intra-Household Analysis.* West Hartford, Connecticut: Kumarian Press.

Sutherland, A.J. 1984. "Rural Sociology and Technology Generation in Subsistence Farming Systems: A Zambian Example." Paper presented at ARPT/CIMMYT Networkshop on the Role of Rural Sociology and Anthropology in Farming Systems Research. Lusaka, Zambia.

Tibaijuka, A.K. 1985. "Intra-Household Resource Allocation Constraints in the Implementation of the Banana-Coffee Development Program in the Kagera Region, Tanzania." Paper Presented at the 1985 Farming Systems Research and Extension Symposium. University of Kansas.

Tripp, R. 1986. "The Planning Stage of On-Farm Research: Developing a List of Experimental Factors." CIMMYT, Draft, September.

Walecka, L. (ed.) 1987. "Techniques for Design and Analysis of On-Farm Experimentation," in *FSR/E Training Units, Volume II.* Gainesville, Florida: Farming Systems Support Project, University of Florida.